# Media
## and the
## CREATIVE PROCESS

Edited by Eric Williams and Beth Novak
*Ohio University*

cognella®
academic publishing

Bassim Hamadeh, CEO and Publisher
Michael Simpson, Vice President of Acquisitions
Jamie Giganti, Managing Editor
Jess Busch, Graphic Design Supervisor
Jill Helmle, Acquisitions Editor
Brian Fahey, Licensing Associate
Mandy Licata, Interior Designer

First published in the United States of America in 2014 by Cognella, Inc.

Trademark Notice: Product or corporate names may be trademarks or registered trademarks, and are used only for identification and explanation without intent to infringe.

Cover image copyright© 2012 by Depositphotos / Roman Khilchyshyn.

Printed in the United States of America

ISBN: 978-1-62661-215-0 (pbk)/ 978-1-62661-216-7 (br)

www.cognella.com      800-200-3908

# Contents

## Section 1: The Creative Process

Creative Lexicon　　　　　　　　　　　　　　　　　　　　3
　　Eric Williams and Beth Novak

## Section 2: Storytelling

Introduction　　　　　　　　　　　　　　　　　　　　　15

Story Basics　　　　　　　　　　　　　　　　　　　　　17
　　Sheila Curran Bernard

Interactivity and Its Effects　　　　　　　　　　　　　31
　　Carolyn Handler Miller

Influences of Sound on Meaning　　　　　　　　　　　47
　　Stanley R. Alten

Why Archetypes are Important　　　　　　　　　　　61
　　Bryan Tillman

Thinking of Structure　　　　　　　　　　　　　　　　67
　　Guy Gallo

Song Production: The Marriage Between Composition
and Audio Production　　　　　　　　　　　　　　　75
　　Danny Cope

Defining Independent Games, Serious Games, and Simulations　　89
　　Nick Iuppa and Terry Borst

## Section 3: Aesthetic Choices

Introduction                                                                97

The Game Consists of Elements                                               101
    Jesse Schell

Aesthetics                                                                  107
    Bryan Tillman

Dialogue                                                                    119
    Robin Beauchamp

The Visual Languages and Aesthetics of Cinema                               129
    Mick Hurlis-Cherrier

## Section 4: Bringing Your Story to Life

Introduction                                                                157

Scene Writing                                                               159
    Elliot Grove

Line and Shape                                                              173
    Bruce Block

Sound Design                                                                197
    Tomlinson Holman and Arthur Baum

Music                                                                       203
    Robin Beauchamp

Animation                                                                   217
    Angie Taylor

Game Play Design                                                            233
    Nick Iuppa and Terry Borst

Image Credits                                                               245

Index                                                                       247

# Section 1

## The Creative Process

# Creative Lexicon

## By Eric Williams and Beth Novak

*H*ere is a well-kept secret: creativity can be learned.

More important, it *has* to be learned. In today's media-rich society, we as creative people have to learn how other creative minds think. We have to learn a vocabulary to articulate our ideas and to understand how others create and define their own work. Once you break it down, though, the job gets a lot easier. Once you break an idea down into fundamental concepts, you can then practice those concepts. You can try them on for size and see whether they fit you and your idea.

You can swap them out like accessories on a fashion model. You can mix and match. It's like playing chess. You need to know how each piece moves, but once you understand the basics, there are infinite ways to play the game. Some people may play a better game on any given day, but if you put time into practicing and learning the game, you play better each day.

Creativity can be learned. It just takes a little time and effort.

## GENRE

If creativity is like a game of chess, "genre" is your king. It is the most important piece on the board, and it defines everything that you do. It influences every play that you make. So, what is genre? *Genre* is the way that we, the audience, categorize things—in our case, a creative work of media. Think about that for a minute. It is not the way in which *the artist* categorizes his or her own work. It is the way in which *the audience* categorizes the work.

Let me give you an example. Some basic genres of music are jazz, rock, and classical. So, when someone says, "Let's listen to some classical music," you, as the potential audience member, get a certain idea in your head of what that genre means. You probably imagine certain instruments (violins, cellos, maybe a viola). You picture certain musician configurations (an orchestra or perhaps a string ensemble). And you probably think of certain musicians (Bach or Beethoven). You probably do not think about The Beatles. But, why not? The famous Beatles song "Eleanor Rigby" was played entirely on violin, cello, and viola—and none of the instruments were played by The Beatles. In fact, the entire instrumentation of the song was played by a string ensemble. So, why is this considered classic rock, instead of classical music?

This answer is *genre*. Genre categorizes work according to *expectations*, and these expectations are developed over a period of time in the minds of a large public audience. Over several decades, the genre of rock music has come to be defined in a variety of ways: typically, a rock band has three to five core members, including at least a drummer, guitarist, bassist, and lead singer. The songs are typically fewer than five minutes in length, with the content being about drugs, sex, and living or dying according to the American Dream. And, most important (in this example), rock music has a long tradition of stealing elements from other genres. So, while the expectation of musical instruments is not met in "Eleanor Rigby," the other elements are: The Beatles are a four-member band, typically playing drums, guitar, and bass. This particular song is fewer than five minutes long and is about dying in loneliness. Because the world recognizes The Beatles as rock musicians who experiment with different musical styles, when they chose classical music instrumentation for the song, it remained in the rock music genre because most of the expectations for that genre were met.

Genre exists throughout media, but it is a term that is often misused or overused. For instance, people often refer to drama or comedy as film genres, but these classifications do not really create any audience expectations (other than being serious or funny). Compare these classifications to a true film genre, such as Western, Horror, or War. Once you begin using true genres, you start having more expectations. As an audience member you expect certain locations, certain types of characters, certain types of stories, and certain types of problems to confront the heroes of the film. Drama and comedy are certainly classifications of film, but they don't provide a deep enough set of expectations to be considered genres.

Calling drama a film genre would be sort of like considering "console game" to be a genre of video games. But the console is just the way by which you might play a wide variety of different genres. Video game genres include shooters, role playing games (RPGs), strategy games, and sports games, just to name a few. The categories can get even more specific when you consider the classification of subgenres. Subgenres for sports games include the actual sports—baseball, football, basketball, and so on—and each of those subgenres has its own set of expectations, just like the subgenres of rock (punk rock, indie rock, grunge, etc.) have their own expectations.

## STORY

If genre is the king of your creative chessboard, story is the queen. She is the most powerful piece and can move in the widest variety of directions. In most cases, story is the central core of your creative production. Whether you are animating and designing the sound for a narrative short, writing songs for an album, or making a documentary video, you are telling a story.

Typically, a story will have a beginning, wherein a character finds herself with a problem, followed by a middle, wherein she tries to solve the problem, and an ending, wherein she either succeeds or fails at solving the problem. By facing this problem—especially in American storytelling tradition—the character goes through a personal change and learns something about herself or about life in general. Sometimes the character does not learn a lesson, but the audience learns a lesson instead.

Not all stories are obvious, especially ones that are simple. Take the video game *Tetris*, for instance. At first, it may not seem like a story, but there is story there. In the beginning, there is a blank space, and you, the main character, must protect that space. You are given instructions to do so. This is the problem that you, the hero, must face. The differently shaped blocks begin to fall, and you attack the problem. In the middle, the task becomes more difficult. The blocks arrive at a faster rate, and they begin to stack up. By the end you will fail. The game is designed so that you fail, but you can succeed by obtaining a high score, or a personal best. Along the way, you have learned that you are getting better (or need to get better) at this challenge. You learn this by comparing your score to previous scores, and these scores are recorded so that others may learn as well. See? Pretty simple, but there is a basic story structure present. And it is a common story in the casual game genre of video games.

With your king and queen standing side by side, you now have a central core on which to build the rest of your team. Some stories fit nicely inside specific genres. For instance, you often find stories of redemption inside a television thriller, tales of loneliness inside a country music genre, or stories with a moral inside an animated fable for children. Story and genre are the building blocks for many, if not most, of the creative decisions that you will make in media. It is best to find those aspects of your project first, then build from there.

## THEME

A theme is an idea that permeates a work of art. A classic theme in stories throughout the history of media explores the struggle between good and evil. Another theme might be the desire to escape. If you listen to the lyrics of Eminem's song "Lose Yourself," you can clearly see how the story is infused with his desire to escape from his trailer park home, his broken family, and poverty. In *Star Wars Episode IV: A New Hope* (also known as "the original" to those who saw it in the theaters in 1977), Luke Skywalker also has a desire to escape his home. It is a common theme in a hero's journey. But the *Star Wars* franchise also explores the theme of good and evil throughout its epic story.

Think of your theme as the bishops on a chessboard. They stand on either side of story and genre, infusing deeper meaning into the story while reinforcing the expectations of the genre. Hopefully, you can see how story, genre, and theme all fit together. Certain themes and certain stories fit more easily into specific genres. A Western often contains a story of a town being taken over by criminal elements. It is often the hero who battles these criminals, and, thematically, the audience sees a battle of good versus evil as the story plays out.

# AUDIENCE

The knights in your creative chess game are the audience. Too often, we spend time processing what is in our own heads, without thinking about how others will perceive our ideas. The problem with that approach is that you've already made the project for yourself: it's in your head, where it is perfect. If that's all you want to do, stop there; you're done. However, most of us want to share our ideas. To do that, you need to get the idea out of your head and into the world. That, I believe, is the true test of creativity: can you take that perfectly formed idea that is in your head and transfer it into someone else's head—or, better yet, into thousands or millions of people's heads? That is the definition of communication, and creativity cannot be expressed without it. So, unless you can communicate your ideas to other people—the audience—your thoughts might just as well be dreams that disappear as soon as you wake up.

The challenge of working with an audience is trying to figure out what will speak to them. But, first, you have to figure out who they are. We often make audience decisions without even realizing that we are making these decisions. For instance, if you write a song and sing it in English, you are already deciding to initially appeal to the 365 million native English-speaking people on the planet. That's a pretty good audience base, but you would have a larger base—by another twenty million people—if you sang the song in Spanish. If you recorded the same song in Chinese, you would nearly triple your immediate audience base. If there were no words at all, you would immediately have an audience base of 7.1 billion people—that is, if everyone had the same interests and taste.

But we don't all have the same interests and taste, thank goodness. Older people see the world differently than younger people do. Religious, ethnic, and racial backgrounds affect our relationships to stories and characters. Themes resonate differently depending on our income levels, our romantic preferences, and our sex. Imagine, for a moment, how a sixteen-year-old boy living in rural Nebraska might respond to a song about tangling with the law and fighting with a girlfriend. That same song might resonate differently with a fifty-year-old gay woman living on the Upper West Side of Manhattan.

It is important to be as specific as possible about the audience, or multiple audiences, that you are trying to address. If you are creating a sitcom television series for a national network such as CBS, ABC, or NBC, you should be thinking about a broad audience base, such as "male and female English-speaking people ages eighteen to forty-five with at least a high school education." But if you are trying to teach children in rural South American regions how to avoid tropical diseases, your audience is much more specific. Your audience is now Spanish-speaking children with an education level below high school. This shift in audience will alter many aspects of your creative process.

# MOOD

Where genre is very specific about its expectations, mood is very broad. But the mood of your piece is also very concrete. It adds strength and direction to your work, like the castles (or rooks) in chess. Mood is the feeling that the audience gets when they experience your work. Mood is more aligned with the definition of comedy or drama than genre is. Mood also lets the audience know whether your piece is serious or sarcastic, whether it is satire or parody, whether it is childish or austere, and whether it is heartwarming or a tearjerker.

Mood is created in a variety of ways. Color, character, and word choice all influence the mood of a piece, but nothing affects mood more than sound design. The sounds that we hear give us permission to laugh. Similarly, music can cue us that this is an important moment of truth. Unless we, as creative minds, know the mood we are shooting for, how can we make the creative decisions that hit a bull's-eye?

# METAPHOR

With genre, story, theme, audience, and mood serving as the back row of your chessboard, think of the amount of creative work that has already been done for you. Imagine that we want to make a television series. We make the following decisions: we want to make a Western (genre) about a cowgirl who wants to become sheriff but has been told that only boys can become sheriffs (story). The story will hopefully show American girls ages eight to fourteen (audience) that they should follow their dreams, because social expectations can change (theme). To make the story fun and exciting (mood) for this audience, we'll make it into a brightly animated musical, filled with crazy characters, and we'll call it *The Good, The Bad, and the Pretty*.

See how we have already created a solid core of creative decisions? Now all we need is support for this core. This support will be provided with metaphors. Metaphors are the pawns out in front that protect your core ideas. Metaphors are a shortcut to more complicated ideas, where one idea stands for something else. For instance, when we said, "Genre is the king of your creative chessboard," you knew that genre wasn't really a wooden carving sitting on a game board in someone's living room. Even if you don't play chess, you knew that we were trying to say that genre was very important. If you know how chess is played, you knew we were saying that chess was vital! A good metaphor gets to the heart of your message very quickly, and it speaks instantly to a wide range of people. By using symbols rather than words, you speak more poetically and creatively about your ideas.

For instance, in *The Good, The Bad, and the Pretty*, a simple way to symbolize the difference between characters is to give the good characters white hats, the bad characters black hats, and the pretty characters pink hats. That way, when we meet a new character, we can instantly tell whether they are good or bad (or just pretty). Of course, characters may change from pretty to bad, then again to good, but their hats will change, too—metaphorically representing the change without having to explain it to the audience.

Another metaphor might be a yellow flower that our main character wears in the buttonhole of her shirt. This flower might represent the innocence of growing up in the fields surrounding her farm. By the end of the TV series, she will replace her yellow flower with a golden sheriff's star. Symbolically, we will know that our hero has accomplished her goal (to become sheriff), but that it has also cost her some of the innocence she had at the start of the series. This metaphor will help end the story because it demonstrates change in our character.

Whether you are creating a song, a documentary, or a video game, metaphor will heighten the artistry and strengthen the emotion of your story.

We've described the key pieces that you will need to play the game of chess in your creative process, but we haven't described the board yet. Whether you are prone to playing

three-dimensional chess with Spock, three-person chess with Sheldon and Leonard, or the standard version with Bobby Fisher, your pieces move along a checkered continuum. Your creative ideas will, too.

Just as a chessboard has eight columns or rows, there are eight binary terms that you will revisit throughout this book and throughout your creative life. As you consider these binary terms, do not think of them as opposites. Instead, think of them as being on a continuum, with each phrase connected to the other.

## CREATOR AND USER

When you write, shoot, draw, record, or make your creative project, you are the creator. Your ideas (or the team's ideas) are being brought to life. Or are they? Some might say that the ideas are not truly brought to life until someone uses your media. What is a song unless someone listens to it? What is a game unless someone plays it? Has your film been brought to life if no one ever sees it?

There is a magical relationship between the creator and the user of art. It is a dance, a beautiful give-and-take. The creator builds a world for the user to enjoy. The user then often creates feedback for the creator, and the creator can use that feedback to create something new. See what I did there? The user *creates* ... and the creator *uses*. ...

It is a symbiotic relationship, wherein both user and creator switch roles, and switch back again, repeatedly. Feedback is just one example of how this relationship works. But think about fan fiction, open-source programming, or sampling music into a new song. In these cases, the users *become* new creators, who in turn garner their own users, who in turn may then become another set of new creators.

## STIMULUS AND RESPONSE

But what motivates us to become a creator in the first place? What motivates anyone to do anything? Typically, there is something that makes you do something. This something is a stimulus. If it gets too hot in the car, you roll down the window. The stimulus (the heat) creates as response (rolling down the window). A fire-breathing dragon forces your character to hide so that she won't get killed. To get your character to hide, you pull the joystick back while pressing the green button twice. Stimulus ... response. It's a pretty cool trick that you can create a character (the fire-breathing dragon) that will make a complete stranger literally writhe around on his or her couch pressing buttons and scream when the character dies. Stimulus ... response.

Unless you, as the creator, know the response that you want to get from your user, how will you know what stimulus you'll need to create? Do you want your audience to tear up at the end of your film? Do you want your crowd to sing along with your encore? Well, you'll need different creative tools to achieve each of these different outcomes. Unless you know your outcome (your intended response), you won't know which tool to use.

## CONSCIOUS AND SUBCONSCIOUS

Often, the user doesn't even know why he or she responded in a certain way to your work. Have you ever looked at a painting or heard a piece of music and it just made you feel uneasy? Maybe it was the colors being used. Maybe it was the instrumentation. But really, you have no idea why you felt the way you did. You were being affected on a subconscious level.

*Subconscious* literally means "below your consciousness." If you are conscious of something, that means that you are thinking specifically about that one particular thing. You know that John Bonham's drumming is what gets you pumped up when you listen to that one Led Zeppelin song. You are conscious of how the drums affect you. But you may be subconsciously affected by other things at the same time. Perhaps the lyrics that you never really paid attention to—but have heard a thousand times—are making you feel a certain way. Maybe Jimmy Page's guitar wailing in the background or the high pitch of Robert Plant's voice is also driving your emotions. You consciously know that it is the drums, but subconsciously you may be affected by other things as well. For instance, there are claims that Led Zeppelin put subliminal messages into their songs to subconsciously affect the audience, and you could only hear these messages by playing the music backward.

## TEXT AND SUBTEXT

An artist communicates with the audience in both direct and indirect ways. We use the term *text* to refer to anything that is actually seen or heard in a piece of media. If one character walks up to another character and says, "Good morning," with a scowl across her face, the words and the scowl are text. What we, as the audience, *interpret* from the text is known as the *subtext*. The woman's scowl may indicate that this character is not having a good morning at all. In fact, her words may mean the exact opposite of what we think they would mean.

Another example of text and subtext can be seen in Andy Warhol's famous painting of thirty-two Campbell's soup cans. The text is simply cans of soup. But the subtext is more of a comment on "what art has become." In the book *Warhol* by David Bourdon, the artist is quoted as saying, "A group of painters have come to the common conclusion that the most banal and even vulgar trappings of modern civilization can, when transposed to canvas, become Art." The subtext of Warhol's famous painting encourages the audience to question the true meaning of art and to ask themselves whether it is the artist or the subject matter that is most important.

## CONTRAST AND AFFINITY

The concepts of contrast and affinity are often used to create subtext. *Contrast* is the pairing of opposites, while *affinity* is pairing things that are similar. For instance, the words "good morning," when paired with a scowl, form a contrast because the words are happy, but the scowl is unhappy. It is this contrast that allows the audience to create a subtextual meaning to the scene. Similarly, the thirty-two cans of soup demonstrate affinity. All the cans are similar in color, shape, and size. The only difference between the cans is the name of the soup they contain (bean, tomato, onion, etc.). Warhol uses the affinity of the cans to make the image repetitive and boring. You can imagine someone saying, "Thirty-two cans of soup? That's not art! That looks like a shelf in the grocery store!" Which is exactly what Warhol wanted you to think. As a media creator, he wanted a specific response from the audience, and used their subconscious reaction to the affinity of shape and color to create that subtext.

When exploring contrast and affinity, nearly any creative decision can be affected. You can compare musical instruments, camera movements, volume, color, shape, word length, languages, and costumes. The list goes on and on, giving us limitless possibilities for creating new and interesting meaning in our work simply by using contrast and affinity.

## TENSION AND RELEASE

Once artists understand how to use contrast and affinity within their work, they can then build patterns using those ideas. Those patterns can create both conscious and subconscious emotions within the audience. For instance, here is a pattern created through contrast: hot-cold-hot-cold-hot-cold-hot-cold-hot-cold-hot-cold-hot-cold-hot-cold. Such sharp contrast repeated over and over tends to create a sense of tension in the audience because they will be constantly shifting from one extreme to the other. Tension is created through conflict. When sharp opposites contrast with one another, there is conflict and, therefore, tension. But as soon as the tension stops, the audience feels a sense of release.

Tension and release are used all the time in media production. It is a very effective way to create a response in the user. How do you make an audience cry? Well, it helps if you make them very uptight first. Imagine the cliffhanger film where you don't know if the hero is going to die. You hope and you pray that the villain won't kill your favorite character, but you just don't know if she'll be able to escape this time. The director is building tension as the ending of the film gets closer. Suddenly, at the last minute, your hero appears. She is safe, she survived, and now she is back home with her family. A sense of relief (or release) washes over you. You are so happy and relieved that you start to cry.

Later, if you recap the story to friends, it is doubtful that you will cry. But why not? You are remembering the same actions. You are telling the same story that was told to you. However, you don't have that same sense of tension and release. Without the tension, you cannot have the release. Without the release, your emotions haven't been primed to respond as they did in the movie theater. Directors and editors understand this phenomenon, and use it to craft very specific responses in their audience by creating the right stimulus at the right time.

You can also create tension without using contrast. Warner Brothers cartoons use tension and release by creating loud noises—a lot of them. There is an affinity of loud noises emanating from inside the coyote after he accidentally eats a bottle full of earthquake pills. These loud noises create tension. The release is actually accomplished through contrast when all of a sudden there is silence. The silence, in contrast with the loud noises, makes us breathe a sigh of relief (and snicker because a huge rock has fallen onto the coyote and squashed him, which is why he is silent).

## ACTIVE AND DIDACTIC

There are two ways to deliver information: the Batman way and the Spider-Man way—or, rather, actively or didactically. *Didactic delivery of information* is when you clearly explain exactly what it is you want your audience to understand. For instance, in the 2002 movie *Spider-Man* (screenplay written by David Koepp), we are told twice—quite didactically—that with great power comes great responsibility. This is also the theme of the film, the lesson learned by both Peter Parker and the audience.

*Active delivery of information* is when you do not explain your meaning to the audience, but, rather, you let the audience figure it out for themselves. Subtext is a form of active information delivery. In the 2008 Batman flick *The Dark Knight*, screenwriters Chris and Jonathan Nolan took a different approach to storytelling. They delivered their information much more actively. For example, there are two scenes where the Joker asks someone, "You want to know how I got these scars?" after which he tells two completely different stories. So, which one was true? It doesn't matter. The point of the stories isn't to didactically tell the audience how the Joker got his scars, it is to actively get the audience to realize that this guy is absolutely insane! The Nolans don't have a character say, "The Joker? He's crazy." Instead, they have you—the audience—make that realization for yourself. Information gathered in an active way has a much stronger resonance because there is more mental stimulation, thus creating a stronger response.

## OBJECTIVE AND SUBJECTIVE

Information can also be delivered in an objective or subjective manner. *Subjective information* is information that is based on someone's opinion or personal point of view. People might say that *Spider-Man* is a better film than *The Dark Knight*, but that is subjective information. It is based on personal criteria of what constitutes a good movie. But if you said that *Spider-Man* made almost $115 million at the box office in its opening weekend, compared to *The Dark Knight*, which made $158 million in its opening weekend, you are sharing objective information. This information is not based on opinions; it is based on fact.

Often, the creative decisions that we make are subjective in nature: "I think this would be the best color for his costume." "That joke is funnier than this joke." "This is a great beat for that reggae song." But, often, subjective decisions can lead to objective rewards: an Academy Award for costume design, a job writing for Conan O'Brien, or your band topping the charts with a new song.

So, there you have it: six concepts and eight binary terms that, together, will help define many of your creative decisions. You will return to these ideas again and again throughout this book, exploring them and turning them over in a variety of ways. As an artist who is shaping your own creative process, it is important for you to create your own relationship with these ideas. Find combinations that work best for you. See how others use them. Use the words to critique and craft the creative world around you. These are just tools for you to use. Learn how to use them.

Remember: creativity can be learned. It is a process. Knowing how these tools can be used to communicate your unique ideas to the minds of others can be very handy. But there is no right way to use them. It's subjective, after all!

# Section 2

## Storytelling

# Introduction

S tories are the central element in many, if not most, media productions. Story is the light bulb that illuminates the room, allowing us to see the architecture, the furniture, and the pictures on the wall. The art of storytelling is central to understanding the creative process of media. If we cannot understand why and how storytelling works, we might as well be stumbling around in the dark looking for the light switch.

Whether you are writing a song, directing a commercial, or designing a video game, you most likely will use some kind of story to engage your audience. In communication, it is the relationship between the media maker and her audience that is of utmost importance. You must know the story that you are trying to tell, and who you are trying to tell it to, before you can make your key creative decisions. Think of *Sesame Street* as an example. If your goal is to educate children, you wouldn't decide to write a 200-page textbook. Instead you would follow the lead of *Sesame Street* and weave one story though a series of short, colorful vignettes using a mixture of live-action puppets, real people, and various form of animation.

We are all part of a rich history of creative decisions. Some have worked, and others have not, and as media makers it saves us valuable time and energy to use our collective creative past to guide us—time and energy we can spend to be more creative in our own choices. What kind of puppets should we build? What sort of fun song should we write? How crazy should that animated cookie be?

Hopefully, what you will realize in this section is that storytelling is a human trait that we all share. In the first chapter, "Story Basics," you will read about documentary storytelling. But the lessons from that chapter can just as easily apply to animation projects, or song writing, or sound design, because all media work in similar ways. Images, whether on the screen or in your mind, work in tandem with sounds. When David Bowie sings the "Lady Stardust" lyrics, "People stared at the makeup on his face / Laughed at his long black hair, his animal grace / The boy in the bright blue jeans jumped up on the stage / And Lady Stardust sang his songs of darkness and disgrace," it is more than just audio that affects the audience—it is an image as well, one that is enhanced by the music that surrounds it.

By juxtaposing a sound with an image, you are communicating with your audience. The juxtaposition, through contrast or through affinity, creates a thought in the mind of the audience—a

thought that is different from either the sound or the image on its own. Only by developing a series of thoughts in the audience's mind do you have the power to develop emotion, create ideas, and tell a story. The second and third chapters, "Interactivity and Its Effects" and "Influences of Sound on Meaning," will elaborate on these concepts by using digital game and sound design examples.

Once you recognize your own ability to create a story, you will soon realize that stories are like anything else: they all share similar attributes for communicating with their audience. As a media professional, you can use established attributes, such as themes, genres, and archetypes, to communicate more quickly and efficiently—leaving you more room for your own creativity. Think about a common theme that we all recognize: good versus evil. On a fundamental level, that theme is carried out by two archetypes: the hero and the villain. If you are working in the Western genre, the hero wears white and the villain wears black. See? Simple. By relying on these common storytelling elements, you can focus more time and energy on the creative side of your story by developing dynamic dialogue and unique plot twists for the audience to enjoy. The chapters "Why Archetypes Are Important" and "Thinking of Structure" will demonstrate how to use these preestablished story elements in your work.

Finally, once you understand how to use storytelling basics to your advantage, you'll want to add complexity and your own layer of creativity to the process. The chapters "Song Production" and "Defining Independent Games" will delve deeper into the storytelling process and explain how the medium you use also connects to your message. Think about it: a song and a documentary both might have the same theme (or even the same story), but you don't fly down the highway listening to a documentary and screaming along to it at the top of your lungs. But why not? Why do we react one way to some media, but not to others? And how can we, as creative media makers trying to tell stories to our audience, use that knowledge to our advantage?

As media professionals, we all want to communicate effectively with people. To do so, we need to understand our audience and the medium we choose to use to connect with them. We need to understand their expectations. We need to understand the tools at our disposal to meet those expectations. Once we know all that—whether in the creation of a video game, a song, a short documentary, a feature film, or an animated clip on *Sesame Street*—we have within us the basic understanding to create a compelling story, a story that will connect consciously and subconsciously with other humans in the very core of their being. We can turn on the light bulb for them. We can illuminate a room that they didn't even know existed. And that is what communication is all about, and why it is so wonderful.

# Story Basics

## By Sheila Curran Bernard

*A* *story* is the narrative, or telling, of an event or series of events, crafted in a way to interest the audience, whether they are readers, listeners, or viewers. At its most basic, a story has a beginning, middle, and end. It has compelling characters, rising tension, and conflict that reaches some sort of resolution. It engages the audience on an emotional and intellectual level, motivating viewers to want to know what happens next.

Strategies for good storytelling are not new. The Greek philosopher Aristotle first set out guidelines for what he called a "well-constructed plot" in 350 BC, and those basics have been applied to storytelling—on stage, on the page, and on screen—ever since. Expectations about how storytelling works seem hardwired in audiences, and meeting, confounding, and challenging those expectations is no less important to the documentarian than it is to the dramatist.

Don't be confused by the fact that festivals and film schools commonly use the term *narrative* to describe only works of dramatic fiction. Most documentaries are also narrative, which simply means that they tell stories (whether or not those stories are also *narrated* is an entirely different issue). How they tell those stories and what stories they tell separates the films into subcategories of genre or style, from cinéma vérité to film noir.

A few storytelling terms:

## EXPOSITION

*Exposition* is the information that grounds you in a story: who, what, where, when, and why. It gives audience members the tools they need to follow the story that's unfolding and, more importantly, it allows them inside the story. It doesn't mean giving away everything, just giving away what the audience needs, when the audience needs it. Exposition is occasionally discussed

Figure 1.1. *Exposition can be woven into a film in many ways. Note how documentary Filmmaker Matthew O'Neil chooses a specific point-of-view while shooting in Egypt's Tahrir Square.*

as something to be avoided, but it's necessary to an audience's understanding of the film, and its presentation, usually in the first act, doesn't have to be heavy-handed.

Exposition in theater used to be handled by the maid who bustled onstage at the start of a play and said, to no one in particular, or perhaps to a nearby butler, "Oh, me, I'm so very worried about the mistress, now that the master has gone off hunting with that ne'er-do-well brother of his, and without even telling her that his father, the Lord of Pembrokeshire, has arranged to sell this very house and all of its belongings before a fortnight is up!" In documentary films, the corollary might be those programs that are entirely front-loaded with narration that tells you information you're unprepared for or don't really need to know—and when you do need the information, you generally can't remember it. Front-loading also frequently occurs when filmmakers decide to put the entire backstory—all of the history leading up to the point of their story's attack—at the beginning of the film.

Exposition can be woven into a film in many ways. Sometimes expository information comes out when the people you're filming argue: "Yeah? Well, we wouldn't even be in this mess if you hadn't decided to take your paycheck to Vegas!" Sometimes it's revealed through headlines or other printed material, as some exposition is conveyed in *The Thin Blue Line*. Good narration can deftly weave exposition into a story, offering viewers just enough information to know where they are. (Voice-over material drawn from interviews can sometimes do the same thing.) Exposition can also be handled through visuals: an establishing shot of a place or sign; footage of a sheriff nailing an eviction notice on a door (*Roger & Me*); the opening moments of an auction (*Troublesome Creek*). Toys littered on a suburban lawn say "Children live here." Black bunting and a homemade shrine of flowers and cards outside a fire station say "Tragedy has occurred." A long shot of an elegantly dressed woman in a large, spare office high up in a modern building says "This woman is powerful." A man on a subway car reading an issue of *The Boston Globe* tells us where we are, as would a highway sign or a famous landmark—the Eiffel Tower, for example. Time-lapse photography, title cards, and animation can all be used to convey exposition, sometimes with the added element of humor or surprise—think of the cartoons in *Super Size Me*.

## THE NARRATIVE SPINE, OR TRAIN

Films move forward in time, taking audiences with them. You want the storytelling to move forward, too, and to motivate the presentation of exposition. In other words, you want the audience to be curious about the information you're giving them. When exposition involves backstory—how we got to where we are now—it's often a good idea to get a present-day story moving forward (even if the story is in the past) before looking back. This overall story—your film's narrative spine—has been described by producers Ronald Blumer and Muffie Meyer of Middlemarch Films (*Benjamin Franklin, Liberty! The American Revolution*) as the film's train.

The train is the element of story that drives your film forward, from the beginning to the end. Get a good train going, and you can make detours as needed for exposition, complex theory, additional characters—whatever you need. Sometimes, these detours let you seed in information that will pay off later in the film; sometimes, the detours are motivated by the train, and the audience wants to take a side track to learn more. If you don't have a train going, those detours will seem unfocused and, more than likely, dull. Your train will be derailed.

Here's an example: You're thinking of telling a story in chronological order about this guy named Jim Jones who becomes a Pentecostal minister in Indiana and has an interracial church and it's the 1950s and—it's not very interesting. But if you pick up this same story much later in time, as a congressman goes to Guyana to rescue some Americans from what their relatives fear is a dangerous cult, and the congressman is killed while members of this cult line up to drink cyanide-spiked juice, chances are the audience will stay with you as you break away from this train to explore the decades of social, political, cultural, and even personal change that created Jim Jones and the tragedy of Jonestown. The drama is already there; it's a matter of finding the "creative arrangement," the strongest way to tell it.

In considering the train, it helps to think about drawing in an audience that doesn't know or care one way or another about the topic you're following. Some people are deeply curious about space exploration, for example, but many people aren't. If you're creating a film that you hope will reach a general audience, whether at a museum, on television, or in theaters, you need to think about how to get a story under way that will grab that audience. Then—and this is what makes you a good documentary filmmaker, not a mediocre one—you want to see how much information that story will allow you to convey even to the disinterested, because you're going to *get* them interested.

In other words, rather than pandering to the lowest common denominator—creating a breathless film about space exploration that's filled with platitudes and exciting music, but little else—your goal is to create a film that's driven by a story, one that will motivate even general viewers to *want* to know more of those details that thrill you. They'll grow to care because those details will matter to the story unfolding on screen. The train of *Super Size Me* is a 30-day McDiet, for example, but look at how much information the film conveys about nutrition and obesity. The train in *Daughter from Danang* is a reunion between an Amerasian woman and

Figure 1.2. *An Inconvenient Truth created a less apparent train by pairing lectures with a dynamic PowerPoint developed by former Vice President Al Gore, pictured above at the Sapphire Now 2010 conference.*

the Vietnamese mother who gave her up for adoption 22 years earlier, but in the telling you learn about social and political history during the last years of the Vietnam War.

An interesting example of a film with a less apparent train is *An Inconvenient Truth*. The film is reportedly built around a PowerPoint presentation developed by former Vice President Al Gore and presented by him to a range of audiences. We see him on a lecture tour, and these speeches (and voice-overs) are intercut with sync and voice-over from a more introspective conversation Gore had with filmmaker Davis Guggenheim about his life, career, and family. The train of this film doesn't come from the subject of global climate change, nor did the filmmakers build a train around any particular lecture tour itinerary. The train builds from Gore's first words, "I used to be the next president of the United States." The personal, introspective essay about Gore drives this film, although in terms of screen time and import, it takes a backseat to the warnings about global warming.

A good exercise is to watch a number of successful documentaries that are very different in subject and style and see if you can identify the train. You also might want to see if, given the same subject and story, you could find another train. How might it change the film's look? Length? Effectiveness?

# THEME

In literary terms, *theme* is the general underlying subject of a specific story, a recurring idea that often illuminates an aspect of the human condition. *Eyes on the Prize*, in 14 hours, tells an overarching story of America's civil rights struggle. The underlying themes include race, poverty, and the power of ordinary people to accomplish extraordinary change. Themes in *The Day after Trinity*, the story of J. Robert Oppenheimer's development of the atomic bomb, include scientific ambition, the quest for power, and efforts to ensure peace and disarmament when both may be too late.

The best documentary stories, like memorable literary novels or thought-provoking dramatic features, not only engage the audience with an immediate story—one grounded in plot and character—but with themes that resonate beyond the particulars of the event being told. *Sound and Fury*, for example, is not only about a little girl and her family trying to decide if she should have an operation that might enable her to hear, it's also about universal issues of identity, belonging, and family.

"Theme is the most basic lifeblood of a film," says filmmaker Ric Burns, "Theme tells you the tenor of your story. *This* is what this thing is about." Burns chose to tell the story of the ill-fated Donner Party and their attempt to take a shortcut to California in 1846, not because the cannibalism they resorted to would appeal to prurient viewers but because their story illuminated themes and vulnerabilities in the American character. These themes are foreshadowed in the film's opening quote from Alexis de Tocqueville, a French author who toured the United States in 1831. He wrote of the "feverish ardor" with which Americans pursue prosperity, the "shadowy suspicion that they may not have chosen the shortest route to get it," and the way in which they "cleave to the things of this world," even though death steps in, in the end. These words presage the fate of the Donner Party, whose ambitious pursuit of a new life in California will have tragic consequences.

# ARC

The *arc* refers to the way or ways in which the events of the story transform your characters. An overworked executive learns that his family should come first; a mousy secretary stands up for himself and takes over the company; a rag-tag group of kids that nobody ever notices wins the national chess tournament. In pursuing a goal, the protagonists learn something about themselves and their place in the world, and those lessons change them—and may, in fact, change their desire for the goal.

In documentary films, story arcs can be hard to find. Never, simply in the interest of a good story, presume to know what a character is thinking or feeling. Only present evidence of an arc if it can be substantiated by factual evidence. For example, in *The Day after Trinity*, physicist J. Robert Oppenheimer, a left-leaning intellectual, successfully develops the world's first nuclear weapons and is then horrified by the destructive powers he's helped to unleash. He spends the rest of his life trying to stop the spread of nuclear weapons and in the process falls victim to the Cold War he helped to launch; once hailed as an American hero, he is accused of being a Soviet spy.

Figure 1.3. As a child, George Donner, above, was trapped with his family in the Sierra Nevada Mountains in 1847. Filmmaker Ric Burns chose to tell the story of the ill-fated Donner Party in his documentary.

In *The Thin Blue Line*, we hear and see multiple versions of a story that begins when Randall Adams's car breaks down on a Saturday night and a teenager named David Harris offers him a ride. Later that night, a police officer is shot and killed by someone driving Harris's car, and Adams is charged with the murder. The deeper we become immersed in the case, the more clearly we see that Adams's imprisonment and subsequent conviction are about politics, not justice. He is transformed from a free man to a convicted felon, and that transformation challenges the viewer's assumptions about justice and the basic notion that individuals are innocent until proven guilty.

In *Murderball*, a documentary about quadriplegic athletes who compete internationally in wheelchair rugby, a few characters undergo transformations that together complement the overall film. There's Joe Soares, a hard-driving American champion now coaching for Canada, whose relationship with his son changes noticeably after he suffers a heart attack. Player Mark Zupan comes to terms with the friend who was at the wheel during the accident in which he was injured. And Keith Cavill, recently injured, adjusts to his new life and even explores wheelchair rugby. All of these transformations occurred over the course of filming, and the filmmakers made sure they had the visual material they needed to show them in a way that felt organic and unforced.

## PLOT AND CHARACTER

Films are often described as either plot or character driven. A *character-driven* film is one in which the action of the film emerges from the wants and needs of the characters. In a *plot-driven* film, the characters are secondary to the events that make up the plot. (Many thrillers and action movies are plot driven.) In documentary, both types of films exist, and there is much gray area between them. Errol Morris's *The Thin Blue Line* imitates a plot-driven noir thriller in its exploration of the casual encounter that leaves Randall Adams facing the death penalty. Circumstances act *upon* Adams; he doesn't set the plot in motion except inadvertently, when his car breaks down and he accepts a ride from David Harris. In fact, part of the film's power comes from Adams's inability to alter events, even as it becomes apparent that Harris, not Adams, is likely to be the killer.

In contrast, *Daughter from Danang* is driven by the wants of its main character, Heidi Bub, who was born in Vietnam and given up for adoption. Raised in Tennessee and taught to deny her Asian heritage, Bub is now estranged from her adoptive mother. She sets the events of the film in motion when she decides to reunite with her birth mother.

As in these two examples, the difference between plot-and character-driven films can be subtle, and one often has strong elements of the other. The characters in *The Thin Blue Line* are distinct and memorable; the plot in *Daughter from Danang* is strong and takes unexpected turns. It's also true that plenty of memorable documentaries are not "driven" at all in the Hollywood sense. *When the Levees Broke*, a four-hour documentary about New Orleans during and after Hurricane Katrina, generally follows the chronology of events that devastated a city and its people. As described by supervising editor and co-producer Sam Pollard, there is a narrative arc to each hour and to the series. But the complexity of the four-hour film and its interweaving of dozens of individual stories, rather than a select few, differentiate it from a more traditional form of narrative.

Some films present a "slice of life" portrait of people or places. With shorter films, this may be enough, particularly if there is humor involved. *Where Did You Get That Woman?*, for example, offers a portrait of a Chicago washroom attendant, and in the light-hearted *Gefilte Fish*, three generations of women explain how they prepare a traditional holiday dish. (The third generation, the filmmaker, unscrews a jar.) With longer films of this type, there still needs to be some overarching structure. Frederick Wiseman's documentaries are

Figure 1.4. Errol Morris, pictured above at a Question & Answer session in Morristown, New Jersey, imitates a plot-driven noir thriller in his documentary The Thin Blue Line.

elegantly structured but not "plotted" in the sense that each sequence makes the next one inevitable, but there is usually an organizing principle behind his work, such as a "year in the life" of an institution. Still other films are driven not by characters or plot but by questions, following an essay-like structure (employed, for example, by Michael Moore in *Fahrenheit 9/11*). Some films merge styles: *Super Size Me* is built around the filmmaker's 30-day McDonald's diet, but to a large extent the film is actually driven by a series of questions, making it an essay.

## DRAMATIC STORYTELLING

Because *dramatic* storytelling often refers more specifically to character-driven stories, it's worth looking at some of the basic elements that make these stories work. As set out by authors David Howard and Edward Mabley in their book, *The Tools of Screenwriting*, these are:

- The story is about *somebody* with whom we have some empathy.
- This somebody wants *something* very badly.
- This something is *difficult*—but possible—to do, get, or achieve.
- The story is told for maximum *emotional impact* and *audience participation* in the proceedings.
- The story must come to a *satisfactory ending* (which does not necessarily mean a happy ending).

Figure 1.5. TV crews shooting a documentary follows the same dramatic storytelling constructs that a narrative production crew might follow, including the search for maximum emotional impact and audience participation.

Although Howard and Mabley's book is directed at dramatic screenwriters, the list is useful for documentary storytellers as well. Your particular film subject or situation might not fit neatly within these parameters, so further explanation follows.

## Who (or What) the Story is About

The *somebody* is your protagonist, your hero, the entity whose story is being told. Note that your hero can, in fact, be very "unheroic," and the audience might struggle to empathize with him or her. But the character and/or character's mission should be compelling enough that the audience cares about the outcome. In *The Execution of Wanda Jean*, for example, Liz Garbus offers a sympathetic but unsparing portrait of a woman on death row for murder.

The central character doesn't need to be a person. In Ric Burns's *New York*, a seven-episode history, for example, the city itself is the protagonist, whose fortunes rise and fall and rise over the

Figure 1.6. *Producer Denise Green explores the Black Arts Movement of the 1960s by viewing it through the eyes and experience of Pulitzer Prize–winning poet Gwendolyn Brooks, pictured above at the Miami Book Fair International in 1985.*

course of the series. But often, finding a central character through which to tell your story can make an otherwise complex topic more manageable and accessible to viewers. We see this strategy used in *I'll Make Me a World*, a six-hour history of African-American arts in the 20th century. For example, producer Denise Green explores the Black Arts Movement of the 1960s by viewing it through the eyes and experience of Pulitzer Prize–winning poet Gwendolyn Brooks, an established, middle-aged author whose life and work were transformed by her interactions with younger artists who'd been influenced by the call for Black Power.

## What the Protagonist Wants

The *something* that somebody wants is also referred to as a goal or an objective. In *Blue Vinyl*, filmmaker Judith Helfand sets out, on camera, to convince her parents to remove the new siding from their home. Note that a filmmaker's on-screen presence doesn't necessarily make him or her the protagonist. In Steven Ascher and Jeanne Jordan's *Troublesome Creek: A Midwestern*, the filmmakers travel to Iowa, where Jeanne's family is working to save their farm from foreclosure. Jeanne is the film's narrator, but the protagonists are her parents, Russel and Mary Jane Jordan. It's their goal—to pay off their debt by auctioning off their belongings—that drives the film's story.

### Active Versus Passive

Storytellers speak of active versus passive goals and active versus passive heroes. In general, you want a story's goals and heroes to be active, which means that you want your story's protagonist to be in charge of his or her own life: To set a goal and then to go about doing what needs to be done to achieve it. A passive goal is something like this: A secretary wants a raise in order to pay for breast enhancement surgery. She is passively waiting for the raise, hoping someone will notice that her work merits reward. To be active, she would have to do something to ensure that she gets that raise, or she would have to wage a campaign to raise the extra money she needs for the surgery, such as taking a second job. Not all passivity is bad: Randall Adams, locked up on death row, is a passive protagonist because he can't do anything, which is part of what makes the story so compelling. In general, though, you want your protagonist to be active, and you want him or her to have a goal that's worthy. In the example of the secretary, will an audience really care whether or not she gets larger breasts? Probably not. If we had a reason to be sympathetic—she had been disfigured in an accident, for example—maybe we would care, but it's not a very strong goal. Worthy does not mean a goal has to be noble—it doesn't all have to be about ending world hunger or ensuring world peace. It does have to matter enough to be worth committing significant time and resources to. If you only care a little about your protagonists and what they want, your financiers and audience are likely to care not at all.

## Difficulty and Tangibility

The something that is wanted—the goal—must be *difficult* to do or achieve. If something is easy, there's no tension, and without tension, there's little incentive for an audience to keep watching. Tension is the feeling we get when issues or events are unresolved, especially when we want them to be resolved. It's what motivates us to demand, "And then what happens? And what happens after *that*?" We need to know, because it makes us uncomfortable *not* to know. Think of a movie thriller in which you're aware, but the heroine is not, that danger lurks in the cellar. As she heads toward the steps, you feel escalating tension because she is walking *toward* danger. If you didn't know that the bad guy was in the basement, she would just be a girl heading down some stairs. Without tension, a story feels flat; you don't care one way or the other about the outcome.

So where do you find the tension? One solution is through conflict, defined as a struggle between opposing forces. In other words, your protagonist is up against someone (often referred to as the *antagonist* or *opponent*) or something (the *opposition*). In Barbara Kopple's *Harlan County, U.S.A.*, for example, striking miners are in conflict with mine owners. In Heidi Ewing and Rachel Grady's *The Boys of Baraka*, the tension comes from knowing that the odds of an education, or even a future that doesn't involve prison or death, are stacked against a group of African-American boys from inner-city Baltimore. When a small group of boys is given an opportunity to attend school in Kenya as a means of getting fast-tracked to better high schools in Baltimore, we want them to succeed and are devastated when things seem to fall apart.

Note that conflict can mean a direct argument between two sides, pro and con (or "he said, she said"). But such an argument can also weaken tension, especially if each side is talking past the other or if individuals in conflict have not been properly established. If the audience goes into an argument caring about the individuals involved, though, it can lead to powerful emotional storytelling. Near the end of *Daughter from Danang*, the joyful reunion between the American adoptee and her Vietnamese family gives way to feelings of anger and betrayal brought on by the family's request for money. The palpable tension the audience feels stems not from taking one side or another in the argument, but from empathy for both sides.

Weather, illness, war, self-doubt, inexperience, hubris—all of these can pose obstacles as your protagonist strives to achieve his or her goal. And just as it can be useful to find an individual (or individuals) through whom to tell a complex story, it can be useful to personify the opposition.

Figure 1.7. *Film actor and former president and spokesman of the NRA Charlton Heston becomes filmmaker Michael Moore's antagonist (or vice versa) in Moore's controversial documentary* Bowling for Columbine.

Television viewers in the 1960s, for example, at times seemed better able to understand the injustices of southern segregation when reporters focused on the actions of individuals like Birmingham (Alabama) Police Chief Bull Connor, who turned police dogs and fire hoses on young African Americans as they engaged in peaceful protest.

## Worthy Opponent

Just as you want your protagonist to have a worthy goal, you want him or her to have a worthy opponent. A common problem for many filmmakers is that they portray opponents as one-dimensional; if their hero is good, the opponent must be bad. In fact, the most memorable opponent is often not the opposite of the hero, but a complement to him or her. In the film *Sound and Fury*, young Heather's parents oppose her wishes for a cochlear implant not out of malice but out of their deep love for her and their strong commitment to the Deaf culture into which they and their daughter were born. Chicago Mayor Richard Daley was a challenging opponent for Dr. Martin Luther King, Jr., in *Eyes on the Prize* specifically because he *wasn't* Bull Connor; Daley was a savvy northern politician with close ties to the national Democratic Party and a supporter of the southern-based civil rights movement. The story of his efforts to impede Dr. King's campaign for open housing in Chicago in 1966 proved effective at underscoring the significant differences between using nonviolence as a strategy against *de jure* segregation in the South and using it against *de facto* segregation in the North.

Note here, and throughout, that you are not in any way *fictionalizing* characters who are real human beings. You are evaluating a situation from the perspective of a storyteller, and working with what is there. If there is no opponent, you can't manufacture one. Mayor Daley, historically speaking, was an effective opponent. Had he welcomed King with open arms and been little more than an inconvenience to the movement, it would have been dishonest to portray him as a significant obstacle.

Remember that the opposition does not have to have a human face. In *The Boys of Baraka*, the goals of the boys, their families, and their supporters are threatened by societal pressures in Baltimore and by political instability in Kenya, which ultimately puts the Baraka program in jeopardy. In *Born into Brothels*, similarly, efforts to save a handful of children are threatened by societal pressures (including not only economic hardship but also the wishes of family members who don't share the filmmakers' commitment to removing children from their unstable homes), and by the fact that the ultimate decision makers, in a few cases, are the children themselves. The audience experiences frustration—and perhaps recognition—as some of these children make choices that in the long run are likely to have significant consequences.

## Tangible Goal

Although difficult, the goal should be *possible* to do or achieve, which means that it's best if it's both concrete and realistic. "Fighting racism" or "curing cancer" or "raising awareness of a disease" may all be worthwhile, but none is specific enough to serve as a story objective. Follow your interests, but seek out a specific story that will illuminate it. *The Boys of Baraka* is clearly an indictment of racism and inequality, but it is more specifically the story of a handful of boys and their enrollment in a two-year program at a tiny school in Kenya. *Born into Brothels* illuminates the difficult circumstances facing the children of impoverished sex workers in Calcutta, but the story's goals are more tangible. Initially, we learn that filmmaker Zana Briski, in Calcutta to photograph sex workers, has been drawn to their children. "They wanted to learn how to use the camera," she says in voice-over. "That's when I thought it would be really great to teach them, and to see this world through their eyes." Several minutes later, a larger but still tangible goal emerges: "They have absolutely no opportunity without education," she says. "The question is, can I find a school—a good school—that will take kids that are children of prostitutes?" This, then, becomes the real goal of the film, one enriched by

Figure 1.8. Zana Briski, pictured above working on a recent project in Japan, uses tangible goals to discuss broader societal problems in her documentaries.

the children's photography and exposure to broader horizons.

Note also that the goal is not necessarily the most "dramatic" or obvious one. In Kate Davis's *Southern Comfort*, a film about a transgendered male dying of ovarian cancer, Robert Eads's goal is not to find a cure; it's to survive long enough to attend the Southern Comfort Conference in Atlanta, a national gathering of transgendered people, with his girlfriend, Lola, who is also transgendered.

## Emotional Impact and Audience Participation

The concept of telling a story for greatest *emotional impact* and *audience participation* is perhaps the most difficult. It's often described as "show, don't tell," which means that you want to present the evidence or information that allows viewers to experience the story for themselves, anticipating twists and turns and following the story line in a way that's active rather than passive. Too often, films tell us what we're supposed to think through the use of heavy-handed narration, loaded graphics, or a stacked deck of interviews.

Think about the experience of being completely held by a film. You aren't *watching* characters on screen; you're right there with them, bringing the clues you've seen so far to the story as it unfolds. You lose track of time as you try to anticipate what happens next, who will do what, and what will be learned. It's human nature to try to make sense of the events we're confronted with, and it's human nature to enjoy being stumped or surprised. In *Enron: The Smartest Guys in the Room*, you think Enron's hit bottom, that all of the price manipulation has finally caught up with them and they'll be buried in debt—until someone at Enron realizes that there's gold in California's power grid.

Telling a story for emotional impact means that the filmmaker is structuring the story so that the moments of conflict, climax, and resolution—moments of achievement, loss, reversal, etc.—adhere as well as possible to the internal rhythms of storytelling. Audiences expect that the tension in a story will escalate as the story moves toward its conclusion; scenes tend to get shorter, action tighter, the stakes higher. As we get to know the characters and understand their wants and needs, we care more about what happens to them; we become invested in their stories. Much of this structuring takes place in the editing room. But to some extent, it also takes place as you film, and planning for it can make a difference. Knowing that as Heidi Bub got off the airplane in Danang she'd be greeted by a birth mother she hadn't seen in 20 years, what preparations did the filmmakers need to make to be sure they got that moment on film? What might they shoot if they wanted to build up to that moment, either before or after it actually occurred? (They shot an interview with Heidi and filmed her, a "fish out of water," as she spent a bit of time in Vietnam before meeting with her mother.) In the edited film, by the time Heidi sees her mother, we realize (before she does) how fully Americanized she's become and how foreign her family will seem. We also know that the expectations both she and her birth mother have for this meeting are very high.

You want to avoid creating unnecessary drama—turning a perfectly good story into a soap opera. There's no reason to pull in additional details, however sad or frightening, when they aren't relevant. If you're telling the story of a scientist unlocking the genetic code to a certain mental illness, for example, it's not necessarily important that she's also engaged in a custody battle with her former husband, even if this detail seems to spice up the drama or, you hope, make the character more "sympathetic." If the custody battle is influenced by her husband's mental illness and her concerns that the children may have inherited the disease, there is a link that could serve the film well. Otherwise, you risk adding a layer of detail that detracts, rather than adds.

False emotion—hyped-up music and sound effects and narration that warns of danger around every corner—is a common problem, especially on television. As in the story of the boy who cried wolf, at some point it all washes over the viewer like so much noise. If the danger is real, it will have the greatest storytelling impact if it emerges organically from the material.

### Raising the Stakes

Another tool of emotional storytelling is to have something at stake and to raise the stakes until the very end. Look at the beginning of *Control Room*. The film intercuts story cards (text on screen) with images of everyday life. The cards read: *March 2003 / The United States and Iraq are on the brink of war./Al Jazeera Satellite Channel will broadcast the war ... / to forty million Arab viewers. / The Arab world watches ... / and waits. / CONTROL ROOM.* Clearly, these stakes are high.

The stakes may also be very personal. In both *My Architect* and *Why He Skied*, for example, the filmmaker sets out to understand the death and life of a close relative. Or the stakes may affect the audience directly: This was the argument driving *An Inconvenient Truth*, Al Gore's presentation about the threat of global climate change. In the hands of a good storyteller, even small stakes can be made large when their importance to those in the story is conveyed. For example, how many people in America—or beyond, for that matter—really care who wins or loses the National Spelling Bee, held each year in Washington, D.C.? But to the handful of children competing in *Spellbound*, and to their families and communities, the contest is all-important. Through skillful storytelling, the filmmakers make us care not only about these kids but about the competition, and as the field narrows, we can't turn away.

Stakes may rise because (genuine) danger is increasing, or time is running out. In *Sound and Fury*, for example, the stakes rise as time passes, because for a child born deaf, a cochlear implant is most effective if implanted while language skills are being developed. How do the filmmakers convey this? We see Heather's much younger cousin get the implant and begin to acquire spoken language skills; we also learn that Heather's mother, born deaf, would now get little benefit from the device. As Heather enrolls in a school for the deaf without getting an implant, we understand that the decision has lifelong implications.

## A Satisfactory Ending

A satisfactory ending, or resolution, is often one that feels both unexpected and inevitable. It must resolve the one story you set out to tell. Say you start the film with a problem: A little girl has a life threatening heart condition for which there is no known surgical treatment. Your film then goes into the world of experimental surgery, where you find a charismatic doctor whose efforts to solve a very different medical problem have led him to create a surgical solution that might work in the little girl's situation. To end on this surgical breakthrough, however, won't be satisfactory. Audiences were drawn into the story of the little girl, and this surgeon's work must ultimately be related to that story. Can his work make a difference in her case? You need to complete the story with which the film began.

Note that there is never just one correct ending. Suppose, for example, that your film is due to be aired months before the approval is granted that will allow doctors to try the experimental surgery on the girl. Make *that* your ending, and leave the audience with the knowledge that everyone is praying and hoping that she will survive until then. Or perhaps the surgery is possible, but at the last minute the parents decide it's too risky. Or they take that risk, and the outcome is positive. Or negative. Or perhaps the doctor's breakthrough simply comes too late for this one child but may make a difference for hundreds of others. Any of these would be a satisfactory ending, provided it is factual. It would be unethical to manipulate the facts to imply a "stronger" or more emotional ending that misrepresents what you know the outcome to be. Suppose, for example, that the parents have already decided that no matter how much success the experimental work is having, they will not allow their daughter to undergo any further operations. You cannot imply that this remains an open question (e.g., with a teaser such as "Whether the operation will save the life of little Candy is yet to be seen.").

Ending a film in a way that's satisfying does not necessitate wrapping up all loose ends or resolving things in a way that's upbeat. The end of *Daughter from Danang* is powerful precisely because things remain unsettled; Heidi Bub has achieved the goal of meeting her birth mother, but even two years after her visit, she remains deeply ambivalent about continued contact. At the end of *The Thin Blue Line*, Randall Adams remains a convicted murderer on death row, even as filmmaker Errol Morris erases any lingering doubts the audience might have as to his innocence.

# Interactivity and Its Effects

## By Carolyn Handler Miller

### WHAT IS INTERACTIVITY?

Without interactivity, digital entertainment would simply be a duplicate of traditional entertainment, except that the medium in which it is presented, such as video or audio, would be in a digital form rather than an analog form. To the audience member or listener, however, the difference would be minimal except perhaps in the quality of the picture or sound. Essentially, the experience of "consuming" the entertainment would be exactly the same.

It is interactivity that makes digital media such a completely different animal from traditional storytelling media, like movies, television, and novels. Traditional stories, no matter how they are told—whether recited orally by a shaman, printed in a book, or projected on a movie screen—have certain universal qualities. They are narrations that employ fictional characters and fictional events to depict a dramatic situation from its inception to its conclusion. Interactivity, however, profoundly changes the core material, and profoundly changes the experience of those who are the receivers of it.

We've all probably heard and used the word "interactivity" hundreds, even thousands, of times. Because of overuse, the word has lost its fresh edge, somewhat like a kitchen knife that has grown dull because it's been utilized so often. Let's take a moment to consider what interactivity means and what it does.

When you stop to think about it, interactivity is one of only two possible ways of relating to content; the other way is to relate to it passively. If you are passively enjoying a form of entertainment, you are doing nothing more than watching, listening, or reading. But if you are experiencing an interactive form of content, you are directly involved with the material; you are a participant. You can manipulate, explore, or influence it in one of a variety of ways.

*Figure 2.1. Interactivity that makes digital media a completely different animal from traditional storytelling media, like movies, television, and novels.*

As the word "interactive" indicates, it is an active experience. You are doing something. And the prefix "inter" means "between," telling us that we are talking about an active relationship between the user and the content. It is a two-way exchange. You do something; the content reacts to what you've done. Or the content demands something from you, and you respond in some way.

## INTERACTIVITY AS DIALOGUE

This dynamic of action-response is something like a conversation, a resemblance that interactive designer Greg Roach pointed out to me during a conversation about the nature of interactivity. Roach is CEO of HyperBole Studios, the company that made such award-winning games as *The X-Files Game* and *Quantum Gate*. He's considered a digital media pioneer, and has given a great deal of thought to the subject of interactivity. "Interactivity is fundamentally a dialogue between a user and the material," he noted. "The user provides the input; the input is responded to." He compared the act of designing interactivity to the act of writing a sentence in a language like English, which uses the grammatical structure of a subject, object, and verb. As an example, he used a simple interactive scene in which you give your character a gun. The interactive "sentence" would be: he (the subject) can shoot (the verb) another character (the object). Carrying Roach's grammatical analogy a step further, the sentences you construct in interactive media use the active voice, and are not weighed down by descriptive phrases. ("He watered his horse" rather than "he was seen leading his dusty old horse down to the rocky creek, where he encouraged it to drink.") These interactive sentences are short and to the point, far more like Hemingway than Faulkner.

*Figure 2.2. Screenshot of Nexuiz, a 3D first-person shooter. Some designers complain that the most common verb set (walk, run, turn, jump, pick up, and shoot) restricts their ability to create more diverse and robust works of interactive entertainment. What do you think?*

Roach is not alone in using grammatical terms to talk about interactivity. Many game designers use the phrase "verb set" in referring to the actions that can be performed in an interactive work. The verb set of a game consists of all the things players can make their characters do. The most common verbs are walk, run, turn, jump, pick up, and shoot. A number of designers complain that the standard verb set is too limited, restricting their ability to create more diverse and robust works of interactive entertainment.

## LEAN BACK VERSUS LEAN FORWARD

Passive entertainment and interactive entertainment are often referred to as "lean back" and "lean forward" experiences, respectively. With a passive form of entertainment like a movie or stage play, you are reclining back in your seat, letting the drama come to you. But with an interactive work—a video game or a MMOG, for instance—you are leaning forward toward the screen, controlling the action with your joystick or keypad.

What the audience does or does not do in terms of relating to the material is one of the most profound differences between interactive and passive entertainment. This relationship is so dissimilar, in fact, that we rarely even use the word "audience" when we are talking about those who are experiencing an interactive work. Instead, we may call upon one of several words to describe this person. If we're talking about someone playing a video game, we will probably refer to the person as a "player" or "gamer," while if a person is surfing the Net, we often use the term "visitor." For simulations and immersive environments, we often call the person a "participant." Some professionals also use the general term "interactor" or another all-purpose word, "user." More often than not, we talk about such people in the singular rather than in the plural. This is probably because each individual journeys through the interactive environment as a solo traveler, and each route through the material is unique to that person.

Because each user is in control of his or her own journey through the material, interactivity can never truly be a mass audience experience. This is the case even when thousands of people are simultaneously participating in an interactive work, as they may be doing with a MMOG or an iTV show. Think how different this is from how a movie or TV audience partakes of a particular narrative. Audience members watch the same unvarying story unfold simultaneously with hundreds—or even millions—of other viewers. Of course, each member of the audience is running the story through his or her own personal filter and is probably having a somewhat different emotional response to the material. Yet no matter how intensely people might be reacting, there is nothing any member of the audience can do to alter a single beat of the tale.

The users/players/visitors who participate in interactive entertainments are given two gifts that are never offered to audiences of passive entertainments: choice and control. They get to choose what to see and do within an interactive work, and the decisions they make control what happens. Less than fifty years ago, such freedom to manipulate a work of entertainment would have been unimaginable.

Unfortunately, liberty always comes with a price. In the case of interactive media, it is we, the members of the creative team, who must pay it. In traditional forms of entertainment, the creator—usually the writer—has God-like powers over the narrative. The writer gets to choose who the characters are, what they are like, and what they do. And the writer controls what happens to them. But in an interactive work, this kind of God-like control over the material must be relinquished and turned over to those individuals who, had this been a piece of traditional entertainment, would have been in your thrall: the audience. Of course, there are trade-offs. Even though we must give up the ability to devise a fixed narrative path and fixed characters, we now have the opportunity to work on a far vaster canvas than in previous media, and with materials never before available.

## IMMERSION

One of the hallmarks of a successful interactive production is that it envelopes the user in a rich, fully-involving environment. The user interacts with the virtual world and the characters and objects within it in many ways and on many levels. Interactivity stimulates as many of the five senses as possible: hearing, seeing, touching—and, in some virtual reality environments, even smelling. (No one seems to have worked out a way yet to involve the fifth sense, tasting.) In other words, the experience is immersive. It catches you up in ways that passive forms of entertainment can never do.

*Figure 2.3. Interactivity stimulates as many of the five senses as possible. Lt. Comdr. Cassidy, center, practices docking the space shuttle with his shuttle commander and pilot in a virtual reality simulator at Johnson Space Center.*

This point was brought home to me by an experience I had during a Christmas season when I was temporarily living in Santa Fe, New Mexico. I'd heard about the city's traditional holiday procession called *Las Posadas*, and I wanted to see it for myself.

*Las Posadas* originated in medieval Spain as a nativity passion play and was brought to New Mexico about 400 years ago by the Spanish missionaries. They felt *Las Posadas* would be a simple and dramatic way to ignite the religious spirit of the local Pueblo Indians, and hopefully turn them into good Catholics.

*Las Posadas*, which is Spanish for "the inns," recreates the Biblical story of Mary and Joseph's search for a place to spend the night and where Mary can give birth. It is performed with different variations in towns all over the Southwest and Mexico, but the basic elements remain the same. In Santa Fe, the procession takes place around the historic town plaza. Mary and Joseph, accompanied by a group of musicians and carolers, go from building to building asking for admittance, but each time the devil appears and denies them entrance, until at last they find a place that will receive them.

On the evening of Santa Fe's *Las Posadas*, my husband and I waited in the crowd with the other spectators, all of us holding candles and shivering in the icy night air, waiting for the event to begin. Finally the first marchers appeared, accompanied by men holding torches to light the way. Mary and Joseph followed, with a group of carolers around them. The group paused in front of a building not far from us and all proceeded to sing the traditional song which pleads for lodging. The devil popped up from a hiding place on the roof and scornfully sang his song of refusal. It was very colorful, very different from anything I'd seen back home in southern California, and I was glad we had come.

By participating in a traditional event like this, one can experience the powerful nature of immersiveness. Photograph by Kathy De La Torre of the *Santa Fe New Mexican*, courtesy of the *Santa Fe New Mexican*.

But then I noticed that a number of people were breaking away from the throng of bystanders and joining in the procession. Spontaneously, I pulled my startled husband into the street after them. In a flash, we went from being observers to being participants, and began to experience *Las Posadas* in an entirely different way. Marching with the procession, we became part of the drama, too, and fully immersed in it.

For the hour or so that it lasted, I became someone else. No longer was I a twenty-first century Jewish writer. I became a pious Catholic pilgrim transported back to a wintry medieval Spanish village. Some of this I experienced on a personal and physical level: I had to watch my step, taking care not to slip on a patch of ice or trip on a curb or get ahead of the Holy Family. I was aware of the scent of burning candles all around me, and the press of the crowd. Much of the experience was emotional and communal: My husband and I would do our best to sing along with the carolers and Holy Family when it came time to ask for a room at the inn. Whenever the devil would appear on a rooftop or balcony, we would join in the hearty boos and derisive shouts of the processioners. The best moment came when Mary and Joseph stopped in front of the heavy gates of the historic Palace of the Governors, the former seat of New Mexico's Colonial government. Once again we all sang the imploring song, but this time the gates swung open! A joyous cheer went up from the processioners, our voice among them, and we all surged into the courtyard. Welcoming bonfires and cups of hot cocoa awaited us Becoming part of *Las Posadas* instead of merely observing it transformed the experience for me. It was like the difference between watching a movie and suddenly becoming a character in it. To me, it vividly demonstrated the power of immersiveness—one of the most compelling and magical aspects of interactive media.

## TYPES OF INTERACTIVITY

The player/user/visitor can interact with digital content in a variety of ways, and different types of interactive media lend themselves to different types of interactivity. For instance, the Internet is particularly good at providing opportunities to communicate with other users; smart toys excel at offering one-on-one play experiences; wireless devices do well at engaging users in short bursts of text or visuals. Each of the interactive media has its limitations, as well. In an immersive environment, a participant's ability to control objects may be limited. Game consoles, unless connected to the Internet, are restricted to just a few players at a time. Interactive TV, at least for now, does not lend itself to interactions with fictional characters or with participating in a

*Figure 2.4. Six basic types of interactivity can be found in almost every form of interactive entertainment, including the one shown here, created in DX Studio.*

narrative story. When it comes to the types of interactivity offered by the various digital media, no one size fits all.

That said, however, six basic types of interactivity can be found in almost every form of interactive entertainment. They are like the basic foodstuffs a good cook always keeps in the pantry, and can be used to make a wide variety of dishes. The basic types of interactivity are

1. The user inputs a stimulus; the program produces a response. The stimulus can be something as simple as clicking on an image and seeing a little animated sequence or hearing a funny sound. Or the user might click on a button and receive a few paragraphs of text information. The stimulus may involve successfully completing a series of steps or solving a puzzle, after which the user is rewarded by the occurrence of some sought-after event: The door to the safe swings open, or a character reveals a secret. The stimulus might also involve a physical act, such as putting a hat on a smart doll. The doll, recognizing the hat, responds with an appropriate comment ("Oh, I just love that pretty pink hat!"). The stimulus-response exchange is a universal component of all interactive programming.

2. The user can move through the program in a free manner; in other words, can choose what to do. Navigation may offer a vast, 3D world to explore, as in a video game or MMOG. Or it may be more limited, restricted to choosing options from a menu offered on a DVD or icons on a website. Navigation, like the stimulus-response exchange, is a universal component of every form of interactive programming.

3. The user can control virtual objects. This includes such things as shooting guns, opening drawers, and moving items from one place to another. While a fairly common form of interactivity, this one is not universal.

4. The user can communicate with other characters, including bots and other human players. Communication can be done via text that the user types in, or via choosing from a dialogue menu, by voice, or by actions (such as squeezing a smart doll's hand). Generally, communication goes both ways—characters or other players can communicate with the user, too. As with #3, it is a common, but not universal form of interactivity.

5. The user can send information. This often involves inputting data into a "community collection box." In turn, the data is generally assembled or tallied and fed back to the users. This form of interactivity is generally found in devices that have a connection to the Internet or to an iTV service.

6. The user can receive or acquire things. The nature of the material can range from virtual to concrete, and the methods of acquiring it can range greatly as well. Users can collect

information (such as news bulletins or medical facts); purchase physical objects (books or clothing); and receive video on demand. They can also collect virtual objects or assets in a game (a magic sword; the ability to fly). This type of interactivity is common in any medium that involves the Internet, wireless services, or iTV, as well as almost all video games.

Using these six basic "ingredients," digital creators can cook up a great diversity of experiences for people to participate in. They include:

1. **Playing games.** There is an almost infinite variety of games users can play: trivia games; adventure games; mysteries; ball games; role-playing games; and so on.
2. **Participating in a fictional narrative.**
3. **Exploring a virtual environment.**
4. **Controlling a simulated vehicle or device:** a fighter jet, a submarine, a space ship, a machine gun.
5. **Creating a character,** including its physical appearance, personality traits, and skills.
6. **Manipulating virtual objects:** changing the color, shape, or size of an object; changing the notes on a piece of music; changing the physical appearance of a room.
7. **Constructing virtual objects** such as houses, clothing, tools, towns, machines, and vehicles.
8. **Taking part in polls,** surveys, voting, tests, and contests.
9. **Interacting with smart physical objects:** dolls, robotic pets, wireless devices, household appliances.
10. **Learning about something.** Interactive learning experiences include edutainment games for children, training programs for employees, and online courses for students.
11. **Playing a role in a simulation,** either for educational purposes or for entertainment.
12. **Setting a virtual clock** or calendar to change, compress, or expand time.
13. **Socializing with others** and participating in a virtual community.
14. **Searching for various types of information** or for clues in a game.

This is by no means an exhaustive list, though it does illustrate the great variety of experiences that interactivity can offer, and the uses to which it can be put.

Figure 2.5. Simulation games are increasingly used for educational purposes for younger and younger audiences.

# HOW INTERACTIVITY IMPACTS CONTENT

These various forms of interacting inevitably affect your content. Users expect to be offered a selection of choices, but by offering them, you give up your ability to tell a linear story or to provide information in a fixed order.

To see how this works, let's compare a linear and interactive version of a familiar story, the Garden of Eden episode from the Bible. The Garden of Eden episode is one of the best-known creation stories in the Western world, and thus seems an appropriate choice to illustrate what happens when you try to adapt a linear story and make it interactive.

As it is handed down in Genesis, the story involves three characters: Adam, Eve, and the serpent. Each of them behaves in exactly the same way no matter how often one reads about them in the Old Testament. And the alluring tree that is the centerpiece of the story is always the Tree of the Knowledge of Good and Evil. God has warned Adam and Eve not to eat its fruit, though they are free to enjoy anything else in the garden. The serpent, however, convinces Eve to sample the forbidden fruit, which she does. She gets Adam to try it, too, at which point they lose their innocence and are expelled from the Garden.

Now let's construct an interactive version of the same story. We'll use the same three characters and the same tree, but offer the player an array of choices. Let's say the tree now offers five kinds of fruit, each with the potential for a different outcome. If Eve picks the pomegranate, for instance, she might immediately become pregnant; if she eats too many cherries, she might get fat; only if she eats the forbidden fruit would the narrative progress toward the results depicted in the Bible.

As for the serpent, let's let the user decide what this character should be: malevolent or kindly, wise or silly. And we'll let the user decide how Eve responds to him, too. She might ignore him, or tell him to get lost, or try to turn him into a docile house pet ... or, she might actually listen to him, as she does in the Bible. We'll give the user a chance to determine the nature of Adam and Eve's exchange, too. Adam might reject Eve's suggestion to try the fruit, or might come up with several suggestions of his own (open up a fruit stand, or make jam out of the tree's cherries). Or they may hotly disagree with each other, resulting in the Bible's first marital spat. Suddenly we have a vast multitude of permutations springing out of a simple story.

Note that all of this complexity comes from merely allowing the player one of several options at various nodes in the story. But what if you gave the players other types of interactive tools? You might

Figure 2.6. *The controversial Grand Theft Auto was one of the first video games to allow players to freely roam the environment in a non-linear fashion.*

allow them the opportunity to explore the entire Garden of Eden and interact with anything in it. They could investigate its rocky grottos, follow paths through the dense foliage, or even snoop around Adam and Eve's private glade. Or what if you turned this into a simulation, and let users design their own Garden of Eden? Or how would it be if you turned this into a role-playing game, and let the user play as Adam, as Eve, or even as the serpent? Or what if you designed this as a community experience, and gave users the chance to vote on whether Eve should be blamed for committing the original sin?

Our simple story is now fragmenting into dozens of pieces. What once progressed in an orderly manner, with a straightforward beginning, middle, and end, has now fallen into total anarchy. If adding interactivity to a simple story like the Garden of Eden can create such chaos, what does it do to a more complex work?

## THE GREAT STORY AND GAME DEBATE

Within the community of interactive media professionals, a vexing question has been batted back and forth for years. The question goes something like this: Is it possible to have a successful work of interactive entertainment that is a pure story and not built on the mechanism of gaming? The question can also be reversed in this way: How much story can you tell in a game? Or even: Is it necessary to have any story components at all to make a good game?

If you examine most interactive works, they are constructed on a gaming model: They involve competition, obstacles, and a goal; achieving the goal is usually a work's driving force. While stories in traditional media use these same elements, they are less obvious, and great attention is placed on other things, such as character development, motivation, the relationship between characters, and so on. Good linear stories also usually have an emotional impact on the audience.

Questions about story and game go to the heart of this book. As digital storytellers, we need to know what kinds of narrations we can construct using interactive tools. It is also important for us to know the similarities and differences between interactive stories and how stories are told in traditional media, such as movies, plays, and novels. And, when we go to create our own digital stories, we need to know which classic narrative tools will still be serviceable, which must be discarded, and what new ones need to be acquired.

## THE DIFFERENCE BETWEEN STORIES AND GAMES

In order to participate in the raging game-story debate, it is helpful to first have a clear grasp of what makes the two forms unique and different from each other, and where they may be alike. Let's hear what a trio of experts has to say about this.

Game designer Greg Roach, introduced earlier in this chapter, has a vivid way of describing what he feels sets stories and games apart. He sees stories and games as two very different types of artifacts—artifacts being objects created by human beings. Roach says, "A story is an artifact you consume and a game is a process you enter into, and create the artifact." In other words, a story is a preconstructed chunk of material, while a game is something more malleable, something that one helps to construct.

Roach regards a linear work like a film as a single artifact, while an interactive work like a game, he says, has "immense granularity." Granularity is a term Roach uses to mean the quality of being composed of many extremely small pieces. "Film is monolithic, like a block of salt," he says, and for interactivity to be possible, the monolith must be busted up into fine pieces. "These granules of information can be character, atmosphere, or action. But if a work is too granular, if the user is inputting constantly, there are no opportunities for story." Roach stresses that in order to have an interactive story, "you must find a balance between granularity and solidarity. You need to find the 'sweet spot'—the best path through the narrative, the one with the optimum number of variables."

Despite the differences between stories and games, Roach believes a middle ground can be found, a place to facilitate story and character development in an interactive environment. As an example, he pointed out that adventure games contain both storytelling and granularity. Roach, like many other game designers and producers, believes that adventure games are the best example of a game genre that is rich in story. Many see adventure games as being on one end of a story/game continuum, with first-person shooters being on the extreme other end in terms of story content. Yet even first-person shooters generally have some sort of story setup to give gamers a context to play in and a goal to strive for, and interactive stories generally have some components of gaming. "When you discard all aspects of gaming, how do you motivate people to move through the narrative?" Roach asked rhetorically. "The fundamental mechanisms of games are valuable because they provide the basic tool sets."

Figure 2.7. *Game designer Greg Roach claims that, "A story is an artifact you consume and a game is a process you enter into, and create the artifact." Do you agree?*

One of the challenges Roach sees in constructing a nongaming interactive story is the task of providing the player with motivation, an incentive to spend time working through the narrative. But he suggests an answer as well. Roach believes that people like to solve problems, the tougher the better, and feels that a major distinction between games and stories is the types of problems they present, plus the tools you can use to solve them. In a game, he suggested, the problem might be getting past the monster on the bridge. In a story, the problem might be getting your son off drugs and into rehabilitation.

As difficult as it may be to construct interactive narratives without relying on game models, Roach feels that creating such stories is not impossible. He says he sees glimmers of such work being produced by students and developers in Europe. There, he says, people take more of a "garage band" approach to creating interactive works, as opposed to the big business approach that dominates software companies in the United States. "I feel confident in saying yes, I have total faith, that interactive media can be a vehicle for fiction," he asserted. And, as we shall see later in this chapter, in the section entitled *Stories That Are Not Games*, we can already find a number of examples of nongaming interactive narratives, and these works are supported by a variety of different platforms.

Figure 2.8. *Game designer Celia Pearce feels that adventure games have done a good job of putting the player in the role of a character. Promotional models at video game trade shows make video game characters even more realistic for the players, and further assist the player in assuming the role of the character.*

## TYING GAMES AND STORIES TOGETHER

Like Greg Roach, game designer Celia Pearce sees similarities between games and stories, as well as certain qualities that tend to push them apart. Pearce, now on the faculty of the University of California at Irvine, and before that, a Visiting Scholar at the University of Southern California, has done a great deal of speaking and writing about interactive media. In an article she wrote for the Winter 2002 issue of *Computers and Graphics*, Pearce suggests that characteristics of games can successfully be tied to a narrative structure. She said this is particularly true if you make " ... the character goal and the player goal synonymous, and motivate the player to move forward the character's agenda, even while discovering what it is." She feels a number of adventure and role-play games have done a good job of putting the player in the role of a character to advance the story. Among her examples are *Resident Evil*, *Deus Ex*, and the *Zelda* and *Final Fantasy* series, as well as earlier games like the Indiana Jones series from LucasArts and the entirely different but enormously popular Myst.

## GAMES AS ABSTRACT STORIES

Janet H. Murray, a faculty member at M.I.T. and the author of one of the best-known books on interactive narrative, *Hamlet on the Holodeck*, takes things a step further than either Roach or

Pearce. She asserts in her book that games and drama are actually quite closely aligned, and that games are really a form of "abstract storytelling."

To underscore the close connection between stories and games, Murray points out that one of our oldest, most pervasive, and popular types of games—the battle between opposing contestants or forces—is also one of the first and most basic forms of drama. The Greeks called this *agon*, for conflict or contest. Murray reminds us that opposition, or the struggle between opposites, is one of the fundamental concepts that we use to interpret the world around us (big/little; boy/girl; good/evil).

Although Murray does not say so explicitly, every writer of screenplays is keenly aware of the importance of opposition, and realizes that unless the hero of the drama is faced with an imposing challenge or opponent, a script will lack energy and interest. For a video game to work, it too must pit opposing forces against each other. Thus, games and dramas utilize the same key dynamic: opposition.

Opposition is not the only way that games and drama are alike, Murray believes. She suggests, in fact, that games "can be experienced as symbolic drama." She holds that games reflect events that we have lived through or have had to deal with, though in a compressed form. When we play a game, she says, we become the protagonist of a symbolic action. Some of the life-based plot lines she feels can be found in games include:

A.  Being faced with an emergency and surviving it;
B.  Taking a risk and being rewarded for acting courageously;
C.  Finding a world that has fallen into ruin and managing to restore it; and, of course,
D.  Being confronted with an imposing antagonist or difficult test of skill and achieving a successful outcome.

Interestingly, Murray finds life-like symbolic dramas even in abstract games—games of chance like throwing dice or playing the lottery, and even in the computer-based puzzle assembly game of *Tetris*. In Tetris, players have to maneuver falling puzzle pieces so they fit together and form a straight row. Each completed row floats off the bottom of the game board, leaving room for still more falling puzzle pieces. "The game is the perfect enactment of the overtasked lives of Americans in the 1990s," she says, "of the constant bombardment of tasks that demand our attention and that we must somehow fit into our overcrowded schedules and clear off our desks in order to make room for the next onslaught."

Games, Murray asserts, give us an opportunity to act out the important conflicts and challenges in our lives, and to create order and harmony where there was messiness and conflict. In many ways, her view of games is much like Joseph Campbell's view of ritual ceremonies—activities that provide us with a way to give meaning to important life experiences and to provide us with emotional release. In its most powerful form, this emotional release is experienced as a catharsis.

## STORIES THAT ARE NOT GAMES

In debating the story/game dichotomy, let us not forget what designer Greg Roach asserted: that it is possible to create interactive stories that are not based on game models. Several different types of interactive stories already exist. One small enclave of such narratives is called, fittingly enough, Interactive Fiction (IF). Works of IF can be found on the Internet and they are also available on CD-ROMs. Though the creators and fans of IF are a fairly small group, often found within academic circles, they are dedicated to advancing this particular form of storytelling.

True works of IF are entirely text-based (although the term is sometimes used for adventure games and other works that are animated or are done on video). To see/read/play a work of IF, you need to be sitting in front of a computer, inputting your commands with a keyboard. The story advances and reveals itself as the user types in commands ("open the door" or "look under the bed" or "ask about the diamond"). Unlike hypertext, you must do more than click on a link; you must devise phrases that will give you the most meaningful and useful reply.

IF stories can be about almost any topic, and can be written in just about any fictional genre, although they work best when the plots call for you to be active, to explore, and to make things happen. They need not be plot driven, however. *Galatea*, written by Emily Short, is an intriguing character sketch that is constructed as a dialogue between the user and a Nonplayer Character (NPC)—a character controlled by the computer. The story is based on the Greek myth of Pygmalion, a sculptor who carves a beautiful statue, Galatea. The statue comes to life after he falls in love with her. It is the same myth that inspired the Broadway hit, *My Fair Lady*. In this interactive version of the myth, you visit the art gallery where *Galatea* is displayed and discover that you are able to talk with her. As you converse with her, you gain insights into her history and troubled emotional state. Her responses to your questions vary, as does her attitude toward you, depending on how you treat her. (See Figure 2.9) *Galatea* won Best of Show at the IF Art Show in 2000.

IF stories resemble text-based adventure games as well as online MUDs and MOOs. Unlike MUDs and MOOs, however, they are played by a single individual rather than with a group. Furthermore, they do not have the win/lose outcomes that are so much a part of adventure games, though they do often include puzzles that must be solved in order to progress. These narratives cannot be as tightly plotted as linear fiction, but they do generally have overarching storylines. Conceivably, the IF genre could be used as a model for interactive stories that are not merely text based, but are told in moving images as well.

Another type of interactive fiction, one that can be found only on the Internet, is the Web soap opera. The most famous of these, *The Spot,* lets users pry into the lives of the fictional characters by reading their journals and poking around elsewhere on the site. *The Spot* provided a two-way experience, giving users the opportunity to communicate back to the show's creators. Their messages often provided ideas for

```
>ask about eyes
"What was it like, having your eyes carved?" you ask.

"He drilled at the corners," she says.  "And that was
agony -- waiting to see whether he would go too deep.  He
never did, but there was always doubt."

>ask about seeing
"When you first begin to see?" you ask.  "Was it when
your eyes were finished, or could you somehow see before
that?"

"Before that," she says.  "Certainly before he began to
drill in the corners.  It was a gradual thing: everything
was dim and shadowed, and it grew brighter and sharper
the closer he came to the surface of my eyes, until I
could recognize colors, and know his face."

>ask about face
She just shrugs.
```

Figure 2.9. *A segment of the IF work* Galatea, *designed and written by Emily Short. It is a character study based on the Greek myth of Pygmalion.*

Figure 2.10. *Other forms of interactive stories can be enjoyed in different settings, such as through animatronic characters at museums or amusement parks.*

plot twists which were then incorporated into future episodes.

*The Spot* might not be high art, but its popularity spawned a wave of imitators and led to successive attempts to tell new kinds of stories on the Web. Some of them have used video and extremely innovative forms of interactivity. A few have incorporated game elements, but many have not.

DVDs are providing one of the newest platforms for interactive narrative. A few digital artists are using DVDs as a vehicle for small screen interactive cinema, and some works of interactive cinema have already been produced for CD-ROMs. How much or how little new stories in this area will lean on game models remains to be seen. One such movie, *Uncompressed*, is a nonlinear drama with six intersecting storylines and contains no gaming elements at all; it is pure nonlinear storytelling. As for large screen interactive movies, the few being made at this time are relying heavily on gaming elements, and also contain robust story content.

But other kinds of interactive stories can be enjoyed in quite different settings. For instance, virtual reality environments and certain types of location based entertainment attractions let you wander through three-dimensional space, interacting with objects you see through a special headset, or with characters projected on a large screen, or with animatronic characters. And a smart doll will tell you a story that is shaped to a large degree on how you interact with her. These interactions are triggered by when and how you use the props and sensors that serve as her cues.

As all these examples illustrate, it is possible to create interactive stories that do not rely on gaming models.

## CONCLUSION

Interactivity, as we have seen, profoundly changes the way we experience a work of entertainment. We go from being a member of the audience to becoming a participant. Instead of passively watching, listening, or reading, we take on an active role. Interactive works are immersive. They involve us in an extremely absorbing and intense way, requiring not only our intellectual attention, but also drawing on most of our senses as well, including sight, hearing, touch, and sometimes even smell.

Interactivity takes many forms, but all of them impact the creator's role in some way: They make the telling of a fixed, sequential, linear story impossible, and have the same effect on the presentation of nonfictional material.

Experts do not see eye to eye on the great story-game controversy, disagreeing on how much story can be told in a game, and whether it is possible to create an engaging interactive story that does not rely on game mechanics. However, we can see that in certain fundamental ways, games and stories are not so very different. Some games certainly have minimal story content, and in some interactive stories, it is difficult to spot anything that is game-like. But in the end, both game mechanisms and story mechanisms play a prominent role in interactive entertainment. Furthermore, they are often used in conjunction with each other. Without either story or game elements, what would make an interactive work entertaining at all? It is hard to imagine how such a work would be able to entice people to participate in it or what about it would keep them connected to the material.

The special qualities of games and stories are equally valuable when it comes to projects that are designed to be more functional—works that marry entertainment to some other task. Such projects are used for education (*edutainment*), information (*infotainment*), and advertising (*advergaming*). They also serve a role in training, promotion, and marketing. Game and story elements can make such interactive works far more palatable to the target users, and more successful at accomplishing their intended mission.

# Influences of Sound on Meaning

## By Stanley R. Alten

Sound influences how we create meaning. While language and the spoken word are in some respects most obvious, nonverbal speech, sound effects, and music also inform our capacity to interpret and understand dramatic intention. The subtleties and nuances of the human voice can communicate more about characters and their motivation than what the words alone might signify. Well-crafted and appropriate sound effects lend realism and convincing illusion to a production while music adds emotional depth and dimension to our experience as an audience.

## CHARACTERISTICS OF SOUND

All sound—speech, sound effects, and music—is made up of the same basic elements: pitch, loudness, timbre, tempo, and rhythm. Furthermore, every sound has its own "life cycle" or sound envelope comprising an attack, duration, and decay. During audio production, everyone involved is dealing with these elements, consciously or subconsciously, and assessing their effects on perception. Because each element contains certain characteristics that affect our response to sound, understanding those effects is fundamental to the art and craft of sound design. The following outlines some of the associations and responses that the different parameters of sound may elicit.

1. *Pitch* refers to the highness or lowness of a sound—its frequency. High-pitched sound often suggests something delicate, bright, or elevated; low-pitched sound may indicate something sinister, strong, or peaceful.

2. *Loudness,* or dynamic range, describes the relative volume of sound—how loud or soft it is. Loud sound can suggest closeness, strength, or importance; soft sound may convey distance, weakness, or tranquility.

3. *Timbre* is the characteristic tonal quality of a sound. It not only identifies a sound source—reedy or brassy—but also sonic qualities such as rich, thin, edgy, or metallic. Reedy tonal qualities produced by a clarinet or an oboe, for example, can suggest something wistful, lonely, or sweet. A brassy sound can imply something cold, harsh, fierce, bitter, forceful, martial, or big.

Figure 3.1. *All sound—regardless of who or what makes the sound—is made up of the same basic elements: pitch, loudness, timbre, tempo, and rhythm. It the combination of these elements—and the sound's attack, duration and decay—that make each sound unique.*

4. *Tempo* refers to the speed or pace of a sound. Fast tempos agitate, excite, or accelerate; slow tempos may suggest monotony, dignity, or control.

5. *Rhythm* relates to a sonic time pattern. It may be simple, constant, complex, or changing. A simple rhythm can convey deliberateness, regularity, or lack of complication. A constant rhythm can imply dullness, depression, or uniformity. Rhythmic complexity suggests intricacy or elaborateness. Changing rhythms can create a sense of uncertainty, vigor, or the erratic.

6. *Attack*—the way a sound begins—can be hard, soft, crisp, or gradual. Hard or crisp attacks can suggest sharpness, excitement, or danger. Soft or gradual attacks can imply something gentle, muted, or blasé.

7. *Duration* refers to how long a sound lasts. Sound short in duration can convey restlessness, nervousness, or excitation; more sustained sounds can create a sense of peace, persistence, or fatigue.

8. *Decay*—how fast a sound fades out—can be quick, gradual, or slow. Quick decays can create a sense of confinement, closeness, or definiteness; slow decays can convey distance, smoothness, or uncertainty.

Of course, these elements are not heard individually but in combination. Other aspects of sound, such as changing pitch, changing loudness, and acoustic interactions, also affect response. That these characteristics are elemental in sonic structure is not to suggest that sound design is prescriptive or developed by applying formulas; the basic components of sound structure do not occur separately but together in myriad forms. Rather, it is to introduce and define the building blocks of sound from which the sound designer shapes aural structure and meaning.

# NONVERBAL SPEECH

For an actor, effectively delivering the words from a page—whether they are in a commercial, documentary, or drama—involves more than just reciting them. It is often not *what* is said but *how* it is said that shapes the meaning. Examples of how nonverbal speech influences meaning include emphasis, inflection, speech patterns, pace, mood, and accent.

## Emphasis

*Emphasis*—stressing a syllable or a word—is important to all speech, whether voiceover, narration, or dialogue. It often conveys the gist of what is said. Consider the question, "What were you thinking?" With no particular emphasis, the question is straightforward and might mean, "What is on your mind?" If, however, any word in the phrase is emphasized, a simple question may become an admonition or an accusation. The words remain the same; the aural emphasis alters the message.

## Inflection

**Inflection**—altering the pitch or tone of the voice—can also influence verbal meaning. By raising the pitch of the voice at the end of a sentence, a declarative statement becomes a question. Put stress on it, and it becomes an exclamation.

## Speech Patterns

*Speech patterns,* cadence, or rhythm are important to natural-sounding speech and creating a believable character. A writer must be equally aware of *what* words mean and *how* they should sound. If the speaker is formal, vocabulary and sentence structure should be precise, and speech rhythms should sound even and businesslike. Informality would sound looser, more relaxed, and more personal.

## Pace

The *pace* or tempo of spoken words can communicate nonverbal information about a character and the emotional tenor of a given situation. Halting, hesitant dialogue conveys a very different sensibility than lines delivered smoothly and slowly or those that are breathless and quick.

*Figure 3.2. Filmmaker David Lynch, pictured here at the Divan du Monde in 2007, has a unique pace and cadence in the way he speaks. Listen to him talk about watching films on your iPhone in this clip: http://www.youtube.com/watch?v=wKiIroiCvZ0*

## Mood

Sound can be evocative and affects the *mood* or feeling of words and sentences. Consider the following line from Keats' *Ode to a Nightingale*, "The murmurous haunt of flies on summer eves."[1] The sounds of the words themselves evoke the din of insects on a summer night.

## Accent

An accent can tell you if a speaker is cultured or crude, a Jamaican from Kingston, or an American from Brooklyn, or someone from China, Spain, or India.

## SOUND EFFECTS

*Sound effects (SFX)* can be classified as anything sonic that is not speech or music. They are essential to storytelling, bringing realism and added dimension to a production. It is worth noting that the art of sound effects design is about creating not only something big or bizarre but also crafting subtle, low-key moments. Good effects are about conveying a compelling illusion. In general, sound effects can be contextual or narrative. These functions are not mutually exclusive; they allow for a range of possibilities in the sonic continuum between what we listen for in dialogue—namely, sound and words to convey meaning—and what we experience more viscerally and emotionally in music.

Figure 3.3. *Sound effects (SFX) can be classified as anything sonic that is not speech or music. Description Foley is the art of recording sound effects in real time to match the picture—as seen here in The Foley Room at the Vancouver Film School.*

### Contextual Sound

*Contextual sound* emanates from and duplicates a sound source as it is. It is often illustrative and also referred to as diegetic sound. The term derives from the Greek, *diegesis,* meaning to tell or recount and, in the context of film, has come to describe what comes from within the story space. If a gun fires, a car drives by, or leaves rustle in the wind, what you see is what you hear; the sound is naturalistic in structure and perspective.

---

1   Sir Arthur Thomas Quiller-Couch, *The Oxford Book of English Verse* (Oxford: Clarendon, 1919, [c1901]); **Bartleby.com, www.bartleby.com,** 1999.

## Narrative Sound

*Narrative sound* adds more to a scene than what is apparent and so performs an informational function. It can be descriptive or commentative.

## Descriptive Sound

As the term suggests, *descriptive sound* describes sonic aspects of a scene, usually those not directly connected with the main action—but key in adding to the compelling nature of the illusion. Descriptive sound for a village scene set in the Middle Ages might include oxcarts lumbering by, the sounds of a tinker repairing a pot, a distant church bell tolling, and the indistinguishable hubbub of human activity in a market square.

**Commentative Sound** also describes, but it makes an additional statement, one that usually has something to do with the story line. For example: An aging veteran wanders through the uniform rows of white crosses in a cemetery. A wind comes up as he pauses before individual markers. The wind is infused with the faint sound of battle, snippets of conversations, laughter, and music as he remembers his fallen comrades.

## Functions of Sound Effects

Sound effects have specific functions in how they influence meaning within the general contextual and narrative categories. They break the screen plane, define space, focus attention, establish locale, create environment, emphasize and intensify action, depict identity, set pace, provide counterpoint, create humor, symbolize meaning, and create metaphor. Paradoxical as it may seem, silence is also a functional sound effect.

## Breaking the Screen Plane

A film or video without sounds, natural or produced, detaches an audience from the onscreen action. The audience becomes an observer, looking at the scene from outside rather than made to feel a part of the action—at the center of an acoustic space. The presence of sound changes the audience relationship to what is happening on screen; it becomes part of the action in a sense. The audience becomes a participant in that there is no longer a separation between the listener-viewer and the screen plane. Therefore, it can also be said that sound effects add realism to the picture.

## Defining Space

Sound defines space by establishing distance, direction of movement, position, openness, and dimension. Distance—how close or far a sound seems to be—is created mainly by relative loudness, or *sound perspective*. The louder a sound, the closer to the listener-viewer it is. Thunder at a low sound level tells you that a storm is some distance away; as the storm moves closer, the thunder grows louder.

## Focusing Attention

In shots, other than close-ups, in which a number of elements are seen at the same time, how do you know where to focus attention? Of course directors compose shots to direct the eye, but the eye can wander. Sound, however, draws attention and provides the viewer with a focus. In a shot of a large room filled with people, the eye takes it all in, but if a person shouts or begins choking, the sound directs the eye to that individual.

## Establishing Locale

Sounds can establish locale. A cawing seagull places you at the ocean; honking car horns and screeching brakes place you in city traffic; the squeak of athletic shoes, the rhythmic slap of a bouncing ball, and the roar of a crowd place you at a basketball game.

## Creating Environment

Establishing locale begins to create an environment, but more brush strokes and textures are often needed to complete the picture. Honky-tonk saloon music may establish the Old West, but sounds of a blacksmith hammering, horses whinnying, wagon wheels rolling, and six-guns firing create environment.

*Figure 3.4. The camera and the microphone do not always have to be recording from the same place. Imagine how you can emphasize space, locale, or action in different ways by altering your sonic and visual recording locations.*

## Emphasizing Action

Sounds can emphasize or highlight action. A person falling down a flight of stairs tumbles all the harder if each bump is accented.

## Intensifying Action

Whereas emphasizing action highlights or calls attention to something important, intensifying action increases or heightens dramatic impact. A car's twisted metal settling in the aftermath of a collision emits an agonized groaning sound. In animation, sound (and music) intensifies the extent of a character's running, falling, crashing, skidding, chomping, and chasing.

## Depicting Identity

Depicting identity is perhaps one of the most obvious uses of sound. Barking identifies a dog, slurred speech identifies a drunk, and so on. But on a more informational level, sound can also give a character or an object its own distinctive sound signature: the rattle sound of a rattlesnake to identify a slippery villain with a venomous intent; thin, clear, hard sounds to convey a cold character devoid of compassion and so on.

## Setting Pace

Sounds, or the lack of them, help set pace. The incessant, even rhythm of a machine creates a steady pace to underscore monotony. The controlled professionalism of two detectives discussing crucial evidence becomes more vital if the activity around them includes such sonic elements as footsteps moving quickly, telephones ringing, papers shuffled, and a general hubbub of voices.

## Providing Counterpoint

Sounds provide counterpoint when they are different from what is expected, thereby making an additional comment on the action. A wounded soldier lying on a bed and looking at a ceiling fan's rotating blades that sound like those of a helicopter suggest the battlefield he has just left.

## Creating Humor

Sounds can be funny. Think of boings, boinks, and plops; the swirling swoops of a pen-nywhistle; the chuga-chugaburp-cough-chuga of a steam engine trying to get started. Comic sounds are indispensable in cartoons in highlighting the shenanigans of their characters.

## Symbolizing Meaning

Sound can be used symbolically. The sound of water swirling down a drain is heard as a murder victim slumps to the floor of a bathtub.

## Creating Metaphor

Sound can create a metaphorical relationship between what is heard and what is seen. A wife leaving her husband after enduring the last straw in a deeply troubled marriage walks out of their house, slamming the door. The sound of the slam has the palpable impact of finality and with it there is a slowly decaying reverberation that reflects a married life that has faded into nothingness.

## Silence

Silence is not generally thought of as sound *per se*—that seems like a

Figure 3.5. Silence is not generally thought of as sound per se, but the silences between words, sounds, and musical notes that help create rhythm, contrast, and power.

contradiction in terms. But it is the pauses or silences between words, sounds, and musical notes that help create rhythm, contrast, and power—elements important to sonic communication.

In situations where we anticipate sound, silence is a particularly powerful element. A horrifying sight compels a scream—but with the mouth wide open there is only silence, suggesting an unspeakable horror. The silence preceding sound is equally effective. A pistol shot breaks the quiet of winter night. Similarly, silence can be dramatic following sound. An explosive device is set to go off in a crowded city square. The ticking of the bomb gets louder as it reaches detonation time. Then, silence.

# MUSIC

Music is elemental. Its sonic combinations are infinite, and its aesthetic values fulfill basic human needs. Therein lies its power in **underscoring**—adding background music that enhances the content of a scene by evoking a particular idea, emotion, point of view, or atmosphere. Music is generally thought of as an art form that evokes emotion. That is true, of course. It provides **affective information**—information related to feeling and mood. But it also provides cognitive information—information related to mental processes of knowledge, reasoning, memory, judgment, and perception.

**Underscore music** is original or library music. Unlike sound effects, underscoring is **nondiegetic sound** in that it comes from outside the story space. Underscoring serves picture in a number of ways. As composer Aaron Copland observed many years ago, and which still holds true today: Underscoring creates a more convincing atmosphere of time and place; it underlines psychological refinements—the unspoken thoughts of a character or situation; it serves to fill pauses between conversation; it builds a sense of continuity; it underpins dramatic buildup and gives finality to a scene.[2]

Figure 3.6. *The band Cake—captured here in concert in 2010—typically plays rock songs that have an upbeat tempo and an expressive melody. See various reactions to their song Short Skirt Long Jacket here:* www.youtube.com/watch?v=X5KmB8Laemg

## Music Characteristics

Music has the same basic structural elements common to all sound, such as pitch, loudness, tempo, tone color, and envelope. It also contains other characteristics that broaden its perceptual and aesthetic meaning such as melody and tonality; harmony and its qualities of consonance, dissonance, and texture; tempo; dynamic range that is quite wide compared with speech and sounds; and style in limitless variety. The characteristics of music are both more

2   Aaron Copland, *Our New Music* (New York: McGraw-Hill, 1941).

and less complex than those of verbal language. Unlike speech (and sound effects), musical structure is both horizontal and vertical and therefore at once linear and simultaneous. That is, linear sound provides melody and rhythm; simultaneous sound provides harmony and texture. The entire audible spectrum of sound can be used in an infinite variety of combinations.

## Melody

*Melody* is a succession of pitched musical tones of varied durations. Because each tone has duration, melody also establishes rhythm. Hence, melody has both a tone quality and a time quality and cannot be separated from rhythm. Generally, if a melody moves in narrowly pitched steps and ranges, it tends to be expressive and emotional. If it moves in widely pitched steps and ranges, it tends to be conservative and unexpressive. Melodies are usually written in keys or tonalities, designated as major and minor. Subjectively, keys in the major mode usually sound positive, happy, bright, and vigorous; keys in the minor mode usually sound darker, tentative, wistful, and melancholy.

## Harmony

*Harmony* is a simultaneous sounding of two or more tones, although three or more tones are usually necessary to be classified as a chord. *Chords* are categorized as consonant or dissonant, and they are important to musical texture. *Consonance* in music is produced by agreeable, settled, balanced, stable-sounding chords. *Dissonance* is produced by unsettled, unstable, unresolved, tense-sounding chords. *Texture*, as the term suggests, is the result of materials interwoven to create a fabric. In music, melody and harmony are those interwoven materials. Undoubtedly, the infinite variety of musical textures that can be designed is a major reason for music's universal appeal and role in human communication.

## Tempo

Tempo provides the pulse and the drive in music. A quick tempo tends to intensify stimulation; a slow tempo tends to allay it.

## Dynamic Range

Because the *dynamic range* of music can be much wider than the dynamic ranges of speech and sounds, it is possible to create a greater variety of loudness-related effects with an equal breadth of emotional impact and response.

Figure 3.7. The band Public Enemy—captured here in concert in 2008—embraced a militaristic style of rap; which became a sub-genre of hip-hop. See them performing My Uzi Weighs a Ton here: http://www.youtube.com/watch?v=mDVJli0aakM

## Style

*Style* is a fixed, identifiable musical quality uniquely expressed, executed, or performed. It is that combination of characteristics that distinguishes chamber music from jazz and hip-hop from rock. Like texture, style is a source of infinite musical variety.

## Functions of Music Underscoring

Music underscoring performs many of the same functions in audio design as sound effects but more broadly and diversely. One essential difference between sound effects and music is that *sound effects are generally associated with action and music with reaction.* This can be argued, of course, but it serves to provide insight into their different roles and effects. The unique language, vast vocabulary, and universal resonance of music also make it so powerful and so widely applicable in aural communication.

Figure 3.8. *Many musical styles are indigenous to particular regions. By recalling these styles, music can establish a locale. In this example, musicians play traditional music in a temple in Siem Reap, Cambodia.*

## Establishing Locale

Many musical styles and themes are indigenous to particular regions. By recalling these styles and themes or by simulating a reasonable sonic facsimile, music can establish a locale, such as an Indian village or Rio de Janeiro during Carnival.

## Emphasizing Action

Music emphasizes action by defining or underscoring an event. For example, a dramatic chord underscores shock or a moment of decision or tempo increasing from slow to fast emphasizes impending danger.

## Intensifying Action

Music intensifies action, usually with crescendo or repetition. The scariness of sinister music builds to a climax behind a scene of sheer terror and crashes in a final, frightening chord. The repetition of a short melody, phrase, or rhythm intensifies boredom, the threat of danger, or an imminent action.

## Depicting Identity

Music can identify characters, events, and programs. Think of John Williams's score for *Jaws* with its distinct musical phrase associated with the menacing shark. A particular theme played during an event identifies the event each time it is heard. Themes also have long served to identify radio and television programs, films, and personalities.

## Setting Pace

Music sets pace mainly through tempo and rhythm. Slow tempo suggests dignity, importance, or dullness; fast tempo suggests gaiety, agility, or triviality. Changing tempo from slow to fast accelerates pace and escalates action; changing from fast to slow decelerates pace and winds down or concludes action. Regular rhythm suggests stability, monotony, or simplicity; irregular (syncopated) rhythm suggests complexity, excitement, or instability. Using up-tempo music for a slow-moving scene accelerates the movements within the scene and vice versa.

## Providing Counterpoint

Music that provides counterpoint adds an idea or a feeling that would not otherwise be obvious. Football players shown blocking, passing, and running are counterpointed with ballet music to underscore their grace and coordination.

## Creating Humor

A sliding trombone, clanking percussion, or a galumphing bassoon can define a comic highlight or underscore its humor.

## Fixing Time

Among the many uses for musical style is fixing time. Depending on the harmonic structure, the voicings in the playing ensemble, or both, it is pos-

Figure 3.9. *If music can be used to fix a period in time, it can also be used to recall a past event or foretell a future occurrence. In this example, musicians use costumes and music to recall the Jazz Age.*

sible to suggest ancient Greece, medieval France, the Roaring Twenties, 1960s San Francisco, the future, times of day, and so on.

## Recalling or Foretelling Events

If music can be used to fix a period in time, it can also be used to recall a past event or foretell a future occurrence. For example, a theme used to underscore a tragic crash is repeated at dramatically appropriate times to recall the incident.

## Evoking Atmosphere, Feeling, or Mood

Perhaps no other form of human communication is as effective as music in providing atmosphere, feeling, or mood. There is a musical analog for virtually every condition and emotion. Music can evoke atmospheres that are thick, unsavory, cold, sultry, and ethereal. It can evoke feelings that are obvious and easy to suggest, such as love, hate, and awe, as well as subtle feelings such as friendship, estrangement, pity, and kindness. Music can convey the most obvious and the subtlest of moods: ecstasy, depression, melancholy, and amiability.

## INFLUENCES OF SOUND DESIGN ON MEANING

The following example demonstrates how *sound design* can affect the meaning of the picture.

FADE IN

INTERIOR. BEDROOM. NIGHT. A LITTLE GIRL IS LYING ON A BED LOOKING AT THE CEILING. A SHAFT OF MOONLIGHT COMES IN THROUGH AN OPEN WINDOW ILLUMINATING ONLY PART OF HER FACE. THE CAMERA SLOWLY ZOOMS IN.

Clearly, the script's story and the director's choices would govern the sound design for this shot. But the intent of this example is to demonstrate sound's significant influence on picture. Consider the shot with the following sound patterns and how each pattern influences its meaning and feel.

1.  The sounds of conversation and revelry coming from another room
2.  The sounds of a man and a woman arguing in an adjacent room and a sudden crash
3.  Two men are heard whispering offscreen
4.  An old woman's voiceover describes childhood memories
5.  The girl breathing, humming softly—almost imperceptibly—to herself
6.  The thrum of an air conditioner and the polyrhythmic din of insects
7.  Gentle breaking of waves and a distant foghorn
8.  The whine of air raid sirens, the rumble of airplanes, and the dull thudding of distant bombs
9.  A single dog howling, building to a scattered chorus of baying hounds in the distance
10. The creaking of floorboards and the sound of a door latch opening
11. The distant sounds of a playground with children laughing and singing
12. Street traffic, the occasional car horn, and the booming bass of music from a passing car

This example has other thematic possibilities, of course.

The choices of dialogue and narration open up numerous avenues for the audience to interpret the scene differently. In addition to what is said, aspects of emphasis, inflection, patterns of speech, pace, mood, and accent also suggest a wide range of dramatic possibilities.

An audience hearing the muffled argument between a man and a woman through the walls may not hear specific words, but the nonverbal dimension of their conversation communicates the tension between them. Their voices rise and lower in intensity, the tempo of the exchange varies, and punctuated silences maintain a level of suspense.

If we think of the scene and hear the voiceover of an old woman reminiscing about her youth haltingly and deliberately with a Russian accent and a twinge of melancholy, it tells us one story. Change the voice to an American from the rural South who speaks quickly with a pronounced drawl and laughs to herself as she pauses between sentences, the scene changes—even though both are talking about childhood memories.

The various ambient soundscapes and sound effects palettes contribute to our understanding of the scene and how we make sense of characters' actions and intentions. The arguing couple heard against the rhythms of a hot summer night in the country carries a different sensibility than that of the inner city—what we hear tells us about time, place, and circumstance.

The Russian woman's reminiscences juxtaposed against the sounds of distant battle as opposed to ocean surf and foghorn convey a different backdrop for the narration. In these examples, what we hear beyond the content of the dialogue in terms of ambience and sound effects informs our capacity to interpret and shape meaning.

Now consider what music underscoring does to the scene, with or without the sound effects and any number of variables with regard to dialogue and/or narration. With music that is, say, celestial, mysterious, sinister, playful, comedic, romantic, melancholy, blissful, animated, or threatening, notice how the idea and the feel of the scene changes yet again. In the same vein as these musical suggestions, consider the wide range of musical styles and how these might influence our interpretation of the scene.

For the man and woman engaged in a heated argument, music can heighten the conflict—whether we are hearing hip-hop, bebop, or a piece of atonal music from a string quartet. With the Russian woman, the plaintive sound of a solo *balalaika* might lend an intimacy to her voiceover, while the strains of an orchestra or choir may give us a sense of pathos. Each choice brings with it a shading of nuance and information that pulls the audience more deeply into the drama of the moment.

The effective interplay of dialogue and narration—quite apart from what the words might signify—along with sound effects and music all contribute to how we create and interpret meaning and dramatic intent.

# Why Archetypes are Important

## By Bryan Tillman

Certain traits are evident in all characters. These traits, called archetypes, allow us to categorize them into specific groups. An archetype is considered to be the original mold or model of a person, trait, or behavior that we as humans wish to copy or emulate. It is the *ideal* example of a character. Archetypes encompass both the good and evil spectrums.

A wide variety of archetypes can be found throughout history, from the works of Shakespeare all the way back to the teachings of Plato. You can spend some time in the library researching archetypes throughout history, but we are going to focus on a specific grouping of archetype. Today, the most prevalent archetypes used are set forth by the Swiss psychologist Carl Jung. Jung, a colleague of Sigmund Freud, studied the idea of the conscious and unconscious mind. He believed that multiple reoccurring innate ideas defined specific characters. It is these reoccurring ideas that we as humans grasp onto in order to define people we encounter in our everyday lives, as well as characters in fictional works. These basic archetypes exist in all literature. The Jungian archetypes are pretty self-evident, but once you become more familiar with the various archetypes and what they mean, they become much more recognizable and thus make character development easier as well.

Jung developed a plethora of archetypes and their meanings, however we will focus only on those most commonly used in storytelling today:

- The hero
- The shadow
- The fool
- The anima/animus
- The mentor
- The trickster

When dealing with character design, always remember that the character exists as a result of the story. The story will dictate that you need a hero. The hero is defined as someone who is very brave, selfless, and willing to help others no matter what the cost.

*Figure 4.1. An archetypal "Hero".*

Now that we have established the hero, we are going to need an enemy for that person to interact with in the story. We are going to need to establish the shadow character. The shadow character is the one who is connected the most with our instinctual animal past. He or she is perceived as ruthless, mysterious, disagreeable, and evil.

*Figure 4.2. An archetypal "Shadow".*

Now that we have a good guy and a bad guy (or gal), we should be able to tell a great story, right? Well, just because you have the two main characters, it doesn't mean that your story is going to be great. You might be able to tell a compelling story with only two people, but that rarely happens. With that in mind, you are going to need a cast of supporting characters to help push the main characters through the story. This leads us to our next character: the *fool*.

The fool character is the one who goes through the story in a confused state and inevitably gets everyone into undesirable situations.

*Figure 4.3. An archetypal "Fool".*

The fool is in the story to test the main character. How that character deals with the actions of the fool tells us a lot about that person—for example:

> *We are following the shadow character, who is followed by the fool character. The fool character flips the switch to the doomsday device early, and now the whole five-month plan goes down the drain. In response to the fool's action, the shadow character destroys the fool character in a fit of rage. This then proves just how unforgiving and ruthless the shadow character is.*

Or, if the same situation happens and the shadow character doesn't act in a fit of rage but instead tries to fix the problem and still uses the fool character. This would show that the shadow character still has some form of humanity and morality. Therefore, the fool adds depth to the story and provides a window into the soul of the main character. No matter how annoying the fool may get, he or she provides the information we need to fully understand the story.

From the fool character we move on to something a little bit more interesting: the *anima/animus*. The anima is the female counterpart to the male, and the animus is the male

*Figure 4.4. An archetypal "Anima".*

counterpart to the female. This character embodies the male and female urges.

Since I mentioned that there is a counterpart to the female:

These characters represent our sexual desires bundled into one character. In other words, the anima or animus represents the love interest in the story. The love interest doesn't have to be just for the main characters; he or she could be for you, the viewer. How many times have you seen a movie or read a comic and thought to yourself:

*"I really have no ideas why that person is in the movie, but they sure are pretty to look at."*

The anima/animus characters exist to draw you into the story. If you or the main character is attracted to the anima or animus character and something happens to that character, it will evoke a wide range of emotions from within. This is another technique to keep you immersed in the story.

Once the main character is emotionally connected to another character—generally the anima or animus—the *mentor* then appears. The mentor is relevant because he or she has the profound knowledge that the protagonist needs even he or she doesn't want to hear it.

Figure 4.5. An archetypal "Animus".

The mentor plays a key role in making the protagonist realize his or her full potential and is often portrayed as an old man or woman. This is because most cultures associate age with having wisdom. The mentor takes on many of the characteristics of a parent. I'll bet that if you think back on your childhood, you can recall that often what your parents told you didn't make any sense, but now that you are older and wiser, you realize they only had your best interests in mind. Remember when I said that the mentor is "often" portrayed as an old man or woman? Well there are many instances where the mentor character is the same age or younger than the main character.

This leaves us with one final character: the *trickster*. The trickster character is the one that is constantly pushing for change.

The trickster can either be on the side of good or on the side of evil. In both situations, the trickster is trying to move the story toward his or her favor or benefit. Just like in the illustration, they are just like puppet masters. The trickster causes doubt to creep into the main character's mind, making that character change the way he or she was going to

Figure 4.6. An archetypal "Mentor".

handle a certain situation. Generally, in the end, it is the trickster's actions that make the main character the type of person he or she is at the end of the story. The trickster is vital to any story because he or she is generally the toughest mental test that the main character has to overcome before the main character can physically and mentally overcome his or her antagonist.

Figure 4.7. An archetypal "Trickster".

So these are the basic character archetypes, but they don't always fit into their stereotypical roles. Take, for instance, the hero and shadow characters. For the most part, these characters are central to the story, but is the hero always the main focus of the story? In this day and age, that isn't always the case. In fact, more and more stories focus on the villain/shadow. That is why the story will focus on the *protagonist*—the main character of the story. Then you also have the *antagonist*, who stands in opposition to the protagonist.

What I am trying to say is that when most people think of a story, they go straight for the hero as the protagonist. That just isn't always the case. If the story is about an evil dictator trying to take over the world, then the antagonist would be the patriot hero standing in the dictator's way of world domination. So, as you can see when you write a story, you need both a protagonist and an antagonist.

I know I have given you examples of each kind of archetype, but I don't know if you understand exactly what each archetype looks like, so, I am going to give you some examples from a very popular movie series: George Lucas' *Star Wars*. I hope that if you are reading this book you have seen all six *Star Wars* movies. If you haven't seen them, hopefully you know a little about them. If you don't know anything about them, you should go watch them. Otherwise this part of the chapter isn't going to help you understand archetypes either.

In all six *Star Wars* movies, I think it is pretty obvious who the hero character is. Luke Skywalker is the true embodiment of the hero character. He stays on the path of good the whole time. Even when he was wandering down the dark path to find out more about his father, his morals and actions were always pure at heart.

He would also put himself in harm's way to help his friends. Even against the wise words of Yoda, Luke went to sky city to help his friends. One of the best examples of why Luke is the hero character, is when he defeats Darth Vader (UHHHHH, hope I didn't spoil that for you!), but still tried to save him. Luke wanted to give him the ability to start over and come to the good side.

The one, the only, true bad guy, Darth Vader, is our shadow character. Darth Vader is ruled by emotions. He believes in survival of the fittest. That goes back to the primitive animalistic nature of humans. This becomes very evident in the third movie, where Anakin Skywalker fully turns into Darth Vader. From that movie on we see that Darth Vader acts on the impulses of his emotions, which makes him very susceptible to the influences of the trickster in *Star Wars*.

Only one character in *Star Wars* can justifiably wear the crown of fool, and that is Jar Jar Binks. That character was able to get under everyone's skin. He would always run into something, drop an important device, or flick some switch that would put the entire cast at risk. Jar Jar was the one character whom everyone had to tolerate. He would change the conditions with almost every step he made, making everybody around him adjust to a new situation.

I know there are characters who fill both of these roles, but the character that both the cast of the movie and the viewers would consider the anima is Princess Leia. If you don't know why this is so, Google her character, and I'm sure you'll understand.

Now, depending on who you want to go with, two characters could be considered the mentor: Obi Wan Kenobi and Yoda. I am going to go with Yoda because he seems to be the one who plays the part of the mentor in most of the movies. Yoda is a good example of the mentor character because he is the one everyone goes to when they need advice. He also always seems to have the right answer, even if he gives it to you in a backward sentence structure.

The trickster character is one many people would argue over, but if you watch all the movies, you will see that Senator Paulpatine/The Emperor is the trickster character. He has a really easy time playing the trickster character because he is literally two different characters. So while he is telling everyone what to do, as the senator he is able to manipulate the outcome of every meeting so it will be to the empire's benefit. He is also able to control young Anakin Skywalker and make him join the dark side without even knowing that he was already slowly turning to the darkside.

I hope this helped you to understand archetypes a little better. Now I must point out that any single character can have multiple archetypal traits.

Combining archetypes can create more complex and interesting characters, but it can also confuse viewers and readers and make events and plotlines hard to follow. In general, a character designer wants to make sure that the archetypes stay clear and singular solely for the purpose of clarity. This way the viewer or reader won't get confused and lose the magic of the story trying to figure out who is who.

Certain types of stories lend themselves to this blurred archetypal character form. These characters fall mostly into mystery and suspense stories, sometimes even horror. By keeping the character archetypes blurred and confusing, the viewer is pulled into the story, trying to figure out "whodunit." Have you ever watched a movie or read a book and thought:

*"That has to be the bad guy. He is just so evil!"*

Just to have that thought changed completely as soon as the story moves on:

*"You know what? She has to be the bad guy because she is just so vindictive!"*

You were just successfully drawn into the story because you were trying to figure out who did what to whom and why. The blurred archetypal characters forced you to become more involved in the story in order to answer questions raised by this intentional blurring of the archetypal lines.

The last thing I want to mention is that archetypes can change at any time. A good guy becoming a bad guy within the course of a book or movie is possible. Even the fool character can become the hero. You need to accomplish this change over the course of the story, not all at once. Your Super Boy Scout hero can't go from saving the day on one comic page to becoming a sadistic mass murderer on the next. All that will happen is that you will lose your reader.

# Thinking of Structure

## By Guy Gallo

## THE PIECES

et's think about how films are constructed, and about the analogues on the page.

## IMAGE

The smallest unit of film composition is the image. Due to the nature of film, the image is dynamic. That is, the visual information within it changes as either the camera or the actors and objects move.

At its basic level, the image conveys any (or all) of three types of information: aesthetic, meaning, emotion. We consume imagery by apprehending at a purely visual level, by comprehending whatever information, and by feeling viscerally.

An image is created on the page with every sentence that you type. And the shape of that sentence determines how the image blossoms in the reader's imagination.

## SHOT

The dynamic nature of the image is approximated on the page by the accumulation of sentences, by the paragraph.

*Figure 5.1. When seen in the context of the story, this single image from the short film* Tears of Steel *conveys all three types of visual information: aesthetic, meaning, emotion.*

So if a sentence is the analogue to a single image, the paragraph stands as the analog for the composed shot.

Again, how the paragraph is composed, its rhythm and tempo and tone, will generate in the reader's mind a sense of the visuals, the movement, the space, even the silence.

# SCENE

There are two types of film scenes: those composed purely of visuals and those where the visuals constitute the arena for dramatic exchange. One of the powerful tools available to the **screenwriter**—and not to the playwright or novelist—is the ability to move story forward silently, via image and spectacle. Remember as you are composing a list of the dramatic scenes in your head—the scenes where characters confront and discuss and argue—that not every scene must, nor should, have the same shape. The rhythm of your screenplay is created by deliberate alternation between dramatic scenes and visuals, scenes with dialogue, and scenes with very little or none.

*The rhythm of your screenplay is created by deliberate alternation between dramatic scenes and visuals …*

Some scenes—those that move quickly, that are mostly dialogue free—can be simple. That is, have a single point, make it, move on. Usually, a series of such small scenes occur sequentially and add up to a shape, a movement forward.

But a dramatic scene recapitulates the shape of the screenplay as a whole. It has (usually) a narrative **structure**: introduction, complication, resolution. It may have more than one thing going on—and more than one conflict. But, for the most part, a dramatic scene has a single and overriding direction, a momentum to a point. That primary shape is what generates expectation, what prepares us for the next scene.

# SEQUENCE

A sequence is a series of related scenes, all concerned with a single portion of the story. There is no set number of scenes within a sequence. Could be three, could be seven. Usually it breaks down to ten to fifteen pages per sequence.

A sequence is to a screenplay as a chapter is to a novel.

It's useful to think in terms of sequences. It helps divide your story into manageable chunks. It gives you something to hold onto, something to shape and manipulate.

As with the individual scenes, a sequence of scenes builds to a dramatic conclusion.

If you look at some of the screenplays of Preston Sturges, *The Lady Eve*, for example, he marked the end of each sequence in the finished screenplay. It's interesting to see the sequences so clearly delineated. However, I'm not suggesting your submission draft should have the sections marked. It may, however, be useful to do so in your working document.

Think of it in terms of outline. If the top level, heading 1, represents the **Act** breaks:

1. Boy Meets Girl
2. Boy Loses Girl
3. Boy Gets Girl

Then the sequence would be heading level 2 (the discrete sequences are the lettered headings):

1. Boy Meets Girl
   A. Meet Boy
   B. Meet Girl
   C. First Date
   D. Running Away
   E. Trip to the Parents

It is at this level of the sequence that outlining can be useful. But I do not mean you need to know all the sequences before you start writing. I actually add these section headings during the course of writing, or after a draft is finished. It's a useful tool for analysis that allows you to easily hold the movement of the script in your head.

This is a case where the point might be helped by taking a well-known film and breaking it down into sequences. Here's an **act**/sequence breakdown of *Amadeus*:

1. **Act** One
   a. Meeting Salieri. Attempted suicide. The priest. Meeting Mozart and Costanza. Desire to stay in Vienna.
   b. *Abduction from the Seraglio.* Katarina. Engagement to Stanzi.

2. **Act** Two
   a. Father to Vienna. Marriage. Seeking help from Salieri. "I will block you," Salieri says to God.
   b. The maid hired to spy. *Marriage of Figaro.* Fight over the ballet. Emperor yawns.
   c. Salieri's opera. Father's death. *Don Giovanni.* Salieri's plan.

  d. Vaudeville *Don Giovanni*. Salieri commissions the *Grand Mass*. Mozart working himself sick.

3. **Act** Three
  a. Stanzi leaves. *The Magic Flute*. Mozart collapses.
  b. Salieri takes dictation of the *Grand Mass*. Stanzi returns. Mozart dies.
  c. Salieri's final condemnation of God.

Bear in mind, this is a breakdown after the fact, and so looks a bit smarter and more finished than a working outline of sequences likely ever would. But it is meant simply to illustrate that we can break the **three-act structure** into smaller units. And that each of those smaller units also has a dramatic shape.

Take your favorite film and look at it again with an eye to sequence. See what you come up with.

Note: Do not confuse this idea of sequences with the chapters into which a movie is divided on the released DVD. There may be some correspondence, but likely not.

## The Well-Made Play

Many of the principals of construction espoused by **screenwriting** How-To books are lineal descendants from a nineteenth-century play-writing formula called The Well-Made Play. Practiced by Frenchmen Scribe and Sardou, adapted by Ibsen, Strindberg, O'Neill, codified by William Archer and George Pierce Baker, the **structural** components of this form are themselves based on Aristotle and his commentators.

The fundamental aspect of The Well-Made Play that has survived in its transmogrification into film is the division of the action into three basic movements: setup, complication, and resolution.

The Well-Made Play was typically in five **acts** (the first and fifth being more prologue and epilogue than full **acts**). The first and second **acts** contain the Rising Action—introductions, interest, minor complications; the third **act** presents a major complication or collision; the fourth and fifth reach a climax of the elements presented in **acts** two and three, and then follows a *dénouement*—an untying (of the plot's knottiness?)—and the falling action of the resolution.

The standard three-**act structure** of mainstream filmmaking simply combines the first and second and fourth and fifth **acts** of the Well-Made Play. So we, in general, and with some variation, follow this dramatic shape:

 I. **Act** One: Introduction of the world and inhabitants; establish the problem.
 II. **Act** Two: A series of complications, false victories, setbacks.
III. **Act** Three: The problem comes to a final crisis, the hero solves the problem (preferably in an unexpected way) and/or achieves insight. Resolution—either closed or open-ended.

The opening of a screenplay presents the status quo of the world of the film—and the hero. It then posits the problem. This is variously called the first complication or the inciting incident. From the status quo, there is a change in direction. The journey begins.

Some examples: Riggs is assigned a new partner (*Lethal Weapon*); the journalist is sent to find the meaning of Rosebud (*Citizen Kane*); the alien life form is discovered (*Alien*); Hans Gruber and gang crash the party (*Die Hard*); a narcissistic corporate yes-man is tasked with purchasing an entire Scottish village for an oil company (*Local Hero*).

In its simplest form, the inciting incident is some external event that crosses the hero or some internal desire that prompts the hero to take action. How it looks and when it happens is dependent upon genre. Action adventure and thrillers often open with the problem already underway. Character driven "slice-of-life" dramas may meander a bit before settling into a journey.

In the second **act**, the consequences of the first complication lead to a series of trials—ups and downs, victories and reversals. It is the body of the film.

The second **act** is usually the longest of the three. A rule of thumb: **Act** two comprises half the length of the screenplay; **acts** one and three, a quarter each. But don't get caught up in page count. Especially for a first draft. It takes as long as it takes to tell the story. You can always cut after the rough draft is complete.

The third **act** presents the final confrontation and conflict between the hero and his antagonist (or the world, or himself). It leaves the protagonist either triumphant (Hollywood), or defeated (French), or chastened ambiguously (Art House). Snideness aside, no matter the victory or defeat, the end of the film leaves the hero with an altered understanding of his place in the world. And the audience with him. It leaves the audience with a sense that something—good, bad, or ambiguous—has been achieved.

The lesson must be consistent with what we have been led to expect in the setup of the problem. Or, perhaps I should say, consistent with character logic, but perhaps different and *better* than what we have been led to expect. That's the best resolution. One that satisfies in ways that were not predicted.

*Figure 5.2. Rembrandt's famous painting* Aristotle with a Bust of Homer *is thought to capture Aristotle in contemplation of how touch and sight can be used to acquire knowledge. Ironically, Homer was a blind poet who penned the epics* The Iliad *and* The Odyssey.

## Back to Aristotle

Aristotle speaks of three important parts of dramatic enactment: *Harmatia*, *Peripeteia*, and *Anagnorisis*. Although he speaks of them as components of the plot, it is important to note that all three are inextricably linked to the main character. They can be mapped to modern concepts of plot construction and character delineation.

## Harmatia

This is often translated as "tragic flaw" or "tragic error." Its root meaning is "missing the mark." Aristotle uses the term to refer to that aspect of the main character without which the plot

Figure 5.3. Polish artist Jacek Malczewski's representation of Hamlet demonstrates the character's internal ambivalence (To Be or Not To Be), while also metaphorically representing Poland's own struggle between the nation's independence (which will result in death due to war) or servitude to Russia (which will avert war and save lives).

would not proceed; the character trait that is most vulnerable to the inciting incident, that predisposes the hero for the journey ahead. It's a character blindness stemming from single-mindedness. I like to think of *harmatia* in the light of *daimon*, the Greek concept that meant both conscience and embraced fate. It is the hero's driving passion and his demon.

Think pride (Oedipus, Lear), an overdeveloped sense of ambivalence (Hamlet), ambition (Macbeth), greed (Scrooge), conviction (Antigone, Creon). It is the mistake—in moral judgment, in personal ambition—that is corrected or amplified in the course of the story, leading to redemption or failure in the final **act**.

Many films have as their initiating engine just such a character blindness, an overwhelming—yet somehow mistaken—desire or purpose. Other films take their archetypal shape from the quest journey (which for Aristotle was the purview of epic rather than drama). In the quest story the hero is given, or assumes, a task to achieve. In this case, the driving character trait is hope or belief. They believe that the successful completion of the quest will result in the overriding desire's fulfillment. For example: *Apocalypse Now* or *Into the West*. In both, the result of the quest is other than what was expected at the outset. Willard, rather than cleansing the world of Kurtz, takes his place. The boys discover their father rather than their mother.

The character blindness, or the object of hope represented by the quest, sets up an expectation for what would constitute success or failure in the course of the story.

## PERIPETEIA

Aristotle defines it thus:

*… a change by which the action veers round to its opposite, subject always to our rule of probability or necessity.*

In colloquial terms it's simply a reversal. In modern dramaturgy there may be many small reversals leading up to the culminating *peripeteia* at the end of the film.

It's a fundamental of dramatic construction that reversal plays on expectation. The best reversal is the one that disappoints expectation. And then, in the disappointing, satisfies in a manner more fulfilling than what was originally desired. The expectation is met in a way that was unexpected.

The audience gets something they didn't know they wanted and their perception of the story takes a major shift.

## ANAGNORISIS

An enlightening discovery or recognition. In its simplest form: mistaken identity is unmasked, the hero discovers the truth of his birth. That is, literal recognition.

More frequently, and more interestingly, the discovery is within the hero. Self-awareness. In such a case it is most effective if the recognition is directly related to the *harmatia*. Scrooge comes to realize that Christmas isn't so bad; Hamlet that action is required; Willard that he is capable of the same extremity as Kurtz.

## JOURNEY

Now let's map this Aristotelian terminology to modern dramaturgy. The term *character arc* or *character journey* is simply another way of naming the movement from *Harmatia* to *Anagnorisis*.

In story conferences and seminars you will often hear the question "What does the hero learn?" or "How has the main character changed by the end of the film?" Aren't these questions really: What is your hero's initial blindness and what does he come to recognize in the end? What is the *harmatia* and *anagnorisis*?

Figure 5.4. In Charles Dickens' A Christmas Carol, the Ghost of Christmas Future provides the anagnorisis for Scrooge—allowing him to recognize that he still has the power to change. Scrooge's character arc can therefore be defined as changing from greed (his harmatia; or tragic flaw) to charity (his anagnorisis or realization).

I would say most times there is too much focus on the lesson—what has he learned, how has she changed—and not enough on the initial character aspect of *harmatia*, the defining blindness or passion that determines behavior. Look first to your hero's driving demon.

If you can get that right, deep and interesting enough, the lesson will follow.

The important point to realize, to internalize, is that all three concepts—*harmatia*, *peripeteia*, and *anagnorisis*—which Aristotle described as aspects of plot, are impossible to conceive without fully understanding your character.

# Song Production: The Marriage Between Composition and Audio Production

## By Danny Cope

## WHAT IS A SONG?

There are numerous ways of looking at exactly what a song is, especially when we see it in its role as part of a production process. For some it tends to be the starting point that kicks the process off, and for others, it's more intrinsically linked into the production process and emerges and evolves along with the sound and vibe of the track as it is built.

Regardless of the manner in which it appears, a song will always consist of several key ingredients. Whether it be conceived by an acoustic guitar-wielding singer/songwriter, a sampling enthusiast, or a combination of similar approaches, a song will always include elements of form, melody, harmony, rhythm and lyrics. The way these elements meet and marry up can vary considerably from writer to writer and producer to producer, but they will inevitably be required to gel to some degree at some point. If we look to a dictionary or encyclopedia for definitions of "song," we will invariably be presented with a definition such as this one from Grove Music.

*... a piece of music for voice or voices, whether accompanied or unaccompanied*

This is a very basic definition, but it has to be. The simple reason for this is that there are so many different kinds of song. They can be so vastly different that it almost seems unsophisticated to use the same word "song" to describe them all. A children's song, for example, is almost always going to be a huge distance from a Death Metal song with regard to its compositional makeup. Similarly, Hip-Hop and Folk songs tend to see very few things eye to eye, but nonetheless, a "piece of music for voice or voices, whether accompanied or unaccompanied" is classed as a song regardless of the genre that it falls within. The marriage of several key ingredients results in a compositional structure that transcends the class of genre and subculture, and it's these

Figure 6.1. PatchWerk Recording Studio, 2007. The recording engineer typically plays a key role in defining the functional purpose of a song and helping to shape it in the studio.

ingredients that give us the most obvious handle when it comes to getting hold of exactly what a song is. However, if we regard a song to be merely a combination of rhythms and sounds, we are missing something very important in what defines them. A song should not be defined purely by what it *is*. What it *does* is also of immense significance. Before we move on to look at the functional purpose of a song, a brief appreciation of each of its ingredients will be beneficial.

## Melody

Regardless of the genre in which it resides, and the degree of effort that went into shaping it, a song's melody is a fundamentally important ingredient. This is because it is usually the part of the song that the listener will be able to get involved in most readily. It is often referred to as the "top line" in a song because it does effectively sit on "top" of most of the other ingredients and is easily accessible regardless of the extent of musical understanding possessed by the listener. Unless the range is way beyond physical limitation, it's likely that someone enjoying any given melody will have a stab at joining in from time to time. It's something that

Figure 6.2. Jazz fusion guitarist Kazumi Watanabe is known for improvising melodies and combining unlikely musical genres to create unique chord progressions in his songs. You can see Watanabe experimenting with a variety of musical genres while in concert here: http://www.youtube.com/watch?v=5vQt0FYk7No

we humans just do. More often than not we feel more comfortable doing it behind closed doors, but getting involved in a song through participation tends to take place when we are enjoying what we are hearing. The melody provides the means to do just that.

It's fair to say that there are plenty of songs that have had a proportionally tiny amount of time spent on the construction of the melody compared to other ingredients. It's also fair to say that this fact has not hindered their success a great deal where the melody was never intended to be the focal point or the reason why the song exists. The "feel," or "vibe," lyrics, or ambient sonic qualities may have been the driving force behind a song's creation, and although these qualities can hold a song up, they cannot completely negate the importance of the position that a melody will inhabit. It may well not be the focal point of composition in all genres, but it will almost always be exposed on the surface nonetheless. Both writers and producers need to be fully aware of this fact. Whether it be a very simple repeating three-note motif or complex labyrinth of inverted and interrupted scales and modes, a melody, no matter how simple or what instrument it is conveyed with, is always going to be a readily accessible element of any song.

## Harmony

In case you haven't come across the term in this light before, the word "harmony" here is not being used to describe just what a backing vocalist sings. Harmony is the term used to describe what many songwriters prefer to call "chord progression." The harmony is the chordal structure that supports or harmonizes the melody and that can convey a great deal of information about the genre of a song. Some styles of music such as Country Music tend to be built on relatively simple harmonic structures, whereas others, including Jazz Fusion for example, usually feature much more elaborate use of extensions and chord substitutions.

There are genres where the supporting role of harmony is very evident. It can simply be conveyed through a realistic and transparent recording of an acoustic instrument or three, and generate a believable representation of a live performance. In other genres, however, the harmony can take its place with confidence at center stage. A song's purpose isn't necessarily to be memorable or singable. These are undoubtedly worthy attributes, but making a song good to dance to, or good to chill out to, or good to experience in any other way are also relevant and appropriate qualities for writers and producers to aspire to. A song can exist primarily to showcase a collection of sounds and the harmony will provide the vehicle to convey a lot of that information. It will also provide a platform on which a Producer may find opportunities to pivot towards varying genres. It's not just a case of recording the right notes. Capturing the right sounds is actually a more pertinent pursuit in some cases. Writers and producers should never lose sight of the purpose of a song, and the way in which the harmony is written and recorded will do a lot to define a song's character and intention.

## Lyrics

From the above definition, it is clear that a song needs to include some words to be sung in conjunction with the melody. Without lyrics, the melody in a song ceases to be part of a song, and becomes just a melody. This would render it more of a "composition" than a "song." Similarly, a lyric without a melody behind it ceases to be part of a song and becomes just a collection of words or prose.

When lyrics are written, they can define genre. At the very least, they can suggest them. There are some themes that are universal and can be found in all genres and styles of production. Songs about love can take many guises and can be found nestling in all sorts of different styles of music for example. However, there are some lyrical themes that will not be particularly welcomed or appreciated in some genres. When a song is written and produced, there needs to be a considered understanding of what it communicates and the manner in which it is communicated. If lyrics can define or limit genre, then they can also do a lot to define production style.

## Rhythm

The previous three ingredients all occur concurrently and are in effect stacked on top of each other in the creative process. Rhythm doesn't quite fit into that club. Owing to our entrapment in the space-time continuum, rhythmical elements all take place after each other, and the timing of each event is just as important as each event itself. The speed of the song, the regularity of the harmonic pulse, variation in stress pattern, and the changes in chord and note length are all incredibly important in defining whether a collection of neatly stacked notes will be magical or plain old monotonous.

## Form

In addition to rhythmical elements, the other linear-based creative decision rests in the construction of the form of the song. The writing of songs is generally categorized through naming each section. Pretty much any song we come across will contain a chorus or pay-off line of some kind, and this moment will be surrounded and usually held up by supporting sections such as introductions, verse, bridges and alike. Editing the form of a song is often massively important in making a song "work." A song can consist of all the right ingredients, but if they are thrown in the pot in the wrong order, then the recipe just won't work and the result will be inedible.

*Figure 6.3. The Talking Heads in Jay's Longhorn Bar, 1978. The Talking Heads were known for building listening complexity from one song to the next. In the rock-u-mentary* Stop Making Sense, *they begins with a solo acoustic number and, by the end of the concert, more than two dozen musicians are on stage playing.*

Cliché phrases such as "Don't bore us, get to the chorus" are often heard and with good reason. The stage of ordering the different sections of a song is where we can carefully present the information as a purposeful chain of events. Things that are generally important to consider in the structuring of a song are the need to make sure it is an appropriate length for its target audience and market, that it contains information that is interesting with as little padding as humanly possible, and that it achieves what the audience wants to hear with regard to listening complexity. Some audiences like songs that consist of ten or more sections. Some don't and would rather have a very safe and predictable passage through the song to a tidy conclusion. Whichever way a song goes about its business, the order in which the different sections appear, and the manner in which they slot together is very important. Reflective editing is in effect the only thing that separates song writing from improvisation, and should therefore be taken very seriously.

Opportunities for the editing of song structure present themselves consistently throughout the production process and should always be confronted head on when they arise. Generally speaking, it's a good idea to ensure that the first draft of any song has the basis of the song all there so that editing can be a process that hones rather than adds. It may be that the composer or composers choose to edit the song before it reaches a producer if the compositional approach makes that a possibility, but even in those cases, the song should still not be above further editing as the process progresses through each stage. Getting the song to fit where it is heading will almost always require some chipping away at the edges that are stopping the substance of the song fitting into the hole it's designed for. Some of these protruding edges are more obvious than others, and it may be a while into the production process before it becomes apparent they are an issue that needs addressing. One of the most valuable things that a producer can bring to a song is objectivity, and it's often in the structural makeup of a song that a producer can make the quickest and most effective changes.

Like a good partner in any marriage, a producer will be able to help a song build in confidence and identify and pronounce good and admirable qualities within in. A good producer will be honest with the composer and composition and help extract the best out of it. This process in itself will invariably lead to hidden gems in the composition coming to the surface.

## IS A SONG JUST A COMBINATION OF ITS INGREDIENTS?

So, what can we do with these ingredients? The main task at hand is to ensure that they all slot together neatly and enhance each other to maximum effect. If we were to visualize the combination of ingredients, it could be easy to see them as being stacked on top of each other. This would certainly seem to work as far as the writing process is concerned, where the melody *may* have been written first, followed by a harmonic chord progression to underpin it and then followed up with some lyrics that work with the melody.

Figure 6.4 is obviously a simplified representation of the manner in which these compositional elements fit together, but it serves its purposes for the time being. The reality is that every writer, regardless of experience or skill, will have a collection of snippets of songs lying around the place. It's likely that there will be the odd few lines of lyrics scribbled down on scraps of paper, melodic phrases sung to death but as yet unfinished, chord sequences that sound "nice" but inconclusive, and possibly a few "vibey" tracks stored away on a tape or hard drive somewhere just waiting to be let loose. Coming up with the occasional idea here and there isn't generally that difficult. What can drive us slowly insane

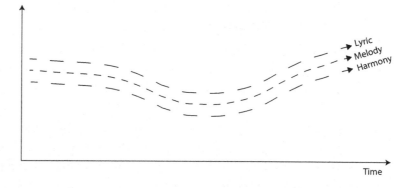

Figure 6.4. Matching song layers.

is figuring out where each of these individual moments of brilliance can find their life partners and make truly beautiful music together. The first thing to remember here is that the writer should never rush this process. If two ideas don't go together in their current form, then they

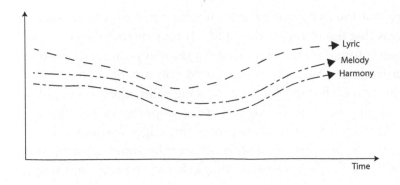

Figure 6.5. *Mismatched song layers.*

don't go together in their current form and that should be the end of it. If a writer is crafting a song on their own, it can be very easy to lose an objective view of the song as it evolves. The goal can get clouded and the composer can get so close to the composition that they really can't see what they have in front of them anymore. One of the benefits of the production process is that it will invariably introduce at least one more pair of ears to the process at some stage. In addition to facilitating the recording and presentation of the song, the person filling these shoes, often the producer, will be able to offer this objective opinion and help keep the crafting process focused and beneficial. Sadly, it's a common problem to see writers who are struggling through on their own marry off incompatible ideas simply so that they can just get shot of them. That will never do anyone any favors other than possibly a short-term favor for the writer, but even that is likely to come back and haunt them (Figure 6.5).

The ingredients we have to play with need to be nurtured and slotted together neatly. On occasions, they will fit together nice and snug. This can happen naturally as a result of writing different elements concurrently such as the melody with the lyric or harmony with the melody, and sometimes the writer can be fortunate enough to have two or more separately fashioned ideas that seem to have been made for each other fall into each other's arms after the event. On other occasions, however, they may not go neatly together in the first instance but will be able to work something out through a little bit of give and take. This may require a lyric to lose a word or syllable here and there, and the rhythm of the melody may have to adjust its run a little bit, but this often happens in the process of writing anyway and is no bad thing.

## Different Measurements

Just as different recipes and tastes require different quantities of each ingredient in food, so too do different genres require different weights of each of these ingredients. The word "weight" has been used here as opposed to "amount" for a simple reason. If a song is 3 minutes long, then there will be 3 minutes of each ingredient present for the most part. There may be moments where the vocal melody departs for a moment along with the lyrics but there will be constant rhythmic and harmonic information at play throughout. The weight is about how important each of these ingredients are at any given time in making the song work. Some genres of music are typically more dependent on some ingredients above others. For example, folk songs tend to rely very heavily on lyrical content because they commonly exist primarily as a platform for the lyric to say something. There may be an age-old story that is being conveyed, supported subtly and sensitively through a simple chord progression and arrangement. In many songs such as this, the harmony is nothing to write home about because it isn't supposed to be the focal point. It can just support and play its part accordingly. If it suddenly got really interesting and all sorts of inversions and extensions were at play, then there is a danger that it would start to fight with the lyrics at the front of the stage and distract rather than compliment. Similarly, there are many "Urban" songs featuring an interplay of rhythmic elements in the production that are more of a focal point than the authenticity and historical grounding of the lyrical narrative. In these cases, the "vibe" of the track is often what the song is really all about, and the lyrics are there more as a means to an end rather than a focal point in themselves.

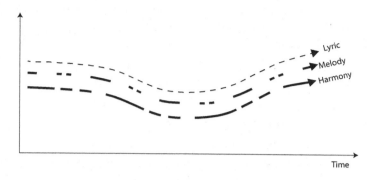

Figure 6.6. *Where lyrics are less of a focal point than other layers.*

The subtle variation in the balance of ingredients needs to be considered carefully, and even though decisions regarding the arrangement and sonic production will frequently come after it has been written, it is still wise to have these considerations in mind when crafting the song in the first place. Some songs will have a fairly even spread of weight right across the ingredients and some will have a very obvious tipping of the balance employed. The significance of each of those ingredients varies according to what the song is trying to achieve, and to a large extent, the genre that it is found within.

## What Does the Song Do?

In addition to looking at the ingredients that go into making up a song, we also need to look at what the song does. Understanding how a song is put together does not necessarily mean that we understand what it is doing or how it does it. We know a lot about the human body these days, but there are still millions of things that we don't

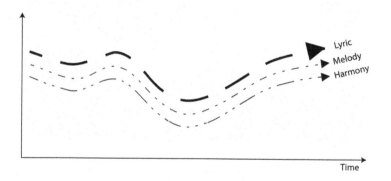

Figure 6.7. *Where lyrics are the focal point.*

quite understand and that scientific analysis is never likely to answer. For example, we understand how the ear works in principle, but can't quite seem to get a handle on why different combinations of waveforms hitting them will generate different emotional responses. Beyond the physical makeup are the emotional and spiritual elements, and this principle applies to songs as well.

We can achieve all our musical grades and get 100% on any music test we ever take, but that will not necessarily make us better songwriters. It means that we know how to control our tools and that we can craft effectively, but it doesn't mean that we have the skill or understanding required to manipulate emotional response in listeners. There are plenty of songs that seem to do everything "right" with regard to compositional makeup, but that leave the listener stone cold. On occasions such as this, it may well be that a producer can make all the difference. In any team creating a recorded product, it can be hugely beneficial to have someone who isn't musically educated. It can be easy to forget that the majority of the listening public will relate to a song on more of an emotive level than an analytical one, and having someone in the team who can offer an "outsider's" perspective in this respect can be massively helpful.

It doesn't matter who that person is or what role they fill. A songwriter with no formal musical training write a song without really understanding it and have a producer focus it a little through applying some core musical principles, or a producer without a traditional musical education can help convert a "correctly" fashioned song into one that goes beyond being competent and into extraordinary.

A song is more than the sum of its parts. In fact, it could be argued that the song exists before any of the ingredients are wrapped around it at all. The ingredients are the tools that enable the writer to give the guts of the song a physical representation. Musical ingredients are essentially an outworking of mathematical principles, and if songwriting was just about combining them, they might be interesting and clever, but they would never really be any more than that. The soul or guts of a song is what can make it magical and wondrous. The ingredients we use to give body to songs are just tools that carry and embody, nothing more and nothing less.

It is fundamentally important to grasp the fact that if the guts of a song aren't in place from the start, the rest of the process will be nothing more than artistic and scientific endeavor. It's all about the song and the vast array of options open to the writer and producer can be so overwhelming that it is easy to forget this point sometimes!

Figure 6.8. *Talking Heads lead singer, David Byrne, has been playing music professionally for more than 40 years. In his 2012 book,* How Music Works, *Byrne theorizes that the process of creating music is shaped by time, place and technology, stating "I believe that we unconsciously and instinctively make work to fit pre-existing formats". Do you agree?*

## WHAT'S THE POINT OF WRITING A SONG?

In seeking to ensure that the quality of the song itself doesn't get neglected under the pile of instruments, plug-ins, monitors and master copies, it's a good idea to start the writing process with the question "Why is this song being written?" It may seem like a mind numbingly obvious thing to ask, but the reality is that this question is often bypassed entirely so that the fun of playing with buttons and automation can begin. The simple truth is that if we don't know why we are writing, the chances are that we won't do a very good job of writing the song in the first place. Even the most basic thoughts such as "What is the song about?" often go unanswered. Nine times out of ten, the reason why writers struggle to finish songs is because they don't actually know what they are writing about. The song has kick-started with a flash of inspiration and got off to a flyer, but that inspiration has not turned into perspiration and has remained the fuel for about 20–30 seconds of promise. There are obviously exceptions to this where songs just seem to appear through just getting on with it, but for every one that works like that, there tends to be a considerable number more that grind quickly to a halt. Knowing the point of a song is massively beneficial. Firstly, it gives us something to work toward and therefore aids the focus and creativity in the writing and production. Secondly, it gives us some kind of meter by which we can assess how successful we have been in achieving our aims.

## What Is It Supposed to Achieve?

We can know what it is about and who it is for without knowing this piece of information. Knowing what the song is intended to achieve enables the writer to be considerably more focused in ensuring that the desired outcome becomes a reality. It will also help set the goal posts for the entire team who will be working on making the product fit for purpose throughout the entire production process. Whether it be to generate an emotional response, to advertise an event, to accompany an occasion, or simply to get something off your chest, a good song will serve some kind of purpose in addition to just existing. The "what," "who" and "where" are all important links between what the song is and the manner in which it will be presented.

## HOW DO WE IDENTIFY WHO THE SONG IS FOR?

This book is all about the process through which a song will make its way through the necessary steps to arrive at someone's ears dressed as *suitably* as humanly possible. Knowing where the song will be "delivered" is useful information to know so as to ensure that the content of the package is right for the recipient. There's no point sending someone something that they don't like. The creator gets to choose whether knowledge of the recipient dictates the creation and treatment of the song, or whether the song's creation and treatment dictates who the likely recipient will be. Songs will appeal to different people on different levels. For some, the compositional makeup of the song is the most important part. For these, the interplay of rhythm and harmony, and of lyric and melody will be where the appeal is grounded. It should be noted here, however, that there are plenty of recipients of songs that will not be attracted on these grounds at all. For many, the attraction to a song is generated not through its content, but the manner in which it is dressed up. The production process is what does this dressing and advertises the song to its full potential. Even if the recipient is able to understand how cleverly crafted a song may be, there is no guarantee that this knowledge will help them get past several other stumbling blocks. One such stumbling block is the production style that the song is wrapped in. When songs are written, the genre that they will fall into can be very obvious even when the song is in its most raw and delicate state. The lyrical theme or groove for example can dictate whether a song is likely to be more suitable for a folk or reggae market straight off the bat. However, it is possible to write a song that facilitates numerous possible routes into all sorts of different genres owing to the fact that its content isn't pushing it anywhere specific. The genre a song lands in isn't always dictated by the song itself. Sometimes it needs to be decided by the producer or arranger at a date after it has appeared in its first form. In fact, there are occasions where a producer may be so sure that the song needs to head to a certain audience that elements of the compositional make up are altered to ensure that its journey into that marketplace is more focused and effective. This marketplace is very important when it comes to viewing the song as a "product" which is essentially what it is when it comes to getting it "out there" to people. Regardless off the impassioned heartache and personal soul-searching that has gone into making a song authentic and "real," the

*Figure 6.9. U2 performing in Ciombra, Portugal, 2002. Having produced a dozen albums between 1980 and 2010, the band U2 continuously reinvents their image and appeals to new subultures by changing the genre of their music from album to album, and realigning their band's identity to address different audiences.*

moment it starts its journey into the big wide world, it becomes a product. For some reason, there are plenty who frown on people "selling out" in this way. It's not "selling out," it's giving out.

The manner in which a song is dressed up and sent out can have a direct effect on whether people will like it at all. When music fits into different genres, which it almost always seems to do to aid marketing and clarification, it also falls into the grip of the subcultures that surround it. When a song and its production gets classed as "Death Metal" for example, it finds its way into the "Death Metal" camp and into the presence of the attitudes and dress codes, etc., that typify that genre. What this then results in is the fact that unwritten rules of taste dictated through fashion and trend above musical appreciation come into play in deciding how accepted that material is going to be. If a song and accompanying production from a foreign camp are thrown into the mix, then there is a real threat that the production itself will get cast aside without a second's thought. The reason for this is that a large number of recipients in the marketplace listen to what they think they are supposed to be listening to above what they can learn to appreciate on a musical level. It happens right across the board in every music genre. Painful though it is to have to acknowledge, there are plenty of recipients who will immediately dismiss a song simply because they can't associate it with how they view themselves and the subculture and accompanying genre or genres of music inherent in that identity. So even if the song is superbly crafted and sent out to breathe with the best upbringing possible behind it, the recipient may cast it aside without a second thought for reasons that are nothing to do with the song at all. Marketing, introduced later in this book plays a massive part in getting the songs to those who will appreciate them, and also in telling them why they will appreciate them. There's a lot more to it than simply combining ingredients as cunningly and effectively as possible. In addition to facilitating a more focused writing and production process, knowing the vision for the product will also enable its marketing and publicity to be more tailor made. If the creator goes with the song first recipient later approach, it could well be that the song is fashioned in such a way that makes it completely undeliverable. As touched upon above, there is no guarantee that the audience will want to hear the song at all if their position has not been considered in its construction. The creators may get lucky and fashion something that fits nicely into a market without much prior consideration, but from a production perspective, it makes much more sense to have the needs and wants of a designated marketplace in mind before or at least at the early stages of a song production.

If knowledge of a target market is useful in focusing the production process, it follows that it makes sense to purposefully glean as much useful information from that target market in ensuring the resulting product ticks all the boxes it needs to.

## What Works?

An obvious place to start in discovering what will work for a designated audience or recipient is just to ask them. Obviously it can't work as simply as this as there will be too many people to ask, and asking them would not provide useful answers as the majority of recipients would not be able to provide the kind of concise musical answers we would require anyway. What we can do is to look at what else that market is listening to. Through identifying the kinds of songs and productions that are popular among the audience that we choose to target, we should be able to get some kind of idea what they will like to hear.

It is interesting to note that target markets tend to identify and present themselves quite coherently whether they mean to or not. It's common for fans of certain artists and their body of songs and productions to share a common interest in other similar artists. Website retailers have got wise to this fact and use it to their advantage in purposefully targeting products at browsers who they have good reason to believe will like what they are pushing. www.amazon.com and www.play.com are just two of many good examples of such sites. Phrases such as "shoppers who bought this also bought ... ," and "like this?, then you'll probably like this too ..." are commonplace and are actually very useful for both the retailer and the buyer. The retailer can count on it as an effective marketing tool to target the most likely demographic to part with some cash, and the buyer can use it as a means to discover new artists that they will probably appreciate discovering. It's not just retailers either. There are plenty of other places where this mentality can be seen at work. Online radio stations are another example where the online community of listeners can introduce other listeners with an identified similar taste to new music whether they do it intentionally or not. The website www.last.fm is a good example of this, and nowhere is it more obvious than at www.audiomap.tuneglue.net. Knowing what people are listening to can be more revealing and more helpful than actually asking them what they want to hear.

Through what they refer to as "Hit Song Science" a company called "Polyphonic HMI" has developed a scientific means of determining the "hit" potential in any song they choose to look at. Through a process they term "Spectral Deconvolution," they have systems in place to analytically assess more than 60 parameters of any given song, and to assess how viable the combination of melody, harmony, rhythm, tempo, octave, fullness of sound, pitch, brilliance, etc., are in giving the song "hit" potential. This may seem a little far-fetched or painfully cold and calculated, or possibly a combination of both, but the principle is actually very sensible and clever. The basic premise behind the technique is to compare the results of the analysis to other songs that have gone on to be hits before. Polyphonic HMI have developed their own "Music Universe" in which they have plotted previous hits like little stars in the cosmos. These songs have been plotted in accordance with the results that came out of their analytical assessment, and it shouldn't be surprising to discover that a lot of the songs assessed actually cluster together in different parts of this "universe." This clustering together reveals that their musical makeup and production sound actually shares a lot in common. We have just acknowledged that this similarity exists in the "real world" where fans of one artist tend to share an interest in other similar artists too, and "Hit Song Science" provides a scientific framework through which the level of this similarity can be quantified.

One of the main sources of inspiration for a budding songwriter is to hear a song and to think something along the lines of "that's a great song and I'm going to write one just like it." The writer then has the option of carefully analyzing the song and trying to replicate something similar as a sort of pastiche, or just going with a similar "vibe" and hoping the result will be pleasing. Generally, the second of these approaches is considered to be more credible as it seems less like cheating, but that isn't necessarily the best way forward. The scientific approach that Polyphonic HMI takes to the assessment of these songs is exactly the same the songwriter will have, it's just that the guesswork is removed and some hard evidence takes its place. Obviously, there is more than just the quality of song and production itself that goes into making a song a "hit" and Polyphonic HMI are keen to state that even a song they assess as having massive hit potential won't necessarily go on to be one. Unless it is marketed appropriately and effectively, a song production will not get the chance to be heard and appreciated regardless of how magnificently constructed it is. Writing a cracking song and making it sound incredible is just a part of the mountain of work that needs to be done.

Figure 6.10. *Beyond musical analysis, marketing to an audience also consists of visual and verbal information conveyed by the album/cd cover and the name of the band. Compare the Jimi Hendrix Experience album cover from 1967 to the 2013 DJ Khalil Westcoast Thang album cover from 2002. Without even hearing the music, can you imagine the genre and the musical makeup of each album?*

Hit Song Science works its scientific magic at the end of the production process. That's all well and good in giving a result once the product has been completed, but what about at the start of the process? Is there something that the writer can do to ensure that the product will start off on the right foot? Emulation would seem to be the most straightforward approach to employ at this stage. Providing alternate versions and adaptations of previously successful models is always a sensible business strategy. If a product seems to be doing well, then it makes sense to "jump on the bandwagon" and to put out something similar. It is certainly the sensible thing to do in the business marketplace where projected sales and forecasts are as close as we can get to predictions of how things will go. It happens in music too. It doesn't take long to think of a song and accompanying artist that came along with a massively successful mold-breaking song, only to be followed by a small but prominent group of artists and/or bands that provided something similar. This happens because those controlling the purse strings at the labels need to make some money, and they are able to do so through following the trailblazer at the front once they have established a new product and paved the way for some new growth in the market. It can seem very unmusical, and that's because it is. At a relatively early stage in the lifespan of a song production, it ceases to be a 'song' to those who market it and becomes a "product" or a "unit" much like any other.

If this pastiche and jumping on the bandwagon happens so often, how is it that new genres and new types of production get a foothold in the market? It tends to be where money isn't a driving factor. The majority of labels endeavoring to survive in the market simply can't afford to take many risks with regard to trying something new. The Internet revolution has hit record labels particularly hard and has resulted in the scaling back of operations, decreased advances and alike. Those in charge have staff to employ and salaries to pay and therefore need at least some products that are almost guaranteed to sell. Whether the chief executive happens to like the product in question personally is rarely of any consequence at all. It's generally where money gives way to a sheer love of creativity and something new that new songs and productions can be given space to flourish. Once that new sound has had some time to develop and invariably grows with popularity, it's then that it can start to turn into more of a commercial viability for some of the big labels. It is at this stage the "underground" nature of the new genres tends to be brought "aboveground" and marketed to the masses. The development and mass marketing of House Music is just one of many good examples of a relatively small and local music phenomenon being taken aboveground and transformed into a mass produced product.

It's not all about creativity free of financial shackles though. There are also times where bands and artists with a massive and passionate following are able to release something completely new and "fresh" relatively safe in the knowledge that a large percentage of their fan base will buy it because it's them and not necessarily because they like the new material. Almost everybody has at least an artist or band or two that they have taken to heart, and whose new album they will always buy. That level of loyalty can lead to new ideas, songs and sounds making their way safely into the public arena too.

What then can the writer and production team do with all of this information? If a song production is going to do a good job of appealing to a target audience, then it needs that target to be identified. It also needs to tread carefully between providing something that the designated audience will want to hear and something new enough to warrant them paying some attention. If all new productions were simply reworks of previous successes, then the musical marketplace would quickly drill itself into the ground through a gradual and gut wrenching decline in variety and adventurous output. A good product will be one that is similar enough to be safe, but at the same time, different enough to warrant it's existence in its own right.

# Defining Independent Games, Serious Games, and Simulations

By Nick Iuppa and Terry Borst

## THE MINEFIELD OF TERMINOLOGY

We'll need to define a few terms before we get going, and none of these terms is easy to pin down. Indeed, even the most trusted media definitions are losing their meanings as technology advances.

For example, what does a term like *television* mean when episodic television is now delivered on iTunes, via broadband, and on DVD? Similarly, the term *videogame* becomes increasingly quaint as we create and play digital games using cell phones and handheld digital "pens" and as we merge the virtual world with the real world via alternate reality games (ARGs).

Nevertheless, we have to work with industry-standard terms even when their boundaries are a little blurry, and we'll find enough general agreement to make these terms meaningful as you navigate these evolving industries.

## INDEPENDENT GAMES

The term *independent games* borrows from the term *independent film*. In the film industry, independent films refer to films not made under the auspices of major studios (Fox, Paramount, Sony, etc.) or "mini-major" studios (Lionsgate, NuImage, etc.). Funded outside the studio system, independent films are, by definition, lowbudget films, with the trade-off being that independent filmmakers usually enjoy more creative freedom than their studio brethren. (In recent years, studios have created their own independent film distribution arms, blurring the line between studio and independent product. But true independent films are still made on very

Figure 7.1. Screenshot of the indie-game Aquaria, developed by Derek Yu and released in 2007.

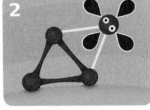
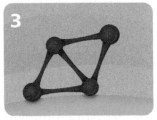

Figure 7.2. Three screen captures of the indie-game World of Goo, demonstrating its gameplay. World of Goo was programmed by Ron Carmel and Kyle Gabler using open-source technologies over the course of two years.

limited budgets, with no studio interference or input.)

Similarly , independent games refer to either entertainment game or serious game titles created by independent companies with limited resources, operating outside the mainstream game publishing industry (Electronic Arts, Microsoft, Sony, Activision, etc.).

As independent game developer Jonathan Blow has noted, "The mainstream industry does not spend much effort exploring the expressive power of games; that's where the Indies come in." Fellow independent game developer Derek Yu has said that independent games are "where the passion is."

Independent games (aka *Indie games* or *garage games*) could only arise when game distribution moved beyond retail shelf space and onto the Internet, thanks to ever-increasing bandwidth and broadband penetration in countries around the world. Often, Indie games are offered as shareware or freeware and sometimes are also "open source," allowing anyone to modify the underlying game code or assets. Some of the most successful independent games produced as of the writing of this book include the following:

- *Portal*, now distributed by Valve Steam (who also distributed *Half-Life* ); *Portal* began as an independent game called *Narbacular Drop*, created by students at the DigiPen Institute of Technology, who entered it into the Independent Games Festival and Slamdance to great acclaim
- *World of Goo*, developed by 2D Boy, an independent game startup
- *Braid*, developed by Jonathan Blow and now distributed via the Xbox Live Arcade service and by Valve Steam

The titles above are the exception that proves the rule about independent games: in general, they have a tough time making "real money." Although the Internet is a tremendous distribution platform, it's also an environment whose users are often reluctant to pay money for a product.

Thus, independent games frequently serve more as calling cards for their creators: they become launch pads for careers and opportunities in the bigger world of mainstream game production and publishing. In this way, independent games are much like independent films: gifted independent filmmakers will almost always "graduate" to studio filmmaking in order to pay the rent as well as to have adequate budgets to fully realize their creative visions.

But while working on its labor of love or seeking licensing on its intellectual property, what can an independent game company do to generate revenue?

Just as some independent filmmakers pay the bills by making commercials or client videos, so can independent game companies now look to producing serious games or simulations for corporate and nonprofit clients. Fittingly (according to Indie game developer Andy Schatz), independent games "spurred the growth of technology that has allowed serious games and persuasive games to be created," bringing us full circle.

The serious games/simulations market isn't easy to break into, clients aren't easy to find, and budgets aren't normally large. But success in this arena can partially or wholly foot the bill for the creation of independent entertainment titles. In addition, the skills and creativity needed to make an engaging serious game or simulation will inevitably be applicable to creating engaging entertainment.

## Serious Games

Early this decade, public policy scholars began to promote a Serious Games Initiative to propel simulation and game development addressing policy and management issues. Gradually, the phrase *serious games* has gained widespread adoption, even though disagreement exists on what they include and exclude.

In general, serious games are designed to act as conduits for each of the following:

1. The transfer and reinforcement of knowledge and skills
2. Persuasive techniques and content aimed at changing social or personal behavior (this would include games that promote, market, and recruit)

Marketing and technology research company Forrester Research broadly defines serious games as "the use of games and gaming dynamics for non-entertainment purposes."

Using "gaming dynamics" for non-entertainment purposes makes a lot of sense in the 21st century. According to University of Wisconsin researchers, videogames are "powerful contexts for learning because they make it possible to create virtual worlds, and because acting in such worlds makes it possible to develop the situated

*Figure 7.3. Grafenworhr Training Area, Germany. The U.S. Army employs serious games to train and teach its soldiers around the world.*

understandings, effective social practices, powerful identities, shared values, and ways of thinking of important communities of practice. "

We might look at serious games as the successors to commercial edutainment games of the 1980s and 1990s ( *Jump Start* , *Reader Rabbit* , and many others), which were aimed strictly at children. Now, with vastly improved videogame technology and more platforms to deliver it on, serious games can be aimed at either children or adults. And we should remember that most adults under 40 are comfortable and accepting of the videogame format. Consequently, serious games have become increasingly popular in education, industrial and emergency training, efforts for social betterment, and marketing. Applications for serious games include occupational training, disaster and emergency preparation, leadership and crisis management, primary and secondary education across the liberal arts and sciences, behavioral and social change, and advertising, recruiting, and activist persuasion.

Because they're built for low-budget development using small teams, independent game companies are ideally situated to develop and produce serious games, which in turn can keep the lights on while an innovative "calling card" entertainment game is under development. But serious games can also be produced by in-house teams, who may outsource some or most of the development and production to small game companies and independent contractors.

Although the two worlds of independent games and serious games are very different, we'll see what independent game developers need to do to win serious game business and succeed in the production of serious games

## Serious Games versus E-Learning Applications

The line between serious games and e-learning applications is becoming increasingly blurry. As learning content began to migrate to digital and online distributions, *e-learning* became the designation for virtual delivery of classroom experiences (lecturing, discussions, assignments, and testing). But simply transferring real-world, real-time classroom pedagogy to the virtual realm has seemed simplistic and sometimes wrong-headed, often ignoring the strengths of each venue while amplifying the weaknesses.

As a result, some e-learning applications have been adopting gamelike features (e.g., quiz show formats, leveling up, lock-and-key mechanisms) to better adapt to the digital realm and better engage the Millennials primarily using the apps.

We have seen e-learning applications labeled as serious games (when they really aren't), and we've seen serious games labeled as e-learning applications (which was sometimes true, but sometimes not).

We continue to separate serious games and e-learning applications, defining serious games as learning, persuasive, or promotional applications that adopt game formats, structure, functionality, and interactions and attempt to be fun to at least some degree. Clearly, a tipping point exists where an e-learning application will adopt so many game tools that it evolves into a serious game.

# SIMULATIONS

In one sense, all games are simulations. But in this book, we'll define a *simulation* as a virtual environment that attempts to accurately replicate (i.e., model) a task or experience for specific training or educational purposes. (Put another way: simulations are models of physical reality combined with models of human behaviors.)

While simulations often use screen-based, three-dimensional, computer-generated environments (such as we see in *Unreal* or *Grand Theft Auto*), simulations may also be delivered through media such as web pages, cell phone text messages, and faxes, or they may be delivered through virtual reality or other physical environments or devices. The question is what exactly we're modeling: navigation, decision-making processes, physical or human interactions, and so on.

We are often asked whether simulations are games. Here's our best answer. Some simulations are extremely open-ended, with little in the way of *game* elements, a game being a closed environment with (1) clearly stated rules, (2) clearly understood goals, and (3) measurements of success or failure in achieving goals.

Other simulations ask users to move through levels, score users for performance, and even offer a winning path through the simulation experience, clearly meeting the test of a serious game.

In the more restricted definition we've offered, simulations with game elements are always serious

Figure 7.4. A common use of simulators is to safely familiarize people with how to fly an airplane or drive large vehicles in hazardous conditions, before placing them in the real-world situation.

games, but serious games do not need to be simulations to succeed, and in fact, the vast majority aren't simulations.

As we might guess, simulations are particularly useful for modeling risky job situations. The airline industry, of course, has used flight simulators for decades, because crashing a virtual airplane is acceptable, while crashing a real one is not. Professional flight simulators cost millions of dollars, but the rapid development of consumer equipment and software means we can now deliver a simulation on a shoestring budget, relatively speaking.

The military, first responders, and industries with potentially dangerous aspects (energy, construction, shipping, etc.) have all begun exploring simulations to better train their personnel. These simulations not only model some of the physical dangers in these endeavors, they often model the leadership and decision-making processes that can either increase or lessen potential dangers.

Simulations of business and financial decision making may not be so life and death, yet the deep 2008–2009 recession demonstrates the high stakes of these realms and the value of simulating these arenas before entering them in reality.

# Section 3

## Aesthetic Choices

# Introduction

**N**ow that you have a story, how do you reinforce that story with your audience? Your aesthetic choices shape the story, creating elements that support the emotion in a song, manipulate the audience into feeling fear, or emphasize a character's evil doings. Aesthetics shape the story, but, of course, you need the story first.

Aesthetics add both textual and subtextual meaning to a story. Remember, the *text* is the direct meaning of the images or words you see or hear, while the *subtext* is how the audience interprets those images or words. What is the textual meaning of the image to the right?

*An elderly man plays chess.*

What is the subtextual meaning of that image?

Paris—Playing chess at the Jardins du Luxembourg

*The man wears a sunhat and a short-sleeved shirt; it must be hot. There are two timers; the man must have an opponent. The pieces are scattered across the board; the game has lasted a long time. The man is playing chess, therefore he must be smart!*

Begin to think about how the aesthetic choices in this image impact the story. What if the character wore a red shirt instead of tan? What if you replaced him with a young woman? What if she played checkers instead of chess? What if there was a beautiful lake in the background instead of a neutral path? All of these are aesthetic choices that change the way the audience interprets the story.

All areas of media arts employ aesthetics, from the characters in a digital game to the layering of sound in music production. Imagine if Lara Croft wore full combat fatigues and used a samurai sword—how would this change the message of the archeologist-adventuress? Lara might seem more interested in combat than discovery and adventure. What if the song "Yesterday" was produced as a punk rock record? Would this change the meaning of the story in the song? You might miss the lyrics, because punk rock uses more instrumentation, a faster tempo, and a stronger "drive."

Most media projects apply audio and video to tell a story. How do the scripted words on the page get translated into aural and visual elements? This section will help you make the aesthetic choices to support your story.

When playing digital games, there is an expectation of gameplay based on the game's genre. If you are playing a first-person shooter, you will play from a perspective where it feels as if you are the main character of the game, and you will be expected to use weaponry to survive and advance in the game. These aesthetics are what set first-person shooters apart.

Similarly, imagine if *Half-Life* used a vintage steampunk style instead of hyper-realistic. The game might not seem as dark and foreboding. Gordon Freeman might not seem as intimidating if his weapon of choice wasn't a crowbar. In the chapter "The Game Consists of Elements" you will learn more about the complexity of game design and how choices such as these impact the user's experience.

The next chapter, "Aesthetics," will take you deeper into the choices you need to make regarding the coloring of your characters and their world. Take, for example, Sully and Mike from *Monsters, Inc.* Character design plays a huge role in how we react to this film. Sully and Mike need to have some complementary attributes to show affinity between them. This is accomplished by using similar values of cool colors. But they also need to have contrasting elements that play to the humor in the film. These include skin texture, height, and, of course, number of eyes. They both need to look scary enough to be monsters, but friendly enough that their interactions with Boo, the young human who finds her way into their world and shows no fear, seem realistic and natural. These are all choices that the filmmakers made that affect you as an audience member on a subconscious level. These choices are not just limited to animated film, but any time visuals need to support a story. Think about the music video for Michael Jackson's "Thriller." Jackson wears his famous red pants and red leather jacket, which makes him the focus of every scene he is in. The sets and backgrounds are always dark, and during the iconic dance scene, the zombies are all in neutral, dark colors, so that your eye immediately follows Jackson. Even his "date" wears all blue denim that contrasts with Jackson's outfit, but she also has pops of red under her jacket and in her jewelry that create affinity with Jackson. All this adds to the story in a way that isn't overt to the audience.

Of course, the emotion you are trying to evoke in your audience is reinforced in other ways, such as through dialogue and framing. The next chapters will touch on both of these areas, which you may not have considered as being impactful to the audience. In particular, you may not have considered how you get visual information about a story from every frame of a film, television, show, or even commercial. Framing gives us the ability to establish location, show emotion, and demonstrate proximity to anything or anyone else in the scene. These images are from a great vintage TV commercial for the 1955 DeSoto (https://archive.org/details/DeSoto5). Notice how the animators begin with a wide shot to establish where are characters are (top). We then see a close-up that shows us the emotion of the characters (middle), and how happy they are to be seeing the product. Finally, we see a medium shot that demonstrates that many people are excited about the product (bottom). It important you have a visual vocabulary for making media, and all of this will be outlined in the chapter "The Visual Languages and Aesthetics of Cinema."

Your aesthetic choices should give your visual story and its characters a basic starting point for communicating with your audience on a deeper, more subconscious level, and should make your story that much more interesting.

*Stills from the 1955 DeSoto television advertisement*

# The Game Consists of Elements

## By Jesse Schell

## WHAT LITTLE GAMES ARE MADE OF

When my daughter was three years old, she became quite curious one day about what different things were made of. She ran around the room, excitedly pointing to things, trying to stump me with her questions:

"Daddy, what is the table made of?"
"Wood. "
"Daddy, what is the spoon made of?"
"Metal."
"Daddy, what is this toy made of?"
"Plastic."

As she looked around for a new object, I turned it around on her, with a question of my own.

"What are *you* made of?"

She paused to consider. She looked down at her hands, turning them over, and studying them. And then, brightly, she announced:

"I'm made of *skin*!"

And for a three-year-old, this is a perfectly reasonable conclusion. As we

Figure 8.1.

get older, of course, we learn more about what people are really made of—the complex relations between bones, muscles, organs, and the rest. Even as adults, though, our understanding of human anatomy is incomplete (can you point to your spleen, for instance? Or describe what it does, or how?), and this is acceptable for most of us, because we generally know enough to get by.

But we expect more from a doctor. A doctor needs to know, really know, how everything works inside us, how it all interrelates, and when something goes wrong, how to figure out the source of the problem, and how to fix it.

If you have just been a game player up until now, you probably haven't thought too much about what a game is made of. Thinking about a videogame, for example, you might, like most people, have a vague idea that a game is this kind of story world, with some rules, and a computer program lurking around somewhere in there that somehow makes it all go. And that's enough for most people to know in order to get by.

But guess what? You're a doctor now. You need to know, intimately, what your patients (games) are really made of, how their pieces all fit together, and what makes them tick. When things go wrong, you'll need to spot the true cause, and come up with the best solution, or your game will surely die. And if that doesn't sound hard enough, you'll be asked to do things that most doctors are never asked: to create new kinds of organisms (radically new games) no one has ever seen before, and bring them to life. Our study of anatomy begins with an understanding of the four basic elements that comprise every game.

## The Four Basic Elements

There are many ways to break down and classify the many elements that form a game. I have found that the categories shown in Figure 4.3, which I call the *elemental tetrad*, are very useful. Let's look briefly at each of the four, and how they relate to the others:

1. **Mechanics:** These are the procedures and rules of your game. Mechanics describe the goal of your game, how players can and cannot try to achieve it, and what happens when they try. If you compare games to more linear entertainment experiences (books, movies, etc.), you will note that while linear experiences involve technology, story, and aesthetics, they do not involve mechanics, for it is mechanics that make a game a game. When you choose a set of mechanics as crucial to your gameplay, you will need to choose technology that can support them, aesthetics that emphasize them clearly to players, and a story that allows your (sometimes strange) game mechanics to make sense to the players.

2. **Story:** This is the sequence of events that unfolds in your game. It may be linear and pre-scripted, or it may be branching and emergent. When you have a story you want to tell through your game, you have to choose mechanics that will both strengthen that story and let that story emerge. Like any storyteller, you will want to choose aesthetics that help reinforce the ideas of your story, and technology that is best suited to the particular story that will come out of your game.

3. **Aesthetics:** This is how your game looks, sounds, smells, tastes, and feels. Aesthetics are an incredibly important aspect of game design since they have the most direct relationship to a player's experience. When you have a certain look, or tone, that you want players to experience and become immersed in, you will need to choose a technology that will not only allow the aesthetics to come through, but amplify and reinforce them. You will want to choose

mechanics that make players feel like they are in the world that the aesthetics have defined, and you will want a story with a set of events that let your aesthetics emerge at the right pace and have the most impact.

4. **Technology:** We are not exclusively referring to "high technology" here, but to any materials and interactions that make your game possible such as paper and pencil, plastic chits, or high-powered lasers. The technology you choose for your game enables it to do certain things and prohibits it from doing other things. The technology is essentially the medium in which the aesthetics take

Figure 8.2. *To achieve a specific tone, you will need to choose a technology that will reinforce the aesthetics.*

place, in which the mechanics will occur, and through which the story will be told.

It is important to understand that *none of the elements is more important than the others.* The tetrad is arranged here in a diamond shape not to show any relative importance, but only to help illustrate the "visibility gradient"; that is, the fact that technological elements tend to be the least visible to the players, aesthetics are the most visible, and mechanics and story are somewhere in the middle. It can be arranged in other ways. For example, to highlight the fact that technology and mechanics are "left brain" elements, whereas story and aesthetics are "right brain" elements, you might arrange the tetrad in a square. To emphasize the strong connectedness of the elements to one another, they could be arranged as a tetrahedral pyramid—it really doesn't matter.

The important thing to understand about the four elements is that they are all essential. No matter what game you design, you will make important decisions about all four elements. None is more important than the others, and each one powerfully influences each of the others. I have found that it is hard to get people to believe in the

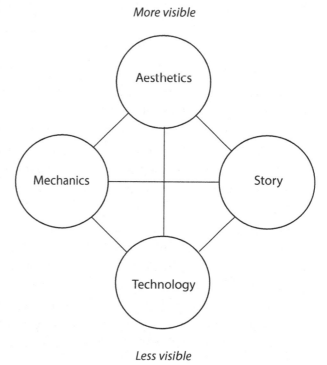

Figure 8.3. *Technological elements tend to be the least visible to the players, aesthetics are the most visible, and mechanics and story are somewhere in the middle.*

equality of the four elements. Game designers tend to believe that mechanics are primary; artists tend to believe the same about aesthetics; engineers, technology; and writers, story.

*Figure 8.4. The cabinet for Space Invaders had a design that was eye-catching and helped tell the story of the evil alien invaders.*

I suppose it is human nature to believe your piece is the most important. But, believe me, as a game designer, *they are all your piece.* Each has an equally powerful effect on the player's experience of your game, and thus, each deserves equal attention.

Consider the design of the game Space Invaders (Taito, 1978) by Toshihiro Nishikado. If (somehow) you aren't familiar with the game, do a quick Web search so that you understand the basics. We will consider the design from the points of view of the four basic elements.

**Technology:** All new games need to be innovative in some way. The technology behind Space Invaders was custom designed for the game. It was the first videogame that allowed a player to fight an advancing army, and this was only possible due to the custom motherboard that was created for it. An entirely new set of gameplay mechanics was made possible with this technology. It was created solely for that purpose.

**Mechanics:** The gameplay mechanic of Space Invaders was new, which is always exciting. But more than that, it was interesting and well-balanced. Not only does a player shoot at advancing aliens that shoot back at him, the player can hide behind shields that the aliens can destroy (or that the player can choose to destroy himself). Further, there is the possibility to earn bonus points by shooting a mysterious flying saucer. There is no need for a time limit, because the game can end two ways: the player's ships can be destroyed by alien bombs, or the advancing aliens will eventually reach the player's home planet. Aliens closest to the player are easier to shoot and worth fewer points. Aliens farther away are worth more points. One more interesting game mechanic: the more of the 48 aliens you destroy, the faster the invading army gets. This builds excitement and makes for the emergence of some interesting stories. Basically, the game mechanics behind Space Invaders are very solid and well-balanced and were very innovative at the time.

**Story:** This game didn't need to have a story. It could have been an abstract game where a triangle shoots at blocks. But having a story makes it far more exciting and easier to understand. The original story for Space Invaders, though, was not a story of alien invaders at all. It was originally a game where you fired at an army of advancing human soldiers. It is said that Taito decided this sent a bad message, so the story was changed. The new story, a story about advancing aliens, works much better for several reasons:

- Several war-themed games had already been released (Sea Wolf, 1976, for example). A game where you could be in a space battle was actually novel at the time.
- Some people are squeamish about war games where you shoot people (Death Race, 1976, had made violence in videogames a sensitive issue).

- The "high tech" computer graphics lent themselves well to a game with a futuristic theme.

Marching soldiers are necessarily walking on the ground, which means the game would have had a "top down" view. Space Invaders gives the sense that the aliens are gradually lowering toward the surface of your planet, and you are shooting up at them. Somehow, hovering, flying aliens are believable, and make for a more dramatic story —"if they touch down, we're doomed!" A change in story allowed for a change in camera perspective with a dramatic impact on aesthetics.

**Aesthetics:** Some may sneer at the visuals, which now seem so primitive, but the designer did a lot with a little. The aliens are not all identical. There are three different designs, each worth a different amount of points. They each perform a simple two-frame "marching" animation that is very effective. The display was not capable of color—but a simple technology change took care of that! Since the player was confined to the bottom of the screen, the aliens to the middle, and the saucer to the top, colored strips of translucent plastic were glued to the screen so that your ship and shields were green, the aliens were white, and the saucer was red. This simple change in the technology of the game worked only because of the nature of the game mechanics, and greatly improved the aesthetics of the game. Audio is another important component of aesthetics. The marching invaders made a sort of heartbeat noise, and as they sped up, the heartbeat sped up, which had a very visceral effect on the player. There were other sound effects that helped tell the story, too. The most memorable was a punishing, buzzing crunch noise when your ship was hit with an alien missile. But not all aesthetics are in the game! The cabinet for Space Invaders had a design that was attractive and eye-catching that helped tell the story of the evil alien invaders.

Figure 8.5. *Some may sneer at the primitive visuals, but the designer did a lot with a little; creating three different characters and a spaceship, each worth a different set of points.*

Part of the key to the success of Space Invaders was that each of the four basic elements were all working hard toward the same goal—to let the player experience the fantasy of battling an alien army. Each of the elements made compromises for the other, and clearly deficits in one element often inspired the designer to make changes in another.

## Skin and Skeleton

It is a wonderful thing to learn enough so that you can see past the skin of a game (the player's experience) into the skeleton (the elements that make up the game). But you must beware of a terrible trap that many designers fall into. Some designers, thinking constantly about the detailed internal workings of games, forget about the player experience. It is not enough to merely understand the various game elements and how they interrelate with one another—you must always consider how they relate to the experience. This is one of the great challenges of game design: to simultaneously feel the experience of your game while understanding which elements and elemental interactions are causing that experience, and why. You must see skin and skeleton at once. If you focus only on skin, you can think about how an experience feels, but not understand why it feels that way or how to improve it. If you focus only on skeleton, you can make a game structure that is beautiful in theory, but potentially horrible in practice. If you can manage to focus on both at once, you can see how it all works while feeling the power of your game's experience at the same time.

# Aesthetics

## By Bryan Tillman

*esthetics* is defined as "the philosophy dealing with the nature of beauty, art, and taste." Hopefully, you can understand why all of these are important to character design. The aesthetic is the first thing the viewer will notice about your character design. No matter what anyone wants to tell you, human beings are attracted to things that look visually appealing. (That's why it's called love at first sight.) Oh come on, you know it's true, and it is no different with character designs. When they see an attractive character, people want to know more about it.

There is no cookie cutter formula that will always make your character appealing to everyone on the planet. People's tastes vary widely, and there is something out there for everyone. You just have to find it. So how can you get the most bang for your buck when it comes to the aesthetics of your characters?

The first thing you have to think about is your audience. If you are creating the character only for yourself, then all you have to worry about is what you like. But if you are trying to reach other people, you have to consider the preferences of the other people who will see your character design. You have to answer two important questions:

1. What is the age group that you are aiming for with your character design?
2. What genre is your character going to be in?

These are the two most important considerations because the aesthetics of your character design depend on your answers.

Let's talk about the age factor first. You will have to do some research to see what the target age group is watching, playing, and reading. This is called "knowing your target audience." Do you know what 0 to 4-year-olds are watching on TV? Do you know why they aren't watching the same programs as 5 to 8-year-olds or 14 to 18-year-olds? You might think you know, but do you really know? Before you answer that question, I'll tell you what I think about the different age groups, and we'll see if you had the same ideas.

I am going to break down the age groups as follows. (This may vary from person to person, but this is generally what I go by.)

**Ages 0–4**   Characters have really big heads and eyes, short bodies, bright colors, and simple shapes.

**Ages 5–8**   Characters still have big heads but less so than characters for the 0–4 age group. Their eyes are smaller, the colors are a bit more muted, and the shapes are more intricate.

**Ages 9–13**   Characters are pulling away from the simplistic. They resemble more believable proportions. The colors are more realistic and have a lot more details.

**Ages14–18**   Characters resemble the real world. They are properly proportioned. The colors are more complicated, and they have the most amount of detail.

Why is this important and why should you care? It's important because it directly influences the design. You don't want to give the viewers too much information if they can't process it. For example, look at what a 4-year-old is watching and then look at what a 14-year-old is watching.

*Figure 9.1.*

Do you notice that the 14-year-old's program has a lot more to look at? There is more they have to process. This is because the older you get, the more information your brain can process. I'm sure that there are cases where that isn't true, but that is the general rule.

Another reason you really want to know your target audience is because you don't want to market a character to the wrong age group. Imagine being the artist who has this great idea about a bloodthirsty mercenary who specializes in killing demons and monsters, and his main quest is to hunt down and kill the devil. It's graphic, gory, and violent, and it even has a little sex in it. Then somebody asks you what age group you plan on marketing this character to, and you reply, "I was thinking 5 to 8-year-olds." Would you let your 5-yearold watch something like this? I know I wouldn't. So you want to make sure that your character is going to ft in with the age group you have in mind. Since we are all visual people, I am going to give you examples of characters placed in the different age groups. First, we are going to look at a character in the 0 to 4-year-old group.

As you can see, this character is very simplistic. There isn't a lot of information to process, just the basics. If we break this character down, you will see that the character is only two heads tall, with the largest part of the character being its head. The idea behind the big head and big eyes is to make the character cute and less threatening. Also, if you look at the lines that were used to define the character, they are very minimalistic. Finally, notice that the colors are very basic—basic in the sense that they are all part of the basic color wheel. There are no shades or tints to any of the colors here. As character designers, we would choose these colors because they are what the age group is learning about.

If you don't believe me, I'll tell you that as a newly minted father, I can tell you out of experience when my child and I are discussing colors, we stick to red, blue, yellow, and so on. Even though I am an artist, I wouldn't tell my 2-yearold that the color isn't really red but burgundy. That would come later if he develops an interest in art.

Which brings us to the 5 to 8-year-old group.

As you can see, the character design has changed a bit. Not by leaps and bounds, but enough to be noticeable. Let's break it down. The head size has become a bit more realistic. Although the character still has a big head compared to the body, it's about three heads high. The line that defines the character is still pretty minimal. The details have become a bit more evident. So we get to see a few more things that define who the character is. The colors are also a bit more advanced and require more of an understanding of color theory. We are getting deeper into what and who the character is.

Now we'll look at the 9 to 13-year-old group. Everything changes in this age group. Kids this age are finding out about the world around them, and they are curious about everything. At this point they should have the mental capacity to

Figure 9.2.

understand and comprehend what is put in front of them. So let's see what a character would look like in this age group.

Do you see how the design has changed to accommodate a more mature level? The line detail and color have become more sophisticated. This is because most artists designing for this age group understand that these kids are well on their way to becoming adults. And you can bet your bottom dollar that this age group doesn't want to be treated like kids anymore.

Some of you might be thinking:

*"At nine, I didn't want to be treated like an adult."*

I'm afraid I have to disagree with you. How many 9 to 13-year-olds have you heard say, "I'm not a kid anymore?" I never said they were adults, just that they didn't want to be kids anymore.

Figure 9.3.

With that in mind, it is fairly easy to design for this age group because you can design stuff the same as you would for the 14to 18-year-olds. Here, let me show you.

Figure 9.4.

Do you see how similar the designs are? At this age people have a fairly decent grasp on what is going on around them. So they want what they are looking at, whether it is fantasy, sci-fi, horror, or whatever, to be rooted in reality as much as possible. There are always exceptions, but as a general rule, you can count on this being true.

So the most important piece of information to obtain from this discussion is that every age group wants to be able to relate to what they are looking at, and as designers one of the big things to relate to is the way a character looks. That is why the younger ages are modeled with childlike proportions and the older age groups want something more adult.

Let's talk briefly about genre. The thing you have to remember is that each genre has very specific qualities that fans of that specific genre want to see every time. So if you are going to be doing a fantasy story, your characters must have some mystical qualities about them. They probably also have to fight dragons, orcs, and goblins. If you are doing a western story, your characters have to be willing to get on a horse and wear a cowboy hat. Once again, there are always going to be exceptions, but genres are based off generalizations. So make sure you know the subject matter of the genre in which you are going to place your characters.

As we continue to look at aesthetics, one of the most important features is color. Color says a lot about a character and his story. It also affects whether a person will have a connection to a certain character. People tend to gravitate toward other people who like the same things they do. Color is one of the things that people tend to gravitate to, it is a mnemonic device that easily works, which you will see later. So it is very important to know the meanings of the colors you use.

First things first; we have to look at the basic color wheel, and then I will convince you that color tells a story about your character.

The color wheel shows the primary, secondary, and complementary colors. Complementary colors are directly across from each other, so red is the complementary color of green, and blue is the complementary color of orange, and so on. I'm telling you this because, well, it isn't labeled on the color wheel and I didn't want you to be confused

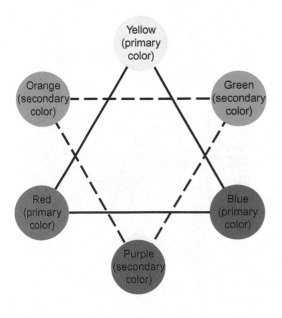

Figure 9.5.

about what complementary colors are. Now here are the colors that we are going to be looking at in depth:

- Red
- Yellow
- Blue
- Purple
- Green
- Orange
- Black
- White

Basically we are going to talk about the color wheel plus black and white. I know there are many more colors in our world, but these are the main colors that we as character designers use. The first thing we have to do is find out what each color says to people.

The color red generally evokes feelings of *action, confidence, courage, vitality, energy, war, danger, strength, power, determination, passion, desire, anger,* and *love.*

The color yellow generally evokes feelings of *wisdom, joy, happiness, intellect, caution, decay, sickness, jealousy, cowardliness, comfort, liveliness, optimism,* and *feeling overwhelmed.*

The color blue generally evokes feelings of *trust, loyalty, wisdom, confidence, intelligence, faith, truth, health, healing, tranquility, understanding, softness, knowledge, power, integrity, seriousness, honor, coldness,* and *sadness.*

The color purple generally evokes feelings of *power, nobility, elegance, sophistication, artifcial luxury, mystery, royalty, magic, ambition, wealth, extravagance, wisdom, dignity, independence,* and *creativity.*

The color green generally evokes feelings of *nature, growth, harmony, freshness, fertility, safety, money, durability, luxury, optimism, well-being, relaxation, optimism, honesty, envy, youth,* and *sickness.*

The color orange generally evokes feelings of *cheerfulness, enthusiasm, creativity, fascination, happiness, determination, attraction, success, encouragement, prestige, illumination,* and *wisdom.*

The color black generally evokes the feeling of *power, elegance, formality, death, evil, mystery, fear, grief, sophistication, strength, depression,* and *mourning.*

The color white generally evokes the feeling of *cleanliness, purity, newness, virginity, peace, innocence, simplicity, sterility, light, goodness,* and *perfection.*

So as you can see, there are many different feelings associated with each color. At this point, you might be asking yourself this question.

*"How can there be so many different feelings evoked by one color?"*

Each color has many tints and shades, and that is where the different feelings come from.

Notice how a different tint or shade applied to the base color changes what the color is saying about itself. The darker red conveys more anger and rage, whereas the lighter red conveys a softer, loving side. I have to mention that if you change the color on a character, it will tell a different story about your character. Here is an example.

Figure 9.6

Do you see how keeping the same character but changing the colors creates a completely new character? This example using a character that is predominately white and one that is predominately black is pretty obvious, but I guarantee it works with all colors. Here is an example.

*Figure 9.7*

Did you see the difference? Are you getting a sense of the character being a bit different? These two are subtle, but the differences are still there. What do you think about the next two?

*Figure 9.8*

Did the character change? Did his story change? What if you look at all four? Are you starting to see that color has an impact on the story of the character? I have one more set of this character to show you.

*Figure 9.9*

I hope these examples helped you to understand the importance of the colors you choose. If you don't put considerable thought into your colors, you could end up with a character that doesn't match the story. Let's look at how characters like Marvel's Spider-man and Hasbro's Snake Eyes and Storm Shadow have colors that match their stories.

With Spider-man, the predominant colors are red and blue. If you look at the colors and the feelings they evoke, you should be able to place some of them on Spider-man's character. If not I am going to break it down for you. Remember we said that blue means loyalty, intelligence, sadness, and power; among other things Spider-man is very loyal to his family and friends, and most of all to New York City. Spider-man is intelligent because Peter Parker is proclaimed to be a scientific genius. He has power because of his spider strength, but the big one is sadness. If I were to pick a primary reason as to why they picked blue I would say it is to represent sadness. Spiderman's life is constantly overshadowed by the death of his Uncle Ben. He became a crime fighter because he believes his uncle's death was his fault.

Let's talk about red. Red means passion, love, courage, confidence, and energy. Spider-man is very passionate about what he does. He believes he can clean up the streets of New York, and let's face it, you have to be pretty passionate to put yourself into the situations he puts himself in. He loves his family and will do anything to keep them safe. Spider-man has confidence in what he can and can't do. It actually borders on being extremely cocky, but it fits with who he is. Finally, if any character has loads of energy, it would be Spider-man. He jumps, flips, swings, and fights—everywhere and anywhere.

See how everything comes together so nicely? You might think this is all just coincidence, but even if Steve Ditko, the designer, didn't do it deliberately, it was still in his subconscious.

Before we discuss Storm Shadow and Snake Eyes, I want to tell you that these two came up at a lecture I gave. An audience member asked me why the colors for Storm Shadow and Snake Eyes were reversed, since Storm Shadow is the bad guy and is wearing white, and Snake Eyes, the good guy, is wearing black. I was glad somebody asked that question because I was able to relate it back directly to both of the characters' stories.

If you look at Snake Eyes, you will notice two things: he is supposed to be a ninja, and he is supposed to be a commando in a military Special Forces unit. So most likely you would wear black for both jobs so you could sneak around undetected, right? Right! That right there would be good enough to suffice for why Snake Eyes wears black. If we were to dig a bit deeper into the character's back-story, however, we would discover another reason why he wears black. Snake Eyes is mourning the death of his ninja master, Hard Master, and as we saw, one of black's meanings is mourning. Now what about Storm Shadow?

We said that white means purity, peace, innocence, goodness, and perfection and is usually associated with the good guy. But when you think about Storm Shadow, these feelings probably don't come to mind. So we have to go back to the character's story to fnd out why this color is appropriate for him. We learn that Storm Shadow was framed for the death of Hard Master. He devoted much of his life to proving his innocence. Also, Storm Shadow constantly strives for perfection. Finally, Storm Shadow always believes that he is doing the right thing, so he feels his motives are pure.

So there you have it! Color can change everything about your character. Just make sure the colors you choose for your characters are saying what you want them to say. The best way to make sure is to ask other people what they think your character is all about. If it lines up with what you had in mind, great! If it doesn't, it's back to the drawing board.

When it comes to aesthetics, another important thing to keep in mind is detail. Detail can make or break a character design. Knowing how much detail to put in your character designs will make the difference between a believable character or one that couldn't possibly exist. There is a saying in the artistic world: The devil is in the details.

What that means is there is a fine line between having too much detail and not having enough. You must always remember that your personal style and the age group of your audience will influence how much detail you need. Even if the age group is in the lowest category, that shouldn't be an excuse to draw unrecognizable and lazy characters or props.

Students often say to me, and I quote, "Oh, that is just my style, and that is why there is a minimal amount of detail." The problem with that statement is that style isn't an excuse. Style is how you perceive the world around you and are able to put it on paper. If we can't tell the difference between your drawings of a gun and a toaster with a handle, it isn't your style; you just don't know how to draw a gun.

I once had a professor who used to say that "L" is the most dangerous letter in the alphabet. It's not a style. It's like reference—the more you draw it, the more it will be engraved in your brain and you will be able to call upon it at any time. That's right, I just made reference to Chapter six. If you don't remember what we talked about there go back and read it again. It is all about reference. But seriously let me show you what I am talking about.

The preceding two drawings can both be classified as guns. We accept them as guns even if one

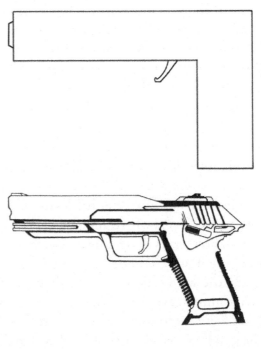

*Figure 9.10*

of them is only the letter "L" with a trigger. But which one do you think is more believable? It won't always be the one that has more details. Depending on your target age group, there must be a balance between realistic and stylistic. Don't get lazy and use the target age group as an excuse to be overly simplistic.

So how much detail is the right amount? The only way to be sure is by trial and error. There is no magic formula. It's a shame, I know, but what are you going do? What I always recommend to my students is that you should show your work to someone who knows nothing about art and your craft. A good person for this is an accountant. Why, you ask?

You probably know that the people in your social circle are only going to give you compliments, and that's not going to help you become a better character designer or artist in general. Thus, somebody who is completely foreign to your craft will at least tell you the truth. The good, the bad, and all the things you didn't want to hear about your beloved masterpiece. Another good person to show your character designs to is someone who doesn't like you. That person will gladly tell you why your work is awful—in excruciating detail—and then it is up to you to take what was said in that verbal bashing and use it to make your designs better.

I am a practitioner of this method of critique. My wife always says she knows nothing about art, so I use her to critique my work. She doesn't hesitate to tell me how awful something is, but, after I swallow my pride, I take a step back, look at my work, and use her remarks to make it better. Believability is the name of the game, and it is very important that it is obtained at all cost. So try this. Show your work to people who will be honest about it. It will make your creations stronger, and that is worth the ego beating.

# Dialogue

## By Robin Beauchamp

## OVERVIEW

Animation has enjoyed a long history of uniquely talented voices infusing personality into their respective characters. One of the earliest known voice artists was Disney himself, serving as the voice of Mickey in *Steamboat Willie* (1928). Artists like Mel Blanc, Daws Butler, and Don Messick devoted their lives to creating the iconic world of talking animals, whereas, Jack Mercer, Mae Questel, and June Foray helped establish the caricature style of voicing humans. As was the case for most voice actors, the characters they voiced would achieve incredible star status yet the public rarely knew the real face behind the voice. Voice actors like Alan Reed (Fred Flintstone) and Nancy Cartwright (Bart Simpson) remain relatively anonymous yet their characters are immediately recognizable throughout the world.

The success of features such as *American Tail* (1986) and *The Little Mermaid* (1989) helped usher in a renaissance of animation. During this period, the reputation for animation improved and "A" list actors once again began showing an interest in animation projects. Perhaps the recent success of directors Seth MacFarlane and Brad Bird voicing characters for their films suggests that we are coming full circle. Like Disney, they demonstrate that understanding the character is essential to finding and expressing a persona through voice. To learn more about the voice actors behind animation, log onto www.voicechasers.org.

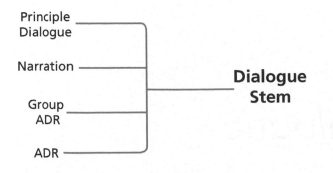

Figure 10.1. Elements of the Dialogue Stem.

## PRINCIPAL DIALOGUE

Dialogue is the most direct means of delivering the narrative, and whenever present, becomes the primary focus of the soundtrack. The speaking parts performed by the main characters are referred to as *principal dialogue*. Principal dialogue can be *synchronous* (lip sync) or *a-synchronous* such as off-screen lines or thoughts shared through voice-over. Some films deliver principal dialogue in a *recitative* (blending of speech and music) style. Two examples of this approach can be heard in the 1954 animation *The Seapreme Court* and the 1993 film *The Nightmare Before Christmas*. With the rare exception of films like *Popeye* (1933), principal dialogue is recorded prior to animating (pre-sync). The dialogue recordings are then used to establish timings, provide a reference for head and body movements, and serve as the foundation for lip sync.

## NARRATION

*Narration* differs from principal dialogue in that the speaker is unseen and cannot be revealed through changes in camera angles. Many animations develop a storybook quality for their projects through the use of narration. Narration is an effective means of introducing the story (*prologue*), providing back-story, and providing closure (*epilogue*). The use of narration as an extension of the on-screen character's thoughts is referred to as *first person*. This technique is used effectively in *Hoodwinked!* (2005) to support the Rashomon style of re-telling the plot from multiple perspectives. The *third-person* narration is told from an observer's perspective. Boris Karloff exemplifies this approach in the 1966 version of *How The Grinch Stole Christmas*. When used effectively, audiences will identify with the narrator and feel invited to participate in the story. Even though narration is non-sync, it is still recorded prior to animating and used to establish the timings.

Figure 10.2. Cory Edwards, the writer/director of the animated film Hoodwinked! is also an actor, and used his talents to voice the character Twitchy in this film and the sequel.

## GROUP ADR AND WALLA

If you listen closely to the backgrounds in the restaurant scene in *Monsters, Inc.* (2001), you will hear a variety of off-screen conversations typical of that environment. These non-sync but recognizable language backgrounds are the product of *Group ADR*. Group ADR is performed by a small group of actors (usually 6 to 8) in a studio environment. They are recorded in multiple takes that are combined to effectively enlarge the size of the group. Group actors perform each take with subtle differences to add variation and depth to the scene. Examples of group ADR can be heard as early as 1940 in the Fleisher *Superman* cartoons and later in the 1960s cartoons of Hanna-Barbera. A more recent example can be heard in *Finding Nemo* (2003) during the scene where a flock of sea gulls chant "mine, mine." In this scene, the words are clearly discernable and as such, are included in the dialogue stem. While group ADR is intelligible, Walla is non-descript. Walla is often cut from SFX libraries or recorded in realistic environments with actual crowds. It can effectively establish the size and attitude of a crowd. Due to its non-descript nature, Walla is included in the FX stem.

## DEVELOPING THE SCRIPT

The script begins to take shape at the storyboard stage where individual lines are incorporated into specific shots. Once the storyboards are sufficiently developed, an animatic (story reel) and recording script are created. At this early stage, *scratch dialogue* is recorded and cut to the animatic to test each shot. Oftentimes it is fellow animators or amateur voice actors who perform these recordings. In some workflows, professional voice actors are brought in at the onset and allowed to improvise off the basic script. With this approach, it is hoped that each read will be slightly different, providing the director with additional choices in the editing room. Once a shot is approved and the accompanying script is refined, the final dialogue is recorded and edited in preparation for lip sync animation.

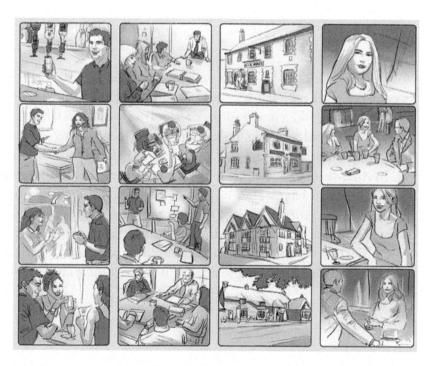

*Figure 10.3. Storyboards are critical to determine where specific character lines will be incorporated into particular shots.*

## CASTING VOICE TALENT

Often when listening to radio programs, we imagine how the radio personalities might appear in person. We develop impressions of their physical traits, age, and ethnicity based entirely on vocal characteristics. When casting voices for animation, we must select voices that will match characters that are yet to be fully realized. We seek vocal performers who can breath life into a character, connect with the audience, and provide models for movement. Voice actors must possess the ability to get into character without the aid of completed animation. Though physical acting is not a primary casting consideration, many productions shoot video of the session to serve as reference for the animation process. It is common practice in feature animation to cast well-known actors from film and television, taking advantage of their established voices. Most independent films lack the resources needed for this approach and must look for more creative means of casting. An initial pool of talent can be identified through local television, radio, and theater.

*Figure 10.4. Spoken word artist Lukas Duczko in 2010. Often, voice actors must possess the ability to get into character without the aid of completed animation.*

## CARICATURE

Voice actors are often asked to step outside their natural voices to create a caricature. Mimicry, sweeteners, and regional accents are important tools for developing caricature. *Animal speak* such as the dog-like vocalizations of Scooby Doo or the whale-like speech in *Finding Nemo* are but a few examples of this unique approach to dialogue. In *Stuart Little* (1999), cat hisses are added (sweetened) to Nathan Lane's dialogue to enhance the character of Snowbell, the family cat. In *Aladdin* (1992), Robin Williams' voice morphs from a genie into a sheep while vocalizing the phrase "you baaaaaaad boy." Regional accents are often used to develop the ethnicity of a character. In *Lady and the Tramp* (1955), the Scottish terrier, the English bulldog, and the Siamese cats are all voiced with accents representative of their namesake. Caricature can add a great deal of depth to a character if used respectfully. It can also create a timbral separation between characters that help make them more readily identifiable in a complex scene.

# RECORDING DIALOGUE

## The Recording Script

Animation dialogue begins with a vetted *recording script*. Each line of dialogue is broken out by character and given a number that corresponds to the storyboard. The recording script can be sorted by character to facilitate individual recording sessions. Some directors hold rigidly to the recorded script while others show flexibility to varied degrees. Many of the great lines in animation are a result of embellishment or improvisation of a talented voice actor. Since the

script is recorded in pre-animation, there still exists the possibility to alter, replace, or add additional lines. Every variation is recorded and re-auditioned in the process of refining and finalizing the dialogue.

Character 1 (Little Orange Guy)
Line 5 (00:03:54:07–00:04:17:12)
I got a plan you see. I'm gonna make a lot more of these machines only bigger. It will make pictures as big as a wall. And they'll tell stories and people will come from all around and give us money to watch them … heh!

*Figure 10.5. Actors that are new to the animation process are often surprised to learn that dialogue is recorded without picture. It is the director's job to help voice actors find the voice best suited for each character.*

Character 2 (Large Blue Guy)
Line 7 (00:04:18:03–00:04:19:22)
You're mad.

*Figure 10.6. Concept art for the lead character in Blender Foundation's short animated film Sintel. Watch the full movie at www.sintel.org*

Character 1
Line 21 (00:04:23:01–00:04:24:17)
What … what what whatabout …

Character 2
Line 22 (00:04:24:23–00:04:38:04)
That is by far the looniest thing I've ever heard. Look mate, no one will ever want to watch little moving pictures dancing on the walls … all right. Much less give some bloody nitwit money for it.

Figure 10.7. *Because most dialogue is recorded from a close microphone placement (8 to 12 inches), any good sounding room can be transformed into a working studio.*

## Directing Voice Talent

Actors that are new to the animation process are often surprised to learn that dialogue is recorded without picture. For many, it is the first time they will rely exclusively on their voice acting to deliver a compelling read. Many arrive at the session prepared to deliver a cartoony voice rather than their natural voice. It is the director's job to help voice actors find the voice best suited for each character. Since their character has not yet been animated, it is important to help the voice actor get inside the character and understand the context for each line. This can be accomplished by providing concept art, storyboards, and a brief breakdown of the script. Directors and/or script supervisors often accompany the voice talent in the live room. Their presence should be facilitative and non-threatening. Directors should resist the temptation to micro-manage the session, allowing voice actors flexibility to personalize the script through phrasing, inflection, and non-verbal vocalizations. In some productions, voice actors are encouraged to improvise off-script. The spontaneity and authenticity resulting from this approach can potentially transform a character or a shot. During the session, it is helpful to record in complete passes rather than stopping in mid-phrase to make a correction. By recording through mistakes, we avoid "paralysis through analysis" and the session produces more usable material.

Figure 10.8. *AKG Perception 120 USB condenser microphone with SH 100 shock mount.*

## The ADR Studio

It is not uncommon for dialogue to be recorded in Foley stages or in facilities designed for music production. Recording dialogue in a professional facility offers many advantages including well-designed recording spaces, professional grade equipment, and experienced engineering. Because most dialogue is recorded from a close microphone placement (8 to 12 inches), any good sounding room can be transformed into a working studio. The essential components of an ADR studio include a digital audio workstation, quality microphones, audio and video monitors, and basic acoustic treatments. The recording software must support video playback with time code. It is important to select video monitors and computers that are relatively quiet. Whenever possible, they should be isolated from the

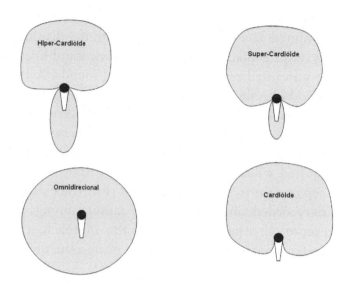

Figure 10.9. Different Types of Polar Patterns

microphone or positioned at a distance that minimizes leakage. If the room is reverberant, sound blankets can be hung to provide additional dampening and sound isolation.

## Microphones

Microphones are the sonic equivalent of a camera, capturing varied degrees of angle (polarity) and focus (frequency and transient response). Most dialogue mixers prefer large diaphragm condenser microphones as they capture the widest frequency range with the greatest dynamic accuracy. There are many condenser microphones that meet high professional standards yet are priced to suit smaller budget productions.

The polar pattern of a microphone is analogous to the type of lens used on a camera (Figure 3.6). However, unlike a camera lens, microphones pick up sound from all directions to some degree. The omni-directional pattern picks up sound uniformly from all directions. Consequently, this pattern produces the most natural sound when used in close proximity to the voice talent. Some microphones are designed with switchable patterns allowing for experimentation. Regardless of the pattern selected, it is wise to be consistent with that choice from session to session. Whether the dialogue is intended as scratch or if it will be used in the final soundtrack, avoid using microphones that are built in to a computer.

Figure 10.10. Tylor Mali performing "What Teachers Make" in 2010. Some directors prefer to keep individual takes intact rather than creating a composite performance. This approach preserves the natural rhythm of the performance while also reducing editorial time.

Principal dialogue is recorded in mono with close microphone placement. The microphone is pointed at a downward angle with the diaphragm placed just above the nose. The recording script is placed on a well-lit music stand lined with sound absorption materials to prevent the unwanted reflections or rustling sounds. Avoid placing the microphone between the actor and other reflective surface such as computer screens, video monitors, or windows. Improper microphone placement can produce a hollow sounding distortion of the voice known as comb filtering. A *pop-filter* is often inserted between the talent and the microphone to reduce the plosives that occur with words starting with the letters P, B, or T. Headphones are usually required when shooting (recording) ADR with three preparatory beeps; many actors like to keep one ear free so they can hear their voice naturally. In some workflows, multiple characters are recorded simultaneously to capture timings of lines interacting and to allow the actors to react to other performers. With this approach, it is still advisable to mike up each character for greater separation and control in postproduction.

## Cueing a Session

In pre-animation, scratch takes of principal dialogue are recorded *wild* (non-sync) and cued on a single track by character. Mixers have the option of recording individual takes on nested playlists or multiple audio tracks. With either approach, all takes can be displayed simultaneously.

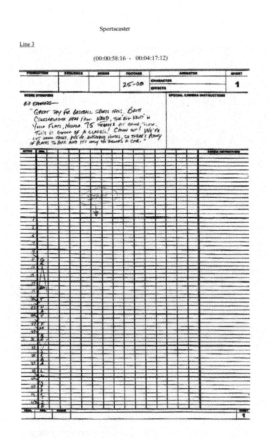

Figure 10.11. Exposure Sheet for Pasttime (2004)

# PREPARING TRACKS FOR LIP SYNC

Some directors prefer to keep individual takes intact rather than creating a composite performance. This approach preserves the natural rhythm of each line while also reducing editorial time. In the second approach, multiple takes are play-listed and portions of any given take are rated and promoted to a composite playlist. When compositing dialogue, the most transparent place to cut is during the spaces between words. With this type of edit, the main concerns are matching the level from take-to-take and developing a rhythm that feels natural. If an edit must be made within a word, cutting on the consonants is the most likely edit to preserve transparency. Consonants create short visible waveforms with little or no pitch variations and are easily edited. It is very difficult to match a cut occurring during a vowel sound due to the unpredictable pitch variations that occur from take-to-take. Regardless of the approach used, once the director settles on a take *(circled take)*, it is delivered to the animator for track reading.

# LIP SYNC ANIMATION

Track reading is an art unto itself. The waveforms displayed in a digital track-reading program represent more sonic events than need be represented visually. Phrases like "Olive Juice" and "I love you" produce similar waveforms unless one places the em fah sis on a different sill ah bull. Animators learn to identify the important stress points and determine what mouth positions are needed to convey the dialogue visually. Track readers map the dialogue on *exposure sheets.* They scrub the audio files and listen for these stress points, marking specific frames where lip sync needs to hit. At the most basic level, consonants like M, P, and B are represented with a closed mouth position. Vowels are animated with an open mouth position. Traditional animators use exposure sheets or applications like Flipbook to mark specific frames for mouth positions.

In 3D animation, the animator imports the dialogue audio files into the animation software, key framing the timeline at points where lip sync needs to hit. Many animators begin lip sync by animating body gestures and facial expressions that help the audience read the dialogue. They view these gestures and facial expressions as an integral part of the dialogue. When effectively executed, this approach leads the audience to perceive tight sync regardless of the literal placement.

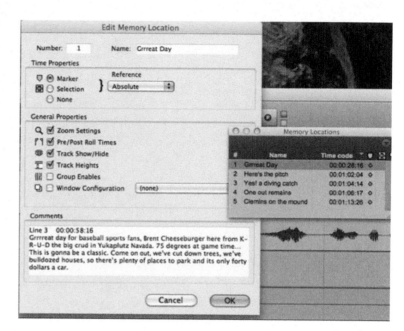

Figure 10.12. Memory Locations for Digital Cues

# ADR

Once the lip sync animation is completed, any changes to the existing dialogue must be recorded in sync to picture in a process known as ADR or replacement dialogue. When recording replacement dialogue, the editor cues each line to a specific time code location within the character's respective track. Three preparatory beeps are placed in front of the cue at one-second intervals to guide the voice actor's entrance. Alternatively, streamers and punches are overlaid on the video to provide a visual preparation for an entrance. Some DAWs provide a memory location feature useful for cueing ADR digitally. With this feature, the location of individual cues can be stored in advance and quickly recalled at the session.

# The Visual Language and Aesthetics of Cinema

## By Mick Hurlis-Cherrier

Film is a medium. ... A medium is based on an agreement, a contract that has developed over a long period during which the speaker and the listener, the picture maker and the viewer, performer and audience, have established a system of meanings: a vocabulary, syntax and grammar of the language being used. For this reason, language emerges slowly, and will continue to evolve for as long as audiences and authors develop new ways of expressing themselves.

Alexander Mackendrick (From On Filmmaking, 2004)

Filmmaking has its own grammar, just as literature does. Everybody knows what basic coverage should be and just because you have some idiosyncratic ideas that might work even though they're breaking rules, the fact remains that there are rules that are there and that work. ... But of course, following the rules does not guarantee that the film will work. That would be too easy.

Ethan Coen (From Moviemakers' Master Class, by L. Tirard, 2002)

## SHOTS, SEQUENCES, AND SCENES

*F*ilm scholars and practitioners alike have long referred to the cinema as a language, which means that it is a shared system of terms, symbols, and syntax used to communicate thoughts, feelings, and experiences. In written language we use letters, words, sentences, and paragraphs. In the visual language of cinema we have four basic elements: the **shot**, the **shot sequence**, the **scene**, and the **dramatic sequence**.

The **shot** is the smallest unit of the film language. A shot is a continuous run of images, unbroken by an edit. Technically speaking, a shot is the footage generated from the moment you turn on the camera to the moment you turn it off—also called a **camera take.** However, these shots are often divided into smaller pieces, which are used independently in the editing stage, and each one of these pieces is also called a shot. Shots can be as short as a few frames or as long as your imaging system will allow before you run out of film or tape or data storage space. The famous shower sequence in Hitchcock's *Psycho* (1960) lasts about half a minute, but contains more than 50 shots, while the film *Russian Ark* (2002), directed by Aleksandr Sokurov and shot on high-definition video, is a 96-minute feature film comprising only one continuous shot!

Crucial to understanding the potential impact of the shot is the concept of **mise-en-scène** (a term derived from a French theatrical phrase that means "put on stage"), which in film terms can be defined as everything visible in the frame of a shot: the subject, actions, objects, setting, lighting, and graphic qualities. The mise-en-scène of a shot contains information, a certain meaning, derived from a combination of what we see in the shot and how it is presented.

Take a look at the very first shot (after the credit sequence) from Darren Aronofsky's 2008 film *The Wrestler* (Figure 11.1.). This shot, unbroken by any edits, introduces us to the main character, professional wrestler Randy "The Ram" Robinson, after a wrestling bout. The choices Aronofsky and cinematographer Maryse Alberti made for this critical shot are precise and convey specific information. The blackboard, toys, and children's drawings which dominate the mise-en-scène tell us that the location is an elementary school classroom, which means that his match was probably in a rented gym and he's forced to use the classroom as a

*Figure 11.1. The mise-en-scène of the opening image from Aronofsky's* The Wrestler *(2008) reveals much about the central character Randy "The Ram" (Mickey Rourke) in just a few seconds.*

locker room. This is not the locker room of a big-time, national pay-per-view championship wrestling arena, so the narrative meaning of this location effectively places him on a very low tier local wrestling circuit, where matches take place in VFW halls, community centers, and school gyms. Randy's hunched posture and the accentuation of the slack aspects of his physique also tell us that this is not a wrestler in prime physical condition. The other aspect of the mise-en-scène that reveals his diminished stature as a wrestler is his position in the frame. Randy is far from the camera and appears very small. He does not command the frame any more than the toy dump truck does. To the right of the truck is another prominent feature of the mise-en-scène, a pair of little kid's stirrup tights. Costume is an important element in mise-en-scène, and Randy is wearing tights too, sequined tights. Sequined tights on big men makes sense in the ring, but in this setting, next to the kiddie's tights, they feel a little like child's play. Finally, the lighting of this scene does not reflect the show-time spectacle and theatrics of big-time wrestling; instead it is as bland and flat as one would expect in this environment, which only accentuates the banality of his dreary circumstances. Everything about the mise-en-scène of this one shot tells us, here is a small time wrestler, isolated and at rock bottom. The crucial concept behind mise-en-scène is that everything you put in a shot has the potential to add story information, so in a very real way you tell much of your story in the shot.

A **sequence** is an expressive unit made up of editing together multiple shots to define a unified action or event, or passage of time or place. Sequences can be designed to make multiple points. The *Psycho* shower sequence just mentioned not only shows us Marion's murder, but Hitchcock, a master of the macabre, also wants us to feel her terror and simultaneously wants to establish a new dramatic question: Who was that woman who killed Marion?

Each shot in a sequence builds on the others, so that by arranging shots in a particular order (or sequence), you can contextualize each individual image to create meaning that is greater than the sum of its parts. Film theorists refer to this concept as **montage** (from the French word "montage," which simply means editing). Broadly defined, montage is the film technique in which meaning is derived from the accumulation of information of the various shots in an edited sequence.

The term **juxtaposition** is often used when talking about sequences. This means placing two or more shots next to each other so that you highlight a link or contrast between the content in each shot. It's essential for a filmmaker to really understand and put to use the fact that a viewer does not simply interpret each image individually but almost instinctively creates additional

Figure 11.2. In Malick's The Thin Red Line (1998), the long shot of a navy ship is followed by a shot of Private Witt (James Caviezel) in a dark location. Although there are no physical clues to indicate exactly where he is, we assume Private Witt is somewhere inside the ship, because of this juxtaposition.

connections between individual shots. If we first show a shot of the United Nations Building, followed by a shot of a group of people seated around a conference table, the audience automatically assumes that this is a conference being held inside the U.N. building. No one needs to announce it; it just becomes a presumed fact. This is a very simple example that, on the surface, seems completely common and obvious, and in fact it is, but on closer analysis you will come to understand the power in the mechanism and the broader creative implications between what's on screen and how an audience assumes connections and actively creates meaning (Figure 11.2.).

Take a look at Figure 11.1 again. We've already analyzed the mise-en-scène information, but add to this the fact that this shot is juxtaposed with a previous shot (as the credits roll). The previous shot is a long, close-up pan over a collection of magazine and newspaper clippings revealing that Randy "The Ram" Robinson was a wrestling superstar in the 1980s; he fought in the biggest arenas, headlined star-studded events, was named "wrestler of the year," and had many fans. Then, when we cut to 20 years later and see that small, hunched, slack figure in the elementary school classroom, the juxtaposition of only two shots effectively traces 20 years of a man's wrestling career from the glory days to the skids. In two shots, without even seeing the man's face, we already know that this is a wrestler who had a glittering career but is now an old has-been.

The "meaning" derived by the juxtaposition of two shots need not only be logistical or expository, but the context created by putting one shot next to the other can also elicit an emotional understanding from the audience. The most famous examples of this phenomenon are the early film experiments of Lev Kuleshov, who in the early 1920s shot the expressionless face of actor Ivan Mozhukhin and juxtaposed the very same, emotionally neutral shot with various other images. When the face was juxtaposed with a bowl of soup, people saw the face as that of a hungry man; when the same shot was juxtaposed with a child's coffin, people read his expression as sorrowful. Each new juxtaposed image inflected Mr. Mozhukhin's neutral expression with a different emotion. It is important to always remember that images and editing are used in tandem to create meaning and communicate your story, in specific terms, to your audience (Figure 11.3.).

Because images and editing function in tandem, they must both be considered as we devise our visual strategy during **previsualization**. That's not to say that we try to precisely edit our film, shot for shot, before we go into production (although Alfred Hitchcock very nearly did just that on most of his films), but it does mean that we need to consider not only what we will

Figure 11.3. *The immovable mask of Darth Vader is sufficiently neutral to take on a variety of emotions, depending on the visual context created through juxtaposition. In this scene from Marquand's Star Wars: Episode VI—Return of the Jedi (1983), we detect feelings of sympathy, concern, and alarm on the ordinarily evil mask of Vader as he watches his son Luke Skywalker get electrocuted.*

shoot (mise-en-scène) but also how these shots might fit together (montage). This is what is referred to as **shooting for the edit.**

Chapter 4 explores these principles in detail. **A scene** is a dramatic unit in which action ostensibly happens in continuous time and within a single location. A scene is usually composed of multiple shots, which guide the audience's attention, and there are principles of visual grammar that we employ in putting these shots together to make coherent sense of time, space, and actions. Depending on the style of the film, a scene, even those that include a variety of camera angles, can also be accomplished in a single shot (Figure 11.4.). This approach has been used throughout the history of cinema, from Bresson to Hou Hsiao-Hsien, but is less commonly used.

A **dramatic sequence** is made up of a series of scenes that create a larger dramatic unit. The relationship between the scenes can vary, because of cause and effect (the result of one scene triggers the beginning of the next) or parallel action (in which the actions in two or more scenes, happening simultaneously, relate to each other), or the scenes can have other associative connections.

Just as in written language, where we put words together to create sentences, and sentences together to create paragraphs, in film we put shots together to create sequences and scenes, and scenes together to create the larger dramatic events of our story. Theoretically, one could certainly shoot any image at all and place it next to any other image, just as one could configure any string of letters to create sounds that resemble a word—for example, *fluugeproit*. This "word" *fluugeproit* doesn't directly communicate anything, and a sentence like "Bilious for at cake one" makes no sense at all either, even though the meaning of each individual word is perfectly understandable. Neither the "word" nor the "sentence" works within our language's shared system of practices.

Likewise in cinema, there are many commonly understood principles that we use for putting the visual pieces together to communicate coherently. **Continuity style** shooting and editing provides tried and true principles for organizing our images to create a coherent sense of space, time, and movement in a way that is recognized and understood by nearly everyone. Keep in mind that, while continuity style is the fundamental cinematic language, there is always room for innovation and evolution. Only a few years ago "smartphone," "blog," "gastropub," and "carbon footprint" meant about as much as *fluugeproit*, but today you'll find them in the dictionary and most of us can actually understand a sentence like, "Today I was at my favorite gastropub and

Figure 11.4. The "Jack/Zak" scene from Jarmusch's Down By Law (1986) is 2 minutes and 45 seconds long and is accomplished in only one shot.

Alfred Hitchcock is known as a master of montage for the way he was able to conjure complex mysteries through visual means—primarily the precise juxtaposition of simple shots that, with a few edits, accumulate complex meaning. In the second scene of Hitchcock's 1937 film Young and Innocent, we are presented with a series of shots that, on their own, don't mean so much, but together they mean murder and mystery! A perfect day, a beautiful beach, a lighthouse, and seagulls. These shots resemble kitsch postcards of a summer vacation spot. Wish we were here (shots 1 and 2)! Waves break along the shoreline and then an arm flops against the water. The shot tells us that there seems to be a swimmer in the ocean. The swimmer, it turns out, is an unconscious woman who is being tumbled by the waves (shots 3 and 4). Now the viewer starts to ask questions. The swimmer washes onto the shore. Her body is limp and clearly lifeless. Did she drown, or was she bitten by a shark? We can't know yet. But a question has been raised, "What happened to this poor woman?" Then, a belt washes up on the shore (shot 5)!

The shot of the belt all by itself simply means that a belt washes up on a beach—no big deal. Juxtaposed only with the first shot it could mean that the beach is more polluted than we thought, given the beauty of the "postcard" shot, but placed here, next to the shot of the woman's body, it seems to answer our question, "What happened to this poor woman?" The belt immediately and clearly becomes a murder weapon and Hitchcock suggests that the swimmer who washed up on the shore was murdered with it! In addition, that idyllic beach becomes an ironic image because, for all its natural beauty, the location has become a sinister crime scene. Suddenly, all those questions, essential to any good mystery movie, flood into the minds of the audience. Who is she? How did she wind up in the ocean? Why was she killed? Whodunit? All in just a few shots (Figure 11.5.).

Figure 11.5. *In this sequence, from Hitchcock's* Young and Innocent, *each image efficiently adds vital visual information that guides the viewer to make specific and complex narrative assumptions.*

used my smartphone to tweet about how staycations reduce your carbon footprint." Cinema, too, is a living language with an ever-expanding vocabulary and ever-evolving syntax—the fundamentals in this chapter are just the beginning of how we speak in film. Just as in writing, the cinematic language can be bland or expressive, prosaic or poetic, utilitarian or profound. The development of visual eloquence and your particular style begins with an understanding of the basic vocabulary and the creative possibilities of the film language. And the best place to begin is with the frame.

> Cinema is a matter of what is in the frame and what is not.
>
> Martin Scorsese

## THE FRAME AND COMPOSITION

### Dimensions of the Frame

Aesthetic considerations concerning the graphic and compositional aspects of your shots begin with the frame. **The frame** has two definitions. The *physical frame* is each, individual, still image captured on film or on video, which, when projected as a series, creates the illusion of motion (see Chapter 8). The *compositional frame* (Figure 11.6.) is a two-dimensional space defined by its horizontal (**x-axis**) and vertical (**y-axis**) dimensions. Within this space we can perceive a third dimension, depth (**z-axis**); however, depth and distance are created through graphic illusion.

The frame is your canvas, the rectangular space in which you determine the parameters of the viewer's perspective. We refer to each of the four edges of the frame as **screen left, screen right, top,** and **bottom.** The frame essentially crops the real-world environment and determines what the audience sees (mise-en-scène) and doesn't see, referred to as **off screen**. Framing your shot, deciding what to show and what *not* to show, is a significant creative decision.

The relationship between the width and the height of the frame is called the **aspect ratio** and is derived by dividing the width of the frame by the height. There are several different aspect ratios used in film and video (Figure 11.7.). The aspect ratio of a full frame of 35mm film, 16mm film, and broadcast

*Figure 11.6. The compositional frame. Although we work with only two dimensions (the x- and y-axes), we can imply depth by emphasizing the z-axis. Still from Mercado's Yield (2006).*

standard video is 1.33:1. In film, this is called **Academy Aperture** (from the technical standards set by the Academy of Motion Picture Arts and Sciences). In video parlance, this ratio is expressed as 4 × 3. In any case, the horizontal (width) is one-third longer than the vertical (height).

Movies intended for theatrical release on film or HDTV broadcast are shot with a different aspect ratio, which elongates the horizontal dimension. The American theatrical release aspect ratio is 1.85:1, the European theatrical release aspect ratio is 1.66:1, and the HDTV broadcast aspect ratio is 16 × 9 (or 1.78:1).

16mm, 35mm full frame and SD video
1.33:1

Super 16,
European theatrical release
1.66:1

HD video
1.78:1

## Shot Composition and the Graphic Qualities of the Frame

Working within the parameters of a given aspect ratio, a filmmaker has a broad pallet of aesthetic choices when designing the composition of a shot. There are no absolute rules concerning visual style except that the choices you make should emerge from the dramatic needs of the script and should reflect your own creative ideas. Each compositional principle is expressed in precise terms, and it's important that you use the proper terminology when applying them to your script and communicating with your crew.

U.S. theatrical release
1.85:1

*Figure 11.7. Aspect ratios. The ratio of the width to the height of a frame depends both on the shooting and the exhibition formats of the film or digital video.*

### Closed and Open Frames

A **closed frame** means that all of the essential information in the shot is neatly contained within the parameters of the frame, and an **open frame** means that the composition leads the audience to be aware of the area beyond the edges of the visible shot (Figure 11.8.). This is not necessarily an either/or choice. A shot can begin as a closed frame and then an unexpected intrusion from beyond the edge of the frame can suddenly disclose the larger off-screen environment. Also, sound or dialogue coming from off screen can serve to open a frame, because it asks the audience to imagine the space beyond the edges of what is visible.

*Figure 11.8. A closed frame contains all essential information within the frame, as shown in Jarmusch's* Stranger Than Paradise *(1984) (left). An open frame has a composition that necessarily implies the existence of space beyond what is contained within the shot, like the gunman's hand protruding into this frame from Melville's* Le Samouraï *(1967) (right).*

## Deep Frames and Flat Frames

We refer to a frame that accentuates the compositional element of depth (z-axis) as a **deep frame** and one that emphasizes the two-dimensionality of the image as a **flat frame.** The graphic factors that are used to create the illusion of depth are the same ones that are minimized to create a flat frame (Figure 11.9.):

1. *Receding planes, overlapping objects, and diminishing perspective.*
   We can achieve a feeling of deep, receding space by creating a mise-enscène in which there are objects placed along the z-axis that define foreground, midground, and background planes. By reducing the z-axis space to two or even a single plane, we flatten the perspective and the space appears shallow. Related to this is the idea of **object overlapping**, which is the understanding that objects nearer the foreground will partially cover or overlap objects farther in the background. Also, related to the notion of receding planes is **diminishing perspective,** which is the perceptual understanding that objects will appear to be smaller the farther they are from the viewer, and conversely, objects will appear larger the closer they are to the viewer. For example, a chicken walking across the foreground of a shot will appear larger than a locomotive far in the background. **Foreshortening** is the same compositional phenomenon but with respect to a single object in which one part of the object appears large because it is very close to the viewer, while another part of the same object appears small because it is farther away, creating a dynamic sense of depth within the frame.

*Figure 11.9. Accentuating depth by using receding planes (left, from Kalatozov's* The Cranes Are Flying, *1957) or by the foreshortening of a subject (middle, from Malmros' Slim Susie, 2003) creates deep frames. Limited number of z-axis planes produces a flatter perspective, (right, from Godard's* Masculin/Féminin, *1966).*

Figure 11.10. *Shooting horizontal lines head on creates flat compositions. Changing the shooting angle so that horizontal lines recede into the distance reinforces the depth of the frame, creating a sense of deep space (frames from Singer's* The Usual Suspects, *1995).*

2. *Horizontal and diagonal lines.*

   Shot head on, horizontal lines or objects in a horizontal arrangement will obviously look, well, horizontal. But shot from an angle, a horizontal line appears to recede into the distance on a diagonal. For example, if we shoot five people standing against a wall for a police lineup head on, the composition will appear flat; if we move the camera 45 degrees (or more) to the side, so that the lineup now recedes diagonally along the z-axis, then we've created depth in the frame (Figure 11.10.). This is a simple yet powerful way to create a sense of deep space. Shooting horizontals head on minimizes the sense of depth.

3. *Deep and shallow focus.*

   The depth of the focus range of a shot can add or eliminate attention to background and foreground information (Figure 11.11.). When focus is deep we can see objects along the z-axis, from foreground to background, in crisp detail. Deep focus gives us an awareness of deep space because it is clearly visible. When focus is shallow, meaning that only a single vertical plane is sharply defined and objects in front of or behind that plane are blurry, our attention is limited to a narrow and flat area.

4. *Shadows.*

   Shadows add depth to just about any image because they accentuate the dimensionality of your subject and their environment (Figure 11.12.). Eliminating shadows, therefore, conceals dimensionality and leads to a flatter image.

Figure 11.11. *Manipulating depth of focus can direct the attention of the audience to selected areas of the composition. The deep focus in Zvyagintsev's* The Return *(2003) (left) lets the audience see the source of the subject's despair (his friends are leaving him behind), whereas the shallow focus used in Leigh's* Naked *(1993) (right) hints at the isolation that exists between the subject and society.*

Although **3D filmmaking** utilizes exactly the same depth cue techniques as standard filmmaking (or 2D cinematography), the difference is that 3D technology replicates one additional element of our ability to visually perceive depth and dimension: stereopsis.

## Balanced and Unbalanced Frames

The principle of compositional balance begins with the understanding that objects in your frame carry a certain visual weight (Figure 11.14.). Size, shape, brightness, and placement can all affect the relative weight of an object in the frame. How you distribute this visual weight within the frame, equally or unevenly, symmetrically or asymmetrically, gives your composition a sense of stability or instability. There is no value judgment attached to balanced

Figure 11.12. Lighting is critical to accentuating dimensionality in the frame. Eliminating shadows conceals texture, creating a flatter image (top). Positioning lights to create deep shadows adds texture and depth to a subject (bottom). Both frames from Coppola's Tetro (2009).

and unbalanced frames; neither is "better" than the other. Like all of the other aesthetic principles in this section, the right choice is the one that is appropriate for the story you're telling and the mood you're creating.

## Rule of Thirds (Looking Room, Walking Room)

Cinematic composition, as with any other art form, has certain classic principles that have developed over time. Film, being a two-dimensional representational art form, developed after painting and photography, has been influenced by many of their ideas of classical form. One such idea is the **rule of thirds**, which is often used as a guide for framing human subjects and for composition in general.

First, we divide the frame into thirds with imaginary lines (sometimes referred to as "sweet spots") along the horizontal and vertical axes and then we place significant objects, focus points, and elements of interest along these lines. For the human form, for example, this would mean placing the eyes along the top third horizontal line. If your subject is looking or moving

Figure 11.13. Although Cameron's Avatar (2009) is a groundbreaking 3D film, it nonetheless uses all the same depth cues as regular cinema. Notice the receding and overlapping planes, the deep z-axis diagonal composition, and the use of shadows to create depth.

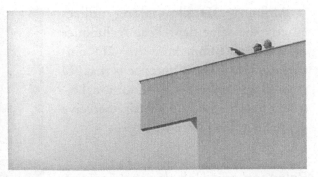

Figure 11.14. *The distribution of objects/subjects in the frame can create a sense of balance or imbalance, according to the needs of the narrative. In Greenaway's* A Zed and Two Noughts *(left), the equal distribution of twins Oliver and Oswald (Eric and Brian Deacon) echoes the film's obsession with symmetry. In Antonioni's* L'Eclisse *(right), the placement of the subjects at a corner of the frame hints at an uneasy relationship with their surroundings.*

toward one side of the screen, then the vertical placement of the figure should be along the left or right vertical third line *opposite* the direction in which the subject is looking or moving (Figure 11.15.).

This extra vertical space, to one side or the other, is called **looking room** (or **walking room** for a moving figure). This space provides a sense of balance because the direction of the gaze, or movement, itself carries a sort of compositional weight. This space also keeps the viewer from feeling like the subject is pushing, or about to go beyond, the edge of the frame. Of course, you may *want* to create that uneasy sense. For example, if you want to accentuate the urgency of a character running, you might want that person bumping up against the front edge of the frame, as if the camera itself can't keep up with them! But this is an expressive deviation (Figure 11.16.), which is made possible by the common application of the rule of thirds. Again, the rule of thirds is just a guide, a convention, and not really a rule at all, and while it is often employed and can be a useful starting point, it is by no means a requirement for a well-composed shot.

Figure 11.15. *Typical use of the rule of thirds. Note how the "sweet spots" created by the intersection of the lines located at the thirds of the image are used to position the subject, giving her proper headroom and viewing room. Still from Mercado's* Yield *(2006).*

## Shot Size

Shot size refers to the size of your subject in the frame. The size of your subject is determined by two factors: (1) the proximity of subject to camera (the closer the subject is to the camera, the larger it will appear) and (2) the degree of lens magnification (the more your lens magnifies the subject, the larger the subject will appear). Dramatically speaking, one selects a shot size based of the narrative emphasis, visual information, and emotional impact needed from a particular shot at a particular moment in the story. As the following figures show, most films are made up of a wide variety of shot sizes.

The frame of reference for any discussion of shot size is traditionally the human form, but the following shot designations work for nonhuman subjects as well:

Figure 11.16. Breaking the rule of thirds for dramatic impact. In this scene from Hooper's 2010 film The King's Speech, Prince Albert "Bertie" (Colin Firth) is boxed in by the bottom left edge of the frame and the corner of the sofa, reflecting his extreme discomfort at having to go to the office of a commoner to receive speech therapy. Notice how the elimination of looking room further accentuates his sense of unease.

- An **extreme long shot** or **wide shot** (ELS) is a shot that shows a large view of the location, setting, or landscape (Figure 11.17.). Even if there are people in the shot, the emphasis is on their surroundings or their relationship to their surroundings.

- A **long shot** (LS) is generally a shot that contains the whole human figure. It's a good choice when you need to show larger physical movements and activity (Figure 11.18.).

- A **medium long shot** (MLS) frames your subject from approximately the knees up (Figure 11.19.). This shot is sometimes called a "cowboy shot" because, as legend has it, of the need to always see a cowboy's gun belt in the western genre pictures. The French call this shot an "American shot" because of its frequent use in genre movies of the 1930s and 1940s.

- A **medium shot** (MS) frames your subject from approximately the waist up (Figure 11.20.). This shot can show smaller physical actions and facial expressions, yet maintain some connection with the setting. However, location is clearly no longer the emphasis of the shot, as the viewer is now drawn closer to the subject.

- A **medium close-up** (MCU) is generally from the chest or shoulders up (Figure 11.21.). The emphasis of this shot is now facial expression, but some connection to the broader physical "attitude" of the body is maintained.

- A **close-up** (CU) places the primary emphasis on the face or other part of the body (Figure 11.22.). Small details in features, movements, and expressions are the subjects of this very intimate shot.

- An **extreme close-up** (ECU) is a stylistically potent shot that isolates a very small detail or feature of the subject (Figure 11.23.).

Figure 11.17. An extreme long shot (Scorsese's Raging Bull, 1980).

Figure 11.18. The long shot (Scorsese's Raging Bull).

Figure 11.19. *The medium long shot (Scorsese's Raging Bull).*

Figure 11.20. *The medium shot (Scorsese's Raging Bull).*

- **Two shots, three shots,** and **group shots:** As these labels clearly state, the two shot includes two subjects, the three shot includes three subjects, and shots that include more than three people are referred to as group shots (Figure 11.24.).

Figure 11.21. *The medium close-up (Scorsese's Raging Bull).*

### Shot Size and Character identification

When framing a human subject, the shot size is especially important in establishing the level of intimacy and identification you wish the audience to have with that character. Obviously, an ELS and an LS cannot show a character's facial expressions with any detail and therefore these shots convey a feeling of distance and remoteness from the subject. With medium shots we are close enough to clearly see them, but we're still at an observation distance, which is why this frame is rather neutral in terms of creating an emotional connection with a character. When using an MCU and CU we enter the very intimate, personal space of a character allowing us see emotions and reactions through facial expressions. At this proximity, audience identification is quite strong. An ECU is so close that it can be either extremely intimate or, in its own way, mysterious and distancing—especially if the ECU obscures a character's eyes. It

Figure 11.22. *The close-up (Scorsese's Raging Bull). Close-up of a person (left) and an object (right).*

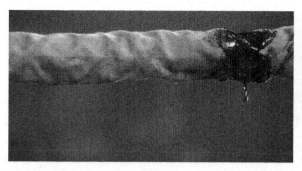

*Figure 11.23. The extreme close-up (Scorsese's Raging Bull). ECU of an object (left) and a person (right).*

depends on the subject and composition of the shot. Understanding this, a filmmaker is able to precisely modulate not only the focus of attention within the frame but also the degree of emotional involvement the audience has with any particular character at any given moment by carefully selecting shot sizes.

## Camera Angles

The orientation of the camera to the subject, the horizontal and vertical angles you are shooting from, has a dramatic effect on your image no matter what size the subject is in the frame. Simply moving the horizontal or vertical position of the camera, relative to your subject, can be a powerfully expressive technique that establishes the viewer's relationship to your subject.

### High And Low Angles

Let's look first at vertical angles (Figure 11.25.). Again, using the human form for our reference, the **eye-level** shot is one in which the lens of the camera is positioned at eye level with your subjects, regardless if they are sitting, standing, or lying down. Raising the camera above eye level yields a **high-angle** shot and below eye level gives us a **low-angle** shot. An eye-level shot can encourage a connection with a subject, while extreme high or low angles tend to be more emotionally remote, but they can make for very dynamic frames.

### Front to Back Angles

The horizontal position of the camera can be anywhere from directly in front of your subjects to directly behind them. A shot in which the subject looks directly at the camera is called **direct address** (Figure 11.26.). Even though music videos use direct address all the time, eye contact with the audience is rare and is especially powerful in narrative films because it shatters the

*Figure 11.24. Two shots, three shots, group shots. These shots are named according to the number of subjects included within the frame (Scorsese's Raging Bull).*

*Figure 11.25. High-angle, eye-level, and low-angle shots. In an eye-level shot, the camera is positioned at the eye level of the subject (middle), regardless if the subject is standing, sitting, or lying down. Positioning the camera above eye level produces a high-angle shot (left), while putting the camera below eye level produces a low-angle shot (right). Examples from Wenders's* Wings of Desire *(1987).*

fictive world by eliminating the separation between the watcher and the watched. Direct camera address is the cinematic version of the theatrical concept of breaking the fourth wall. Much more common are **frontal shots**, in which the camera looks directly at the face of your subject but the subject's sightline glances just off the edge of the frame. Moving the camera along a horizontal arc, we progressively move through **three-quarter frontal, profile shot, three-quarter back** (Figure 11.27.), and finally to **shooting from behind** (see Figure 11.30.). As we move the camera angle from frontal, to profile, to the back of the subject, we drastically change the relationship of the viewer with the subject. Looking directly at a subject's face (frontal and three-quarter frontal) is an intimate perspective and can elicit strong engagement; a profile shot is a somewhat neutral point of view, and hiding the face by shooting from behind can create a sense of distance, remoteness, or mystery. However, shooting from three-quarter back position can also encourage the audience to identify with a character by aligning their visual point of view with that of the subject.

One other camera angle that we can consider adjusting is the lateral positioning of the camera. Tilting the camera laterally so that the horizon of your composition is oblique is called a **canted angle** (or **Dutch angle**) (Figure 11.28.). This sort of shot can create a feeling ranging from slight imbalance to extreme spatial disorientation, depending on the extremity of the lateral tilt of your camera. A canted shot can infuse tension, imbalance or disorientation into a scene.

*Figure 11.26. A character who looks straight into the camera appears to address the audience directly. Each time Amélie (Audrey Tautou) speaks to the camera, she is inviting the viewer into her thoughts and schemes as a secret accomplice to her acts of kindness. (from Jeunet's* Amélie, *2001).*

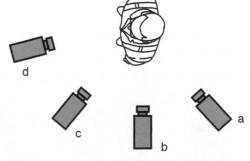

*Figure 11.27. Front to back camera angle positions: (a) three-quarters back, (b) profile shot, (c) three-quarters |frontal shot, and (d) frontal. Unless you want direct camera address, actors should look slightly off the side of the lens in a frontal shot.*

## Creating New Frames And Aspect Ratios

So far, we have been looking at working within the given aspect ratio of the film and video frame (1.33:1, 1.85:1, etc.), but you are not entirely restricted to these compositional dimensions. Many filmmakers find interesting ways to alter the aspect ratios of the area that frames their subjects. Because we cannot physically change

Figure 11.28. In The Crying Game (1992), director Neil Jordan uses a canted angle when a desperate Jody (Forest Whitaker) shows Fergus (Stephen Rea) a picture of his "girlfriend" Dil. This imbalance adds to the sense of precarious tension as Jody struggles to survive.

the aspect ratio of the film or video frame, this technique involves using some element of the location or lighting to crop the existing frame to new proportions. This is called a **frame within a frame** (Figure 11.29.).

## THE MOVING FRAME

A shot in which the framing remains steady on the subject without moving or shifting perspective is called a **static shot** (or **fixed frame**). We can certainly use two static shots edited next to each other to shift the viewer's perspective from, say, a man working at his desk, to the dark window behind him. But there are often important dramatic and stylistic reasons to shift the perspective of the frame and therefore the viewer's attention, horizontally, vertically, or even along the z-axis, during the course of a shot. This is called a **camera move**. Shifting the viewer's perspective, in one continuous motion—from the man at his desk, across the empty room, to the dark window behind him—might provide extra information or a visual connection, which could be vital to fully develop that particular dramatic moment. For example, by scanning the room between the man and the window, we can see that he is completely alone.

Figure 11.29. Frames within frames. The filmmaker is not restricted to the aspect ratio of the shooting format. Through careful use of composition or lighting, it is possible to alter the dimension of the frame to create a dramatically compelling way of presenting a subject. Left from Fassbinder's Ali: Fear Eats the Soul (1974); Right from Hausner's Lourdes (2009).

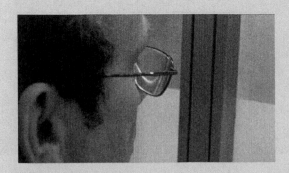

*Figure 11.30. Shots taken from behind Olivier (Olivier Gourmet) in the Dardenne brothers' The Son (2002) bring the audience into the point of view of the lead character but also serve to obscure his emotional response, because we can't make out his facial expressions.*

In their film *The Son* (2002), the Dardenne brothers tell the story of Olivier, a carpentry mentor at a rehabilitation center for juvenile delinquents. One day the boy who killed Olivier's son during a botched robbery is released from prison and winds up in his carpentry shop as one of his apprentices. On the boy's first day the camera follows Olivier, who is following the boy, as he tries to get a glimpse of the kid who killed his son years ago. For extended sequences the camera remains behind Olivier, shooting from a three-quarter back angle or completely from behind (Figure 11.30.). This camera angle choice allows the audience to feel like they're peering over Olivier's shoulder, seeing the world from his perspective; however, this angle does not allow us to see how Olivier is reacting to seeing his son's killer. Through this camera angle, the Dardenne brothers and director of photography Alain Marcoen build enormous tension and suspense by frustrating our need to see what emotions are playing across Olivier's face.

## Camera Moves

There are two kinds of moves: stationary camera moves and dynamic camera moves.

### Pivot Moves

**Pivot camera moves** (also **stationary camera moves**) involve pivoting the camera, horizontally or vertically, from a stationary spot while the camera is running. This can be done on a tripod or with a handheld camera as long as the location of the camera doesn't change, just its horizontal or vertical angle.

A **pan** scans space horizontally by pivoting the camera left or right (*pan left* and *pan right*). A **tilt** shifts the camera perspective vertically, with the lens facing up or facing down (*tilt up* and *tilt down*) (Figure 11.31.). A pan or a tilt that moves from one subject to another is called **panning from/to** and **tilting from/to**. For example, you pan *from* the man at his desk, *to* the dark window across the room. A pan or a tilt that follows a subject as they move within the space is called a **pan with** or **tilt with** (this move is also called a **follow pan** or **follow tilt**). For example, the man at his desk thinks he hears a funny noise outside. We can pan *with* him as he walks from his desk to the window to look outside (Figure 11.32.).

It is also possible to move in closer or farther away from a subject while your camera remains in a stationary spot. **Zooming in** or **zooming out** requires a variable focal length lens. This lens is common on DV cameras but less common on film cameras. Just as with any other move, one can *zoom from/to* subjects or *zoom with* a moving subject.

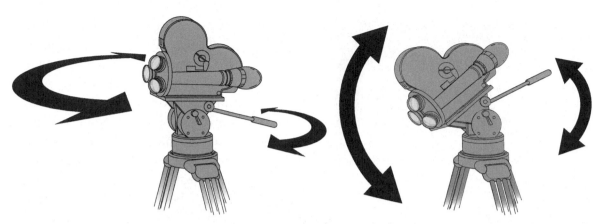

*Figure 11.31. Panning and tilting. In a pan, the camera scans space left or right on the tripod's axis. A tilt shifts the camera's perspective vertically on the tripod's axis.*

### Dynamic Moves

**Dynamic camera moves** involve a mobile camera, which means literally moving the entire camera in space, horizontally (left or right), closer or farther (forward or backward), or even vertically (up and down). These moves can be accomplished with special camera mounting equipment or with a handheld camera.

A **tracking shot** is a term used when you move the camera in order to *follow* or *track with* a subject (Figure 11.33.). You can *track* left, right, forward, or backward to follow along with the movement of your subject. Gus Van Sant's film *Elephant* (2003) makes frequent use of long tracking shots, following characters as they walk through the hallways of their high school. Tracking shots can also be from/to shots. **Dolly shots** are generally moving shots in which the camera moves closer or farther away from the subject (Figure 11.34.). To *dolly-in* or *dolly-out*

*Figure 11.32. Pan with and pan to. In Cocteau's* Beauty and the Beast *(1946), the camera pans from right to left with Beauty (Josette Day) as she explores the Beast's castle. The camera keeps her centered in the frame as she moves from the door to the window (top frames). In a later scene, the camera pans from Beauty to the Beast (Jean Marais) standing across the room. The camera move follows Beauty's look and reveals the Beast, which heightens the surprise and tension of their encounter.*

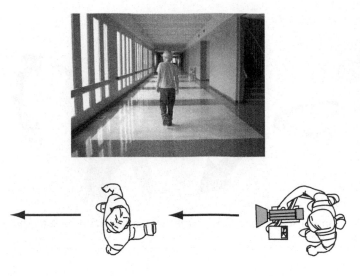

Figure 11.33. *Tracking is when the camera follows a subject as it moves. Tracking shots can be accomplished with dollies, wheelchairs, vehicles, handholding the camera, or, in the case of Van Sant's* Elephant *(2003), with the use of a Steadicam system.*

means to move the camera closer to or farther away from, respectively. Dolly, however, is a slippery term because it also refers to the wheeled apparatus on which we mount the camera to move it. We can certainly move a camera closer or farther away from our subject without using a dolly, for example, with a handheld camera. So you'll also hear people say *push-in* or *pull-out* for this camera move, especially when an actual dolly isn't being used.

Lifting the camera up and down is called **booming** (*boom up* or *boom down*). This can be done with a handheld camera or mechanically with a boom or jib arm (Figure 11.35.). A **crane shot** is one in which the camera is raised very high in the air, certainly above a human subject's head. This usually requires a special, and expensive, piece of equipment called a crane. The specific equipment and techniques used for dynamic camera moves are discussed in more detail in Chapter 11.

All of these moves—pans, tilts, dolly, tracking, booming, and zooming—are often combined. For example, following the trajectory of a helium balloon just as a child lets go of it would require panning and tilting simultaneously—one might even want additionally to zoom in. Executing more than one move at a time is referred to as a **combination move** and is very common.

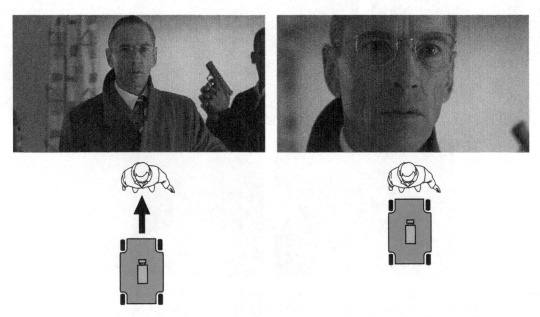

Figure 11.34. *In a dolly shot, the camera is moved away or closer to a stationary subject. In this example, from Demme's* The Silence of the Lambs *(1991), a dolly-in move was used to underline the dramatic moment in which Jack (Scott Glen) realizes they've just seized the wrong house and put Clarice (Jodie Foster) in grave danger.*

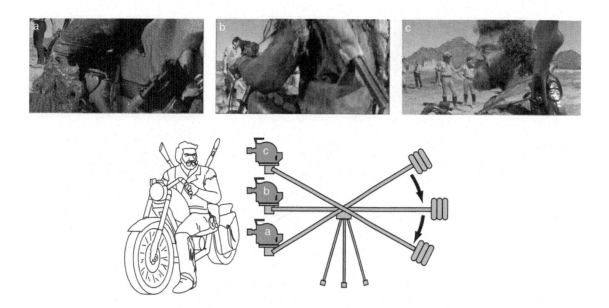

Figure 11.35. This boom shot, from Coen's Raising Arizona (1987), reveals the bounty hunter Leonard Smalls (Randall "Tex" Cobb) from boots to beard. The camera move not only scans his arsenal of weaponry but also emphasizes his fearsomeness.

## The Moving Frame and Perspective

Although the general directions of the frame shifts are similar (i.e., left to right or up and down), there is a big difference between stationary camera moves (pans and tilts) and dynamic camera moves (dolly, track, and boom). Think of the camera as essentially the seat from which an audience member views the world of your film. With pivoting camera moves this perspective point of reference remains fixed. Panning or tilting the camera is the equivalent of placing the Steadicam system viewer in one spot and then having them turn their head left and right or up and down. Their viewer's seat becomes the pivot point as they scan the world horizontally or vertically. With a mobile camera, you are essentially moving the viewer's seat through the space of the fictive world of the film. This makes for an extremely dynamic feeling of traveling through space.

Here's an example of the difference. Let's say we are filming a runner, jogging down a street. First, let's shoot the run with a follow pan, placing the camera at the halfway mark along his path (Figure 11.36.).

The beginning of the shot is quite frontal, looking into the runner's face. When he hits the midpoint mark, directly in front of the camera, he will be seen in profile and, continuing, when he reaches the end of his path, we will be looking at his back. It's the perspective of a stationary spectator—as if we were sitting on a bench watching him run past us.

Now, let's go back to the beginning of the runner's path and shoot his run with a tracking shot (Figure 11.37.). We begin alongside the runner, in profile, and as he moves, our camera tracks along with him. As he reaches the midway point and then the end of the path, the runner remains in profile all the way because we have been following parallel to him. In this shot, the viewer, like the camera, is a runner too, a participant—moving through space just like the runner.

*Figure 11.36. In a pan, a subject is seen from different angles from a stationary point as the shot progresses. In this example, the runner is facing the camera at the beginning of the shot and is seen from behind at the end of it.*

## Motivation and the Moving Camera

Camera moves can look very cool, and because they do, they are one of the most over used techniques in film. Your film, after all, should be about what happens to the characters and not about what's happening with the camera. So like all film techniques, you need a good reason to employ a moving camera. Camera moves should be **motivated** in two ways. First, conceptually speaking, a camera move must have a narrative function, meaning that it serves as an important storytelling technique. If it is included just because it looks snazzy, then it will be a distraction rather than and enhancement. Second, the moment the physical camera move actually begins needs to be motivated within the scene.

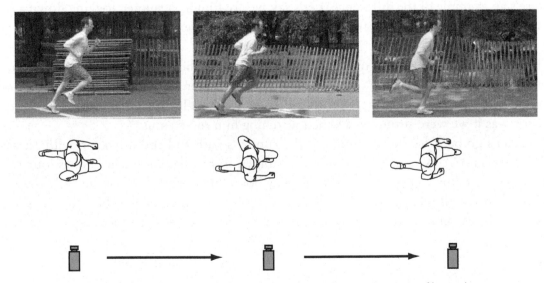

*Figure 11.37. Here the camera tracks with the runner, maintaining a consistent profile angle.*

## Narrative Motivation: Reveal, Conceal, or Dramatic Punctuation

A camera move, whether it's a pan, track, or zoom, is a promise—it promises the viewers that they are going to get a new piece of information, a new perspective or a new understanding by the end of the camera's little trip. Let's say we're shooting a wide shot of a mountain range and we pan right; the pan promises the viewer that we'll see something in addition to those

Figure 11.38. The short dolly push-in underscores a particularly dramatic and pivotal moment in a scene from von Donnersmarck's The Lives of Others.

mountains: maybe the pan reveals a forest fire raging on the south slopes or maybe a cowboy comes into view in the foreground, or perhaps the pan of the mountains goes on and on and on and the move reveals that our character is surrounded by mountains on all sides. But if you just pan from some mountains to a few more mountains and the move accomplishes nothing more than a static shot would, then the move breaks its promise of showing something else, and it is considered an unmotivated move. Although camera moves are often used to **reveal** new (and sometimes startling) information within a single shot, they can also be used to **conceal** actions and details for dramatic effect. What, how, and when you reveal or conceal details are very important factors to consider when you devise camera moves of any sort (see the "Reveal Conceal Camera Movement" box).

Short camera moves, like a short dolly-in to a character's face or a short arc around a character can be used to punctuate an important or highly emotional moment. These shots do not change the image composition very much; rather, they infuse a little jolt of energy at critical points in the narrative. Florian Henckel von Donnersmarck's 2009 film *The Lives of Others* revolves around East German Stasi (secret police) officer Captain Weisler (Ulrich Mühe) and his covert surveillance of a couple: the playwright Dreyman (Sebastian Koch) and his lover Christa-Maria (Martina Gedeck), an actress. Early in the film Captain Weisler starts to feel sympathetic toward the two "subversives" he's spying on and actually comforts Christa-Maria at a local bar as if he were just a friendly stranger. However, later in the film Weisler is asked by his superior to interrogate her directly. Weisler knows that she will recognize him as the stranger

## Reveal and Conceal Camera Movement

The 2009 film *Creation*, directed by Jon Amiel and shot by Jess Hall, is about Charles Darwin as he struggles to complete his life's work on the origin of species. Although he believes absolutely in the scientific evidence of his theory of evolution, his inability to reconcile the death of his beloved daughter Annie with the brutal natural cycle of survival of the fittest, which he is espousing, has caused serious trauma to his health and his ability to complete the manuscript. The opening frame of this scene shows Darwin alone, procrastinating with research he doesn't really need to finish his book, but as the camera dolly-arcs around him (frame right), it reveals another figure in the room with him—the spirit of his deceased daughter. This small perspective shift effectively moves us right into Darwin's psyche. At first, Annie remains out of focus, but as Darwin shares deeply personal thoughts with her, she comes into sharper focus. Through this surprising dolly "reveal," Amiel manages to imbue a flesh-and-blood actor with the aura of an apparition who has just appeared, conjured by Darwin's troubled mind (Figure 11.39.).

Camera moves that conceal space or action have been used since the very early days of cinema primarily to conceal a violent or sexual encounter that might run afoul of the censors. We've all seen it. A man and a woman enter a passionate embrace, kiss, and recline onto a bed as ... the camera pans away to the window where a thunderstorm is raging. Quentin Tarantino and his director of photography Andrzej Sekula slyly wink at this tradition in *Reservoir Dogs* (1998). In this scene Mr. Blonde (Michael Madsen) has been dancing and taunting a captured cop with a straight edged razor. We know he'll use it, we just don't know when. The buildup to the horrific moment when Mr. Blonde moves in to slice off the officer's ear is nearly unbearable, but when the act finally happens, Tarantino dollies left, away from the action, to show a doorway with a sign along the top that reads, "watch your head." The conceal is humorously coy for a director who obviously has no qualms about showing graphic blood and brutality, and the sign above the door encourages us to chuckle at the little joke, but we also know that a man's ear is being sliced off. With this ironic, concealing camera move Tarantino reduces the gore but exaggerates the sadism of the moment (Figure 11.40.).

 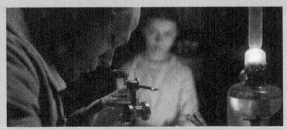

*Figure 11.39. A subtle dolly-arc to the right in Amiel's Creation serves to reveal the presence of Darwin's (Paul Bettany) deceased daughter Annie (Martha West) in such a way that we understand her to be an apparition from his imagination.*

*Figure 11.40. This dolly-left in Tarantino's Reservoir Dogs serves to conceal the physical torture in this scene, yet manages to emotionally amplify this horrifically violent moment.*

who spoke kind words to her in her hour of despair and this recognition could put them both in grave danger. The scene is already suffused with tension, but the short dolly-in electrifies the exact moment he reveals himself to her in his official capacity as a Stasi officer (Figure 11.38.). Notice also that as the camera pushes in, Weisler does not make eye contact with Christa-Maria until the very end of the movement, thus motivating the cut to her reaction.

## Move Motivation

The moment the camera begins to move also needs motivation within a scene. A move that begins arbitrarily can feel artificial and make the camera apparatus itself very apparent to viewers, causing them to become aware of the filmmaker manipulating the world of the film. Camera moves can be motivated by the physical movements of a character or even simply by their gaze. In the example from Cocteau's *Beauty and the Beast* (Figure 11.32., *top*), which was photographed by the inimitable Henri Alekan, the pan-with is motivated by the movements of Beauty who crosses from the door to the window prompting the camera to follow her. Narratively speaking, the purpose of the pan is to reveal more detail of the Beast's castle, particularly Beauty's room at the castle. During the pan we see that this is a magical place, with mist and flora obscuring walls and ceiling this is neither inside nor outside, but more like a fantastical dream space. The pan-to example from the same figure (Figure 11.32., *bottom*) is from the scene where Beauty sees the Beast for the first time. The physical pan move is motivated by her seeing something off screen and the move follows her gaze to reveal the Beast. In cases like this we say that we "pan off her look." The purpose for a pan like this is to place the camera, and therefore the viewers, closer to the subject's point of view—we see what she sees because it is the force of her gaze that moves the camera.

# CONCLUSION

It is essential that anyone hoping to tell stories with moving images develop a deep working appreciation for the concepts of mise-en-scène and montage, because it is here where we truly connect with an audience on the level of story information, meaning, and emotion. In addition, being aware of the expressive power of camera angles and camera moves allows one to conceive of shots, sequences, and scenes that are narratively and emotionally eloquent. When it comes to the aesthetics of the frame—still or moving—we have only laid the groundwork in this chapter.

# Section 4

Bringing Your Story
to Life

# Introduction

Congratulations! You now have the foundations of an excellent story with aesthetic support. Now that you understand the basic building blocks, we can begin to add complexity into the story. This is typically accomplished by communicating with the audience on both a conscious and subconscious (or subtextual) level. This communication with the audience could rightly be called *manipulation*—and you are manipulating the text and the subtext of your artistic work. The term *manipulation* has negative connotations, but it is the basis for entertainment. Think of how happy you feel when Buzz and Woody are reunited with Andy at the end of *Toy Story*, or how sad you feel when listening to "Everybody Hurts" by R.E.M., or how frightened you become when you hear the main musical motif from *Jaws*. All of this is accomplished by layering story with visuals and music in a way that creates a complex experience. By adding complexity to a story, a media artist is able to manipulate an audience into feeling a certain emotion.

Lucky for us, artists have been attacking the problem of manipulation for years, and they have developed some standard concepts that you can build on. In the first chapter of this section, Elliot Grove will teach you how words in the mouths of actors can make you cry. Dialogue is more than just transcribing how people talk; it's making the audience believe that the dialogue is natural, when really it has been crafted and rehearsed by experts over weeks or months. Imagine watching *Game of Thrones* and hearing Daenerys Stormborn say, "Yo, dragons, get 'em." It doesn't quite have the same ring as "I am the blood of the dragons!"

Bruce Block teaches us how to manipulate the most common elements of a visual frame (line and shape) in order to manipulate the audience. Superman, for example, whether animated or live-action, always has a rectangle-shaped head with a square jaw. This visually identifies him as strong. Transversely, the villain from 1941's *Superman: The Mechanical Monsters* (https://archive.org/details/superman_the_mechanical_monsters) has a triangle-shaped head, giving him an evil, rat-like appearance. While line and shape don't apply just to animation, they are the basis for drawn shapes, and ever since Walt Disney and his "nine old men" started exploring the science and art behind animation, certain concepts have been applied. Angie Taylor's chapter expands on line and shape to discuss key animation concepts, such as anticipation, exaggeration, and timing.

Tomlinson Holman dives into the world of sound design, perhaps the most subconscious element of the visual medium. Layers of sound add depth and meaning to the images they support. Imagine a scene from a film without music, sound effects, dialogue, background noises, and ambience. The scene begins to feel flat without it. When Luke confronts Darth Vader in *The Empire Strike Back*, the audience encounters sound effects from the ship, the light sabers, and Vader's breathing, as well as musical score and dialogue from both characters. All of this creates an atmosphere that manipulates the audience into feeling suspense, apprehension, and anticipation. In the absence of visuals, there are layers to music as well. Some songs have dozens of separate tracks, with each track adding depth and subtext to the song. Imagine the different "dialogue"

*Stills from 1941's* Superman: The Mechanical Monsters

that a violin adds compared to that of an electric guitar, or the harpsichord versus an organ. You will learn more about the impact of musical styles in the "Music" chapter.

While games seem to be open-ended, there are many elements that need to be incorporated into their design. Nick Iuppa and Terry Borst will explain the role and the function of designing gameplay using all these elements. Gameplay creates tension and a sense of immersion for the user. Have you played a game with impossible or nonsensical gameplay? Was it an enjoyable experience? Making a game challenging but engaging is part of the goal of Iuppa and Borst.

Complexity is what will give your media depth and meaning, and what makes an experience resonate with an audience. Whether your medium is film, music, or video games, connecting with your audience should be a priority. With these techniques, you should be well on your way to creating your vision!

# Scene Writing

## By Elliot Grove

A screenplay has two parts—the dialogue and the descriptive passages. The descriptive passages in a screenplay are called the *black stuff* referring to the amount of space they take up on the page. Dialogue margins are much narrower.

Script readers frequently reject scripts because they contain too much black stuff. A script with a high percentage of black stuff appears verbose and ponderous.

But script writing is a visual medium and your script will probably have more description than dialogue.

The irony is that in the trade they say that agents and producers (hopefully the first two people to read your script) will never read the black stuff. Instead they read the dialogue, and when they don't understand what is happening through the dialogue, they push their eyes up the page and through the descriptive passages until they understand what is going on, and then they drop back down the page to the dialogue.

It would be a little bit like going into a cinema and requesting a screening of, say, *Gone With The Wind,* and asking the projectionist to put a board in front of the lens, and turn a magic switch and play you the entire movie without the pictures, the sound effects track or the movie track. When the story is not carried by the dialogue alone, then you would go to the projection-ist, rewind a minute (page) or two and replay with the pictures until the dialogue made sense.

Script readers always approach a script with the three 'ums'.

When they pick up a new script, the first um is when they check the length of the script. The next um is as they open the script at random to see if it is properly and professionally typed. The last um, they flick through the pages for an idea of the amount of black stuff to dialogue.

There is no science to this, but by fanning the pages one can get a rough idea of whether or not the script is a talking heads movie, or a descriptive piece.

We do this ourselves when we browse through a bookstore. You probably did this when you first saw this book. Did you not pick it up, and flick through it to see how dense the type was, how long it was, and how many illustrations it contained? Maybe you started to read a chapter to judge the writing style and quality of the ideas.

The next irony is that screenplay is a very sparse, honed down art form and you are denied any of the literary tools used by novelists, lyricists and poets. Simile, alliteration, metaphors and rhymes have little or no place in a screenplay.

## THE BASIC RULES

**You can only write what you physically can see on the screen**

You cannot write:

```
Elliot is depressed.
```

How would you show that visually? It's impossible. Think about how you can show Elliot depressed. You could say:

```
A tear splats at Elliot's feet.
```

---

**Hint:** If your screenplay has too many internal thoughts, you are writing a story better suited to the novel form.

---

**A writer's job is to describe all the action on the screen**

I often get the following line of descriptive action:

```
They make wild passionate love.
```

Remember that a page of screenplay is a minute of screen time. The writer assumes that this love scene will take a minute or two, yet it occupies a single line, making it last a few seconds. I always ask the writer for more detail: Who is on top, what are their hands doing, where are their lips? I also want to see the choreography of the scene—any trick pelvis moves—who knows, I may learn how to improve my sex life!

With your minute, or page of screentime, you now have to decide how long you are going to take to describe this love scene, or car chase. How long is it going to last in your mind's eye of the movie? A minute is a very long time. And if your car chase or love scene is two minutes long, you now have two minutes/pages in which to show us a chase scene from hell or the poke of the century. Don't wimp out. Show us every visual idea you have. Inspire us, titillate us.

---

**Hint:** When you start writing a new scene, sit back and try to imagine yourself sitting in a cinema in front of a blank screen. What would you like to see?

---

## BEWARE OF OVERWRITING

A common mistake new writers often make is to overwrite the descriptive passages.

I recently read a script as a favour for a friend. If you had an extra $25,000 to spend on a venture, would you write a cheque for this:

```
Elliot sits on the stool, his left leg crossed and supported
on the rung. He reaches for a coffee in a shiny blue mug with
the word HOLLYWOOD in gold sitting on the shelf to his left.
He brings the coffee forward to his lips. He suddenly passes
the coffee from his left hand (elbow bent) to his right as the
telephone RINGS …
```

Not only is description such as this overwritten, it is confusing to follow and gives the actors too much detail. It is also dry and boring, and fails in the writer's first task — to inspire everyone on the shoot.

I rewrote the passage as:

```
ELLIOT fidgets on a stool.

Coffee splashes from his cup.

The phone RINGS.
```

## DEVELOPING A STRONG PERSONAL STYLE

The knack of writing descriptive passages distinctively is acquired through practice, and through reading scripts of commercially successful movies that you admire. Once you have achieved the ability of writing compelling descriptive passages, your career as a writer will develop rapidly. Remember too, that you are at all times writing for the reader — the person with a cheque book. It is this person that you must inspire first.

Let's consider the following example of an excellent descriptive passage. It is the opening of *Shawshank Redemption* written by Frank Durabont from the novella by Stephen King:

This scene doesn't appear for nearly a minute (a page), and when it does it is cross cut with the courtroom scene. But it is the opening of the screenplay.

```
A dark empty room.

The door bursts open. A MAN and WOMAN enter, drunk and horny
as hell. No sooner is the door shut than they're all over
each other, ripping at clothes, pawing at flesh, mouths locked
together.
```

```
He gropes for a lamp, tries to turn it on, knocks it over
instead. Hell with it. He's got more important things to do,
like getting her blouse open and his hands on her breasts. She
arches, moaning, fumbling with his fly. He slams her against
the wall, ripping her skirt. We hear fabric tear.
```

There are four movies that are created during the filmmaking process:

- the one you write
- the one the director makes
- the one the actors create
- the one the editor makes

Now imagine again you have a spare twenty-five grand to invest in a movie. Can you see the difference from the example above? Did this scene turn you on? Did you get images of the setting, the action in the scene? Most importantly, would you like to read more?

## THE METHOD OF SCENE WRITING

This is a plan I have developed for writing a scene. It involves getting a piece of paper for each scene and drawing a chart.

**Hint:** Keep description brief. Make every word count. Be very clear about what the point of the scene is.

Write the scene from start to finish. Remember we are not writing dialogue yet. If you have an idea for dialogue, make a note of it on the back of a piece of paper, or write it in the margins.

Do this for the entire script. Then look at the script and ask yourself of each scene: is there a briefer, faster, fresher way that I can say the same thing?

Make the necessary revisions until the entire script flows. Have you ever been typing into a long document when suddenly you feel that you may be repeating yourself but you can't remember whether or not you have typed these words before, and so now you have to scroll up and down a lengthy document? If you are like me, this is one of the most boring and irritating jobs to be confronted with as a writer.

You may want to use the action flowchart.

## ACTION FLOWCHART

Your story is not just about one character trying to reach their goals. It is about numerous characters all trying to achieve their goals, sometimes working together, and sometimes working against each other.

| Scene no. | 12 |
|---|---|
| Previous endpoint | Bob hits the bottle in the local bar |
| Cast members in scene | Bob, Mary |
| Point of scene | Mary and Bob break up |
| Goal of main character | Bob goes to Mary's office to propose |
| Endpoint | Mary tells Bob that it's over |
| Conflict | Mary is tired of waiting for Bob to propose |
| Twist | Bob shows Mary a ring |

Write the scene, what happens, without dialogue

*Figure 12.1. Scene Writing Chart*

This chart is a visual aid that can assist you in keeping track of the actions of the different characters.

List actions that the reader or audience cannot see, so that you can fully flesh out each character. Each character must be fully motivated and active throughout the story. You can also tag scenes to keep track of how many violent scenes/loves scenes you have, for example. The result is a story with multiple lines of action perfectly choreographed with well-defined characters.

Make up a chart with the following headings:

**Tag**
The type of scene: conflict, love, violence etc.

**Scene**
A short description of the scene.

| | Tag | Scene | Hero | Character | Character | Character | Character | 1 | 2 | 3 | Symbol |
|---|---|---|---|---|---|---|---|---|---|---|---|
| 10 | Tears | Bob spills his guts to Joe, the bartender and gets very drunk | Bob / to get drunk | | Joe / to be a friend to Bob | | | | Bar | | |
| 11 | Fight | Bob goes to Mary's office to propose | Bob / to give mary the ring | Mary / to break up with Bob | | | | Office | | | Ring |
| 12 | | | | | | | | | | | |

Figure 12.2. Action Flowchart

**Hero**

The actions the hero takes to reach their goal.

**Four character columns**

The actions of the main opponent and other key characters.

**Three open columns**

For tracking the actions or objects of any character or story element.

**Symbol**

List up to three symbols that can be found in that scene.

Which hurts more: banging your head on a corner of a cupboard, or being zapped by a raygun? Obviously, the laser blast. But what exactly does that feel like? Have you ever been hit by a raygun blast? On the other hand, how many times have you banged your head? When you see an actor bang their head you go 'ouch'. If you see an actor being melted by a raygun, you have no connection with the pain.

Always try to write personal pain. A good example is in *Die Hard* when John MacLean played by Bruce Willis steps on broken glass.

# THE EIGHTEEN TRICKS AND TRAPS OF SUCCESSFUL DESCRIPTION

## 1. Write action, not description

Don't think of writing description, think of writing action—movement. Describing an inanimate object is boring to write and boring to read. And especially boring to a reader with a chequebook!

Remember, your job is to inspire the entire cast and crew. One of the key people on the crew who has to visualize your script is the Production Designer. It is the Production Designer's job to create the actual sets you have described. Sometimes the log line of the scene will do it:

Most screenplays are static and the scenes do not flow. Writing movement into a scene makes your script more interesting to read, immediately distinguishing it from ninety-five percent of all the other screenplays in circulation.

INT. RAINDANCE OFFICE—DAY

From this simple line, the Production Designer will know to create a room with desks, telephones, and computers. The Props Master will add further details, like the clutter and knick-knacks. Here is where you, as a writer with the biblical quote, can use your creativity to inspire.

It is not your job to describe the clutter, the furniture and knick-knacks, unless required by the plot.

If the slugline says INT. RAINDANCE OFFICE—DAY the reader will imagine desks and office furniture. You do not need to mention them.

If the slug line doesn't convey all of the information necessary, then you need to add some simple description.

INT. RAINDANCE OFFICE—DAY.

```
    A puddle of water is growing in the middle of the floor.
```

Now we start to get a more detailed picture of the set, but it is still ambiguous enough to allow for the collaboration of the Production Designer and Props Master.

Once you have all the necessary description of the scene you move on to action. You are still writing description, but you are creating pictures with movement in them—your characters and objects moving in their world. By creating movement you will also enable the reader to visualize the scene. Achieving visualization in your reader will enable them to watch your movie.

You aren't describing things, you are describing things happening. When we use our words to paint pictures, we are painting moving pictures—and that is interesting to a reader. Which means that you have a better chance of selling your script.

---

**Hint:** Action is the element between patches of dialogue.

---

## 2. Attention to details

There are times when INT. RAINDANCE OFFICE—DAY is too generic. The reader needs additional information. The trick is not to bore the reader by completely describing the setting. This could lead you to an overwritten scene—one of the fatal flaws of scenewriting (see overwriting below). Instead, find the one (or two) details which give us clues, and let the reader's imagination fill in the rest.

INT. RAINDANCE OFFICE—DAY

```
    Files and half empty coffee cups litter the room.
```

Or

INT. RAINDANCE OFFICE—DAY

```
    A lonely paperclip partners a vase of flowers on the boardroom
    table.
```

These are two very different offices. How is the first office different from the second? Imagine yourself as a Production Designer. What sort of table lamp would you use in the first office? How would that differ from a lamp in the second office? The carpet is different, the curtains are different, the pictures thumb tacked to the wall in the first are very different from the lithos and expensively framed posters in the second.

---

**Hint:** Carefully select a detail which implies other details. Try to distil the entire situation. Then you can sum up an entire room in one short sentence which also explains character as well. Notice how there are two very different Elliots in the following two scenes.

---

## 3. Paint movement

If you describe people and objects as moving pictures, you can hide the descriptive passages within action, within movement.

Instead of a boring, static still life, you give the reader the excitement of action. You can hide the description within the action.

INT. RAINDANCE OFFICE—DAY

```
ELLIOT slumps amongst the cluttered files and trash.
```

The reader is focusing on Elliot, and doesn't even notice you write the description of the office. No static words in this scene—just movement.

---

**Hint:** Good descriptive writing does three things at once—it shows things happening, describes the location, and illuminates character.

---

## 4. High school English

Readers in the industry are accustomed to an easy read. The language used is of the same level as a high school English essay. Avoid complicated words and convoluted descriptive passages.

## 5. Maximize your vocabulary

The key to economical and dynamic writing is word choice.

During your first draft, you may write a dozen words to explain a situation. Later, you may hone it down to one or two words which explain exactly what you mean. You have hit two birds with one stone—you create quick, easy-to-read sentences coupled with greater impact than your puffed-out original.

## 6. Avoid wimpy verbs

```
Elliot walks into the room.
```

*Walks* is not specific. *Walks* is too general. How many words can you think of for the word *walk*? Does Elliot limp in, stride in, jump in, sneak in, jog in, slide in?

If Elliot saunters in, strides in, struts in, strolls in, marches in, paces in, or bounces in, not only does this give us a specific type of walk, but adds to the action and character while removing clichéd words from your script.

## 7. Classified ad

Screenwriting is a very pared down and sparse art form. The challenge for a writer is to create the greatest possible impact with the fewest possible words. A novelist can spend pages and chapters describing the minutest of details. A screenwriter has just ninety to one hundred and twenty pages to get a complete story across.

---

**Hint:** Economy is the creative challenge.

---

Economy is not only the most important part of a screenwriter's job, it is the most difficult to learn.

How do you learn lean, compact and dynamic writing?

One of my tasks at Raindance is to write copy for the various ads we use to promote the film festival. As you know, newspapers charge by the word. A good trick when you start to write a scene is to imagine that you are writing a classified ad for a newspaper, and you only have a limited budget—say $10. This particular newspaper charges 0.75 per word. Try to see if you can describe the scene and leave yourself enough change to buy yourself a coffee! While writing or rewriting, I will take apart every single sentence and try to find a bolder, fresher, quicker way of saying the same thing. In a first draft, I might have six or seven words that end up being replaced by one. I try to recognize every time I have used unnecessary words or beat around the bush. You will learn how to get directly to the point.

Try to write scene description like you are writing a classified ad.

---

**Hint:** Scenewriting is like writing haiku where you have a very limited number of words. Try to use words that imply other words.

---

## 8. Find the emotion

Don't describe how something looks, but how it feels. The Production Designer will decide how the set looks, the Casting Director decides on how each character will look.

The writer describes the attitude of the scene, the feel, the emotion.

One of my favourite writers, William C. Martell, writes dynamic description that seeps with emotion. Consider the opening of *Hard Return:*

```
EXT. URBAN JUNGLE, 2019 AD—EVENING

The wreckage of civilization. Crumbled buildings, burned out
cars, streets pockmarked by war. Downed power lines arc and
spark on the street.
```

```
This place makes Hell look like Beverly Hills …

Except the battered twisted metal sign reads BEVERLY HILLS.

Night is falling. Fingers of shadow reaching out to grab
anyone foolish enough to be in this part of town.
```

The only time the future is mentioned is in the slug line. Every other word in this scene describes how the future, this scene, feels: frightening, ugly, dangerous.

Did your skin on the back of your head crawl when you read this? Did you get a visual image of the scene? If you were the Production Designer, how many different possibilities would you have in order to recreate this scene?

Suppose you were an actor who had to walk down the street? How would you do it?

---

**Hint:** Well-written descriptive passages describe the scene's emotion.

---

## 9. Avoid poetry

Too much imagery, alliteration, homonyms and other forms of word play can make your script more interesting. But overuse these tools and your script will end up looking cutesy.

Avoid asides to the reader. Your job is to involve the reader in the story, not impress them with your verbal dexterity.

Good screenwriting is both interesting and invisible. Word play should service the script, not show what a good education you have.

## 10. The four-line rule

If you want to *whiten* your script, a good rule is the four-line rule. No passage of action should last longer than four lines.

If you have a big action scene which lasts a page or more, break it up with spaces. Every four lines, put in a blank line. This instantly adds more *white stuff* to your script!

Another quick trick for long action passages is to have at least one line of dialogue on every page … even if it's just a character yelling 'Watch out!' This breaks up the page, and gives the reader a break from reading actions described.

## 11. Style on the page

Try to make each page look attractive and easy to read. Develop your own personal style of writing descriptive passages.

Experiment. After a few scripts, you will develop your own style and your own *voice* in descriptions. Developing a voice is an important step in taking command of the page (more on that, later).

## 12. Character

Do you think you could completely describe a character in three words? John Dahl managed that amazing feat in his script for *Buffalo Girls*, made as *The Last Seduction*.

This is a wonderful example of clear, succinct writing.

```
BRIDGET GREGORY, bitch-ringmaster-goddess.
```

He manages to convey Bridget's occupation and attitude, which allows us to imagine details about everything from the number of tattoos to hair length, personal grooming and wardrobe in a mere three words.

## 13. Active verbs

Use active verbs. Elliot doesn't *try* to sit on the chair, he *sits* on the chair. Better yet, he *crashes* into the chair. *Try* is an energy-sapping verb: it saps power from the active verb. Other pitfalls to avoid are *starts to, begins to* and *… ing*—*walks* is stronger than *walking*.

There are two ways to make a character's quest for global destruction personal:

Make sure your hero has a stake in the outcome, and make sure the audience's identification with your hero is very strong. For example, in *Ransom*, the hero loses his child; in *Patriot Games* and *Gladiator*, the hero loses his family.

Have the villain's plan threaten the audience. Buying a cinema ticket allows you to sit in a cinema. You are minding your own business when suddenly you see that a deadly virus has been spawned, and is rapidly spreading throughout the civilized world (i.e. the USA). The villain, usually a British actor like Alan Rickman, demonstrates how quickly the virus will spread in an hour, a day, two days! Suddenly, sitting in the audience munching your popcorn, you see that your own existence could be threatened unless someone (Arnold Schwarzenegger) stops the virus. The story has become personal. If the hero does not stop the virus, we will perish! Successful films that operate this way include *Deep Impact, Twelve Monkeys, Jaws, Terminator* and *Star Wars*.

At the time of writing, foot and mouth is ravaging the UK. For a movie about this to work, one needs to find a personal story around which the impending doom of foot and mouth could be told.

## 14. Avoid widows

Typesetters call the last word of a sentence that carries over onto a new line of print a *widow*. A single word which takes up an entire line of space. In the rewrite process, kill all the widows. Rework the sentence until it fits entirely on one line. You should aim for a widow-free script. Another benefit is that this discipline will force you into choosing the correct words and eliminate any unnecessary words. As a result, your widow-free script will look cleaner on the page.

## 15. No ands or buts

*And* and *but* are almost always unnecessary. You can almost always delete them.

In real life, pain hurts. Screen writers merit the attention of an audience by making an emotional connection with them. By making an emotional connection with the audience, you allow them to participate in your story.

## 16. Confidence

An experienced writer knows exactly what each page has to say, and knows how to say it. Write strong sentences with strong visual images, and remember that the page belongs to you. Write with such clarity that anyone can open your script at random, read a passage and know exactly what is going on. Don't fill your pages with energy-sapping verbs in long, run-on sentences. It's your script. It's your idea. You are the writer. Write with confidence.

---

**Hint:** Remember the three reasons you won't write a screenplay: lack of Confidence is number one!

---

## 17. Page turners

View each page as its own unique drama. At the end of each page, you must have built up enough suspense that the reader is actually willing to exert the energy to raise his or her hand, grab a hold of the page and turn it.

Build a page turner into each page of your script.

Add extra spaces or trim entire lines just to end a page on a moment of suspense. If there's a moment where the hero is about to be killed but saves himself, put the 'about to be killed' at the end of one page so you have to turn the page and keep reading to get to the saves himself part.

William C. Martell even adds artificial suspense to the end of a page to keep those pages turning. One of his thriller scripts has a scene where the hero comes home, and his girlfriend suggests they go out to dinner.

Boring! The hero enters his apartment on the second to last line on the page. So he added:

```
Hands reach out from behind the door and grab him!
```

At the top of the next page, we find out it's his girlfriend. Lines like this not only turn your script into a page turner, they add suspense, reversal, and excitement.

## 18. Editing

If you think your description is a little overwritten and could use some trimming, be brutal. Kick out every word that is not earning its space.

Design the page so the eye is drawn down, and make sure that you have a page turner at the end of each page.

# EXERCISE FOR WRITING; DESCRIPTIVE PASSAGES

This simple exercise is one you can use in a variety of situations, and will enable you to hone your descriptive passage writing skills.

1. Take a careful look around the room you are in at the moment and describe everything and everyone in it, including yourself.
2. List the movement in the room. If there is no movement, try to recall how you entered the room.
3. See if you can include some of the objects in the room in the description of movement.
4. What is the emotion of the room?
5. Imagine you are sitting in front of a blank cinema screen. What must you tell the production designer to achieve the look of the room?
6. See if you can sum everything up in four lines—the look, the movement and the feel of the room, including any character description.

# SUMMARY

1. Organise yourself. Know which scene comes when, and what the source of conflict is. Use the charts provided, if they improve clarity.
2. Write out the action and keep it as brief and dynamic as possible.
3. Develop your own individual style.
4. Never forget to draw on your instinctive storytelling ability.

# Line and Shape

## By Bruce Block

*L*ines are everywhere in the real world. For example, doorways have two vertical lines, and a volleyball has one curved line. The real world is also full of shapes. A door is a rectangle and volleyball is a sphere. Lines and shapes are closely linked because they define each other.

## LINE

Line differs from the other visual components, because lines appear only due to tonal or color contrast. Depending on this contrast, a line can be revealed or obscured. Lines exist in an infinite number of ways in the real world and in the screen world. To make recognizing them easier, lines can be divided into seven perceptual types: edge, contour, closure, intersection of planes, imitation through distance, axis, and track.

## Edge

The apparent line around the borders of any two-dimensional object is called *edge*.

These four lines are a drawing of a piece of paper. Obviously, a piece of paper is not truly two-dimensional, but for our purposes it can be considered two-dimensional. When you look at this drawing of four lines, you imagine a piece of paper. Examine a real piece of paper, like this book page. There aren't actually any lines around the page, but the edges of the page are similar to lines. We accept this drawing of four lines as a representation of the edges of the page, but actually, a piece of paper, or any two-dimensional object, has no lines.

Lines will appear only if there is tonal or color contrast. A piece of white paper on a black background is easily seen. When the same paper is placed on a white background, the paper and its lines practically disappear. Without tonal contrast, lines don't exist.

A shadow cast onto a two-dimensional wall is an example of edge. We see an edge or line around the two-dimensional shadow, even though there's no actual line there at all.

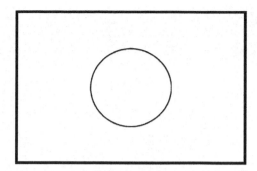

## Contour

The apparent line around the border of any three-dimensional object is called contour. Most objects in the real world are three-dimensional, having height, width, and depth. We perceive a line around these objects.

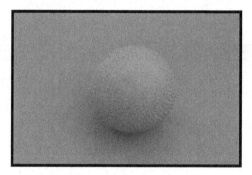

A basketball is a three-dimensional object. We accept the curved line around the ball as the border of the ball itself, but a real ball doesn't have a line around it. Our perception creates the line.

If the ball and the background are the same tone, the lines (and the ball) will disappear, because line needs tonal contrast to be seen.

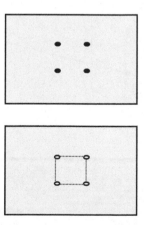

## Closure

Primary points of interest in a picture create imaginary lines.

This is a drawing of four dots, but a viewer imagines lines that create a square.

The viewer connects the dots, or the primary points, in the picture to produce lines. The primary points can be important objects, colors, tones or anything that attracts the viewer's

attention. The dots can connect to form any variety of curved or straight lines, triangles, squares, or other shapes.

Here, the primary points are people's heads. The closure creates a triangle and a diagonal line.

## Intersection of Planes

When two planes meet or intersect, they appear to create a line.

Every corner of every room can create a line if there is tonal contrast between the two planes.

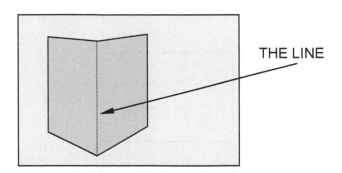

THE LINE

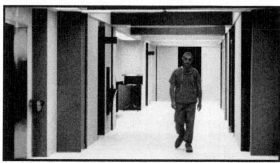

If the tonal range is changed to remove the contrast between the two walls (or planes), the lines disappear. As the tonal contrast is exaggerated, the lines become more apparent.

Intersection of two planes is an extremely common way to produce lines. The corners of furniture, windows, doorways, and the intersection of walls can all create lines if there is tonal contrast between the two planes.

## Imitation through Distance

Imitation through distance occurs when an object appears to reduce itself to a line or lines because it's so far away.

The girders of this tower are not lines; they're large steel beams, yet at a distance, they look like lines. The same is true for the telephone poles or the distant desert road. When viewed from a distance, the objects appear thin enough to imitate a line.

## Axis

Many objects have an invisible axis that runs through them, and this is perceived as a line. People, animals, and trees are examples of objects that have an axis.

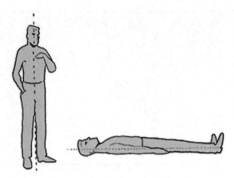

A standing person has a vertical axis. A reclining person has a horizontal axis.

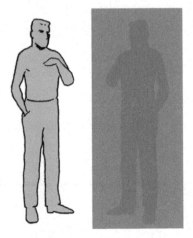

An axis, like most other types of lines, needs contrast to be seen. The axis becomes difficult to define when the tonal contrast between the object and the background is reduced.

This shot has two vertical axis lines.

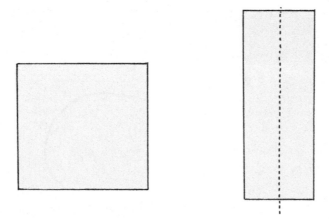

Not all objects have an axis. A square has no definite, single axis, but a rectangle does.

## Track

Track is the path of a moving object. As any object moves, it will leave a track or line in its path. There are two types of tracks: actual and virtual.

### Actual Tracks

When certain objects move, they actually leave a visible track or line behind them.

A skywriting airplane leaves a line of smoke behind it as it flies, and skiers moving down a snowy hillside will produce a line in the snow with their skis. The smoke and the indentations in the snow aren't actually lines, of course; they're imitation through distance or contour, creating a track left behind by the moving object.

### Virtual Tracks

Most objects don't create an actual track or line when they move, but they do generate a virtual or invisible line. A virtual track is a line we must imagine.

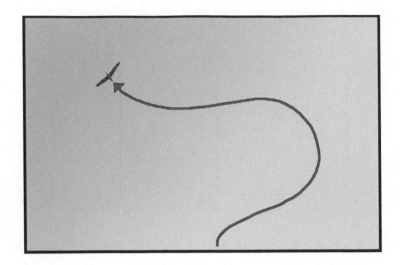

A flying bird or a moving car, for example, generates virtual tracks. The lines left behind by the bird or the car exist only in the viewer's imagination. Since tracks deal with moving objects, we'll return to line and track in Chapter 7, "Movement."

# LINEAR MOTIF

Any picture can be reduced to simple lines. This is called the linear motif. A picture's linear motif can be any combination of circular, straight, vertical, horizontal, or diagonal lines.

Here's a picture and a high contrast version of it that simplifies the tonal range, and reveals the linear motif. The linear motif is found by emphasizing the tonal contrasts in the picture.

There are two ways to reduce any picture to simple tonal contrasts and reveal the linear motif. Many cinematographers use a contrast viewing glass to light their shots and check tonal contrasts. A contrast viewing glass is used like a monocle, but its glass is extremely dark, usually a dark brown or blue color. Looking through the viewing glass increases a picture's contrast and reveals the linear motif. Another way to see the linear motif is simply to squint. Squinting increases a picture's contrast, reduces detail, and emphasizes the lines that create the linear motif.

Squint at this shot. The linear motif is diagonal.

It's essential when evaluating or defining a linear motif that you analyze the line on the two-dimensional screen, not the line in real life.

In the real world, the fountain in this picture has two round bowls. In the screen world, the bowl's curved lines are not curves at all. The diagram reveals that the lines of the fountain bowl are nearly straight. The only curves in this picture are the arches.

## CONTRAST AND AFFINITY

Line is used to produce contrast or affinity in three ways: orientation, direction, and quality. Remember that contrast and affinity can occur within the shot, from shot to shot, and from sequence to sequence.

## Orientation

Orientation is the angle of lines created by nonmoving or stationary objects. Most lines created by edge, imitation through distance, and the intersection of two planes are stationary lines. This includes room corners, doors, windows, furniture, sidewalks, curbs, trees, buildings, etc.

The three angles of line orientation are horizontal, vertical, and diagonal.

Linear motif is usually created by the orientation of lines. The linear motif of each picture is diagrammed in the accompanying drawing. If you can't see the linear motif created by orientation, squint at the picture to remove extraneous details that camouflage the lines.

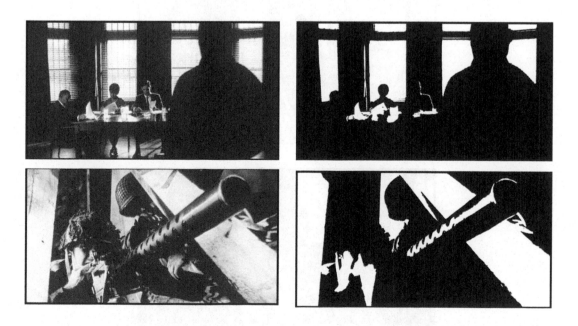

The diagonal line is the most intense, the vertical line is less intense, and the horizontal line is the least dynamic or intense line. Contrast of orientation can occur within a shot, from shot to shot, or from sequence to sequence.

This shot illustrates contrast of line orientation within the shot.

This shot illustrates affinity of orientation within the shot.

These two pictures illustrate affinity of orientation from shot to shot, because the angle of the stationary lines is the same.

These pictures illustrate contrast of orientation of line from shot to shot.

## Direction

Direction refers to the angle of lines or tracks created by moving objects. In the following drawings, the arrow indicates the direction of the track made by the moving object.

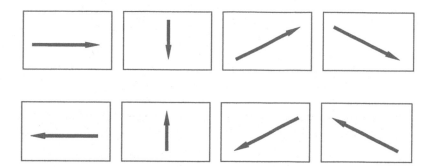

There are eight directions in which an object can move on the screen.

Affinity of direction within the shot is created when two (or more) objects move in the same direction.

In this example of contrast of direction of line within the shot, objects move in different directions.

Contrast or affinity of direction of line can also occur from shot to shot.

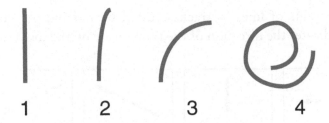

## Quality

Quality of line refers to the linear (straight) or curvilinear (curved) nature of a line.

Lines 1 and 2 have affinity of quality of line, because they're both nearly straight.

Lines 1 and 4 have contrast, because one is straight and the other curved.

Certain adjectives and emotional moods often are associated with quality of line. Most of the other basic visual components don't have preexisting emotional characteristics associated with them, but straight and curved lines often do.

Generally speaking, a straight line is associated with these characteristics: direct, aggressive, bland, honest, industrial, ordered, strong, unnatural, adult, and rigid. A curved line often is associated with these characteristics: indirect, passive, pertaining to nature, childlike, romantic, soft, organic, safe, and flexible. These characteristics can create predictable stereotypes and are only a general guide. Your own feelings about straight and curved lines will affect how you use them. Chapter 9 explains how any descriptive characteristic can be assigned to any basic visual component.

These pictures illustrate contrast or affinity of quality of line within the shot. The contrast of straight and curved lines increases the overall visual intensity. The affinity of the straight lines keeps the visual intensity low.

This pair of shots illustrates affinity of line quality. All the lines in both shots are straight.

There are many other ways to apply the Principle of Contrast & Affinity to line including thick and thin, continuous and broken, long and short, and in-focus and out-of-focus lines. These are important considerations in a drawing class, but it becomes difficult for an audience to notice these aspects of line during a story filled with moving images and sound. It is also difficult for a filmmaker to control them. Occasionally these secondary aspects of line become visually important in film and video, but usually they have little effect on contrast and affinity. Orientation, direction, and quality are visual aspects of line that are immediately useful to the picture maker, because they are quickly recognizable by an audience.

## SHAPE

Just as there are basic types of spaces and lines, there are basic shapes. The basic shapes are the circle, square, and equilateral triangle. Shapes exist in a visual space that can be flat or deep. Therefore, shapes can be classified as two-dimensional (flat space) or three-dimensional (deep space).

The circle, square, and triangle are two-dimensional.

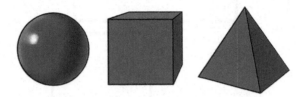

The sphere, cube, and three-sided pyramid are three-dimensional.

A shape can be classified as basic only if its unseen sides can be predicted correctly by examining the visible sides. A three-sided pyramid reveals all the information needed about the shape of its hidden sides. The cube does the same, and of course a sphere's shape remains identical no matter how it's turned.

Many other shapes including the cylinder and cone often are incorrectly classified as basic shapes. When viewed from below, the cylinder and cone appear identical and give no clue that one is pointed. This disqualifies them as basic shapes, because they hide their true shape identities.

Another reason why many shapes aren't classified as basic is because it makes shape recognition too complicated. Basic shape differences must be easy to see. Visually speaking, it's too difficult to notice small differences in the shapes of objects. An audience can't easily see the shape difference between a three-sided pyramid and a four-sided pyramid, for example. The circle, square, and triangle are visually different, useful, and within the perceptual reach of an audience. Simplification makes structuring the complex visual component of shape possible.

## Basic Shape Recognition

The real world is filled with millions of objects, and each one seems to have its own unique shape. The basic shape of any object can be revealed by reducing it to a silhouette. Any object, no matter how apparently unique, can be categorized into one of the three basic shapes.

Here are the basic silhouettes of three cars.

The first car is based on a circle. The circle is the most benign of the basic shapes. It doesn't have an up or down or any sides. A circle has no direction or intrinsic visual dynamic. Most people describe cars with a circular shape as friendly or cute. This middle vehicle is obviously based on a square shape. It is less friendly than the circular car, but it seems to possess a visual stability and solidity that the circular car lacks. The fastest of the three cars has the shape of a triangle. It may be a high performance racecar, but its basic shape is a triangle. The triangle is the most dynamic of the three basic shapes, because it's the only shape that contains at least one diagonal line. A triangle is an arrow. It points in a particular direction, which is something the square and circle can't do.

Every object has a basic shape that can be discovered by reducing the object to its silhouette.

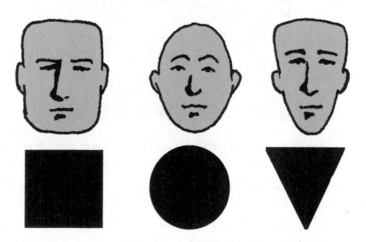

Faces can be categorized as basic shapes.

Trees come in three basic shapes, too.

Furniture and everything else can be classified into one of three basic shapes that can easily be seen by looking at the object's silhouette.

Light patterns and shadows can also produce circles, squares, and triangles.

The same emotional characteristics associated with curved and straight lines can be linked to round, square, and triangular shapes. Rounded shapes often are described as indirect, passive, romantic, pertaining to nature, soft, organic, childlike, safe, and flexible. Square shapes are direct, industrial, ordered, linear, unnatural, adult, and rigid. Because of their diagonal lines, triangles often are described as bold, aggressive, dynamic, angry, menacing, scary, chaotic, disorienting, and unorganized. Remember, these emotional associations are not rules and can lead to stereotypes. Chapter 9 will explain how almost any emotional characteristic can be attached to any line or shape.

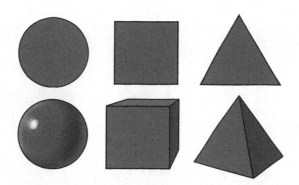

## CONTRAST AND AFFINITY

Among the two-dimensional shapes, the circle and triangle have maximum contrast. Using three-dimensional shapes, the sphere and the three-sided pyramid have maximum contrast. If the two- and three-dimensional shapes are grouped together, maximum contrast is best created by the sphere and the triangle or the circle and the three-sided pyramid. These two combinations create contrast in the basic shape, as well as in their two- or three-dimensional properties.

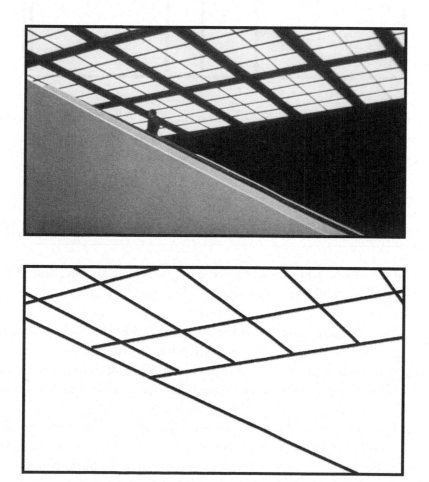

Here's an example of contrast of shape within the shot. The triangles contrast with the squares.

This picture illustrates affinity of shape within the shot. All the basic shapes in the shot are squares. Contrast and affinity of shape can also occur from shot to shot or from sequence to sequence.

## CONTROLLING LINE AND SHAPE DURING PRODUCTION

Here is a practical situation. Tomorrow you're going to direct a scene, and you've decided to emphasize lines and shapes. How can you control them on the set?

1. **Squint**. Most lines in the modern world are vertical and horizontal because they're created by architecture. Doors, windows, and walls tend to be vertical and horizontal. The same thing often is true with furniture. What is the linear motif of the shot? Use a contrast viewing glass or learn to squint properly so recognizing the lines in your locations and pictures becomes easier.

2. **Evaluate the lighting**. Since line exists because of tonal or color contrasts, line can be controlled through lighting. As a picture gains tonal contrast, more lines will appear. Brightening or darkening an object can create or obscure lines to alter the linear motif.

3. **Stage movement carefully**. When an object moves, it creates a horizontal, vertical, or diagonal line or track. Each of these three lines communicates a different visual intensity to the audience.

4. **Create a linear motif storyboard.** Line is an important factor in planning shots. A storyboard is a series of drawings illustrating the composition of shots. But the following storyboard plots the linear motif of line orientation from shot to shot.

The linear motif will decrease or increase the visual intensity of any sequence. It doesn't matter if the sequence is a violent car chase or a quiet conversation; the contrast or affinity of line can orchestrate the intensity changes of the scene.

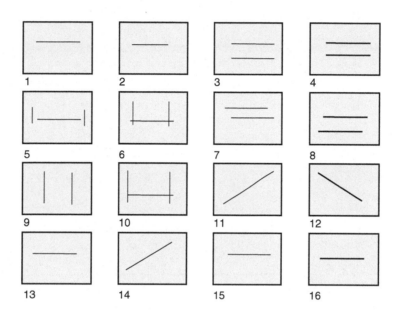

The most intense frames of this storyboard are 12-13-14, because they have the greatest visual contrast. The line orientation moves from diagonal (12) to horizontal (13) to diagonal (14). This is an extremely useful storyboard, not because of realistic drawings of people and objects, but because it uses the Principle of Contrast & Affinity to structure the linear motif of the sequence. Visually, this sequence will build in intensity toward a climax. In Chapter 9, this concept will be reviewed in relationship to a story structure.

Shape control requires careful examination of an object's silhouette:

1. **Evaluate the shapes:**
   a. **Actor.** If the actor and wardrobe are reduced to silhouettes, what is the basic shape?
   b. **Scenery.** Define the lines to discover the shapes in your picture. Horizontal and vertical lines usually create squares and rectangles. Diagonal lines create triangles.
   c. **Set dressing.** Define the basic shape of the furniture and other set dressing.
2. **Control the lighting.** Lighting can change or emphasize the basic shapes of objects in the picture. A pattern of light can create a circular, square, or triangular shape.
3. **Simplify.** Shape works best if it's easy for the audience to see similarities and differences. Use the lens choice and camera angle to emphasize, or remove lines and shapes in the shot.

# Sound Design

## By Tomlinson Holman and Arthur Baum

S ound design is the art of getting the right sound in the right place at the right time. This chapter concentrates on defining what the right sound is. The right place can be defined as placement of a sound into the correct track out of many possible tracks, an organizational skill exercised during editing that anticipates and strongly affects mixing. The right time defines the placement of sounds in a time line, often with a synchronous relationship to the picture or to other sound effects. The right place and time have to do with the details of editing and are covered in the next chapter.

One concept that filmmaking borrowed from theater is called *mise en scene*, defined as what the director puts into the scene. The scene in film is the frame that we see—what is in it and what is excluded, the lighting, costumes, and blocking of the actors; that is, their massing and movement. When first applied to cinema, the concept meant simply everything in front of the camera: the set, costumes, composition of the shots, patterns of light and dark, and so forth. More recently, the term has been broadened within its use in film studies to include cinematography and its effects such as depth of field, as well as editing and sound. Thus sound stands in modern critical thinking as one principal ingredient of the film art. Reading a film means understanding the role that each of these ingredients plays in its perception, including sound.

The first notion of film sound influenced by the *mise en scene* idea is that somebody somewhere has decided what you hear, moment by moment, within a movie; as with any creative work, there is an author, and what you hear in a film is not accidental but planned. What you hear could be just the sound of what the camera sees in documentary fashion, but it is often a more constructed sound, built out of bits and pieces by professionals to simulate a desired overall sound impression. Sometimes, just to portray reality, sound may have to be changed from that which was captured during production. Off-screen sound recorded during production may include inappropriate noise, in which case constructed or substituted sound is more appropriate. At other times, various film sound styles may dominate during different parts of

*Figure 14.1. Establishing shot from the film* Tears of Steel. *Science fiction relies heavily on mise en scene to set the mood and history of the story. What sort of sound design to you imagine for this highly visual scene set in the future?*

a single film, extending from the real to the surreal to montage, for instance, across a range representing increasing levels of abstraction.

In most mainstream pictures, certain film sound conventions prevail that are perhaps stereo-typical, but that also have the advantage of transmitting emotional information quickly. At the end of the climactic scene after the Ark of the Covenant has been closed in *Raiders of the Lost Ark*, Indy and Karen are left exhausted, but happy. The ambient sound we hear is that of crickets, a quiet and peaceful sound that ends a remarkable sonic sequence. The fact that all is at peace is transmitted quickly to the audience by the use of such stereotypical sound.

We come to understand the conventions of film sound through exposure to a great many examples; we are all trained through listening to films, whether we know it consciously or not. Thus a scene with a particular piquancy for us is that of lovers gazing into one another's eyes accompanied by orchestral score. The camera dollies back to reveal— an orchestra playing in the foreground. What

*Figure 14.2. John Williams scoring* Raiders of the Lost Arc. *A balance must be struck between the musical score and the sound design so one does not detract from the other.*

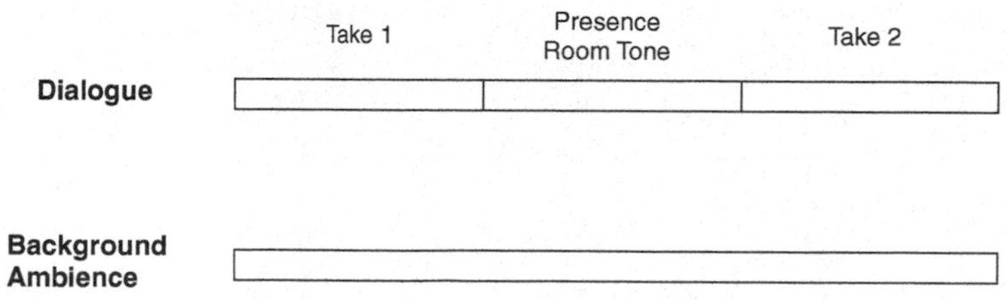

could be more likely? The literalness of this sound joke is funny thanks to the confusion between whether the music heard is source music or score. It is a play on film sound conventions.[1] Another example occurs at the beginning of *Diva*, when we hear score over the titles, but the mail carrier shutting off the radio on his motorcycle

|  | Take 1 | Presence<br>Room Tone | Take 2 |
| --- | --- | --- | --- |
| **Dialogue** | | | |
| **Background<br>Ambience** | | | |

Figure 14.3. The difference between presence, which is intercut with dialogue tracks, and ambience, which exists on its own track(s).

kills the score. For this film, the fact that music is going to play a major role is highlighted by the effect of this character's action in the opening seconds.

One of the basic film sound conventions is that keeping sound constant across a picture cut implies that while we may have changed our point of view, we are nonetheless still in the same space. This job of improving overall continuity is most often handled by presence (also called *room tone*, or in England *atmosphere*). Presence is defined as sound that matches the sound captured during production so well that it may be intercut with production dialogue tracks without discontinuity. It is the sound of relative quiet for the space being portrayed. Note that it is not silence, because cutting to silence is instantly noticeable and leaves us in an auditory void as opposed to a quiet location. It may well be very, very quiet, though, and hopefully this will often be the case because we want the best dialogue intelligibility possible most of the time, and the fact that the background is quiet rather than loud helps intelligibility. Sometimes it is impossible to get precisely matching presence, and the result is a bump at an edit. Dialogue editors smooth dialogue using such tactics as cross-fading between recordings or hiding a sound edit by delaying it until the beginning of the next utterance after the corresponding picture cut.

If dialogue tracks can't be perfectly smoothed, or if the director and sound designer wish to create a new sonic space for the scene to exist in other than the one captured on set, ambience tracks, also known as backgrounds, can play a similar role (Fig. 14.1.). They provide continuity across picture cuts, as well as substitution of a new space for the original. If presence in the production track is low enough in level, backgrounds may be able to cover up or mask discontinuities at edits, in addition to providing a storytelling element of their own. Think of *Star Trek*:

Each part of the ship has its own background sound, and part of cutting from Engineering to the Bridge, or to 10 Forward, is the change in ambience that accompanies the cut. We as the audience are taught by the filmmakers what each space sounds like as well as looks like, so we can orient ourselves quickly in a scene change, using both auditory and visual cues.

By using dialogue intercut as necessary with presence, and potentially one or more ambience tracks, a realistic-sounding dialogue scene may be constructed whether or not it was shot in a single day or at a single location, even if the background sounds that would be expected for creating verisimilitude were not actually present on set during shooting. The next element that is often used to help sell the reality of a scene is Foley. Named for the person who invented it at Universal,[2] Jack Foley, it is a series of sound effects made while watching the edited picture in a quiet, acoustically dead recording stage.[3] The mic is typically operated close to the sound source. Recordings of footsteps, chair squeaks, clothing rustle, and small physical effects like pouring a drink, or large ones like a body hit or those of a dinosaur brushing up against foliage, may all be Foley effects. Given the close mic perspective and the quiet, dead room used to

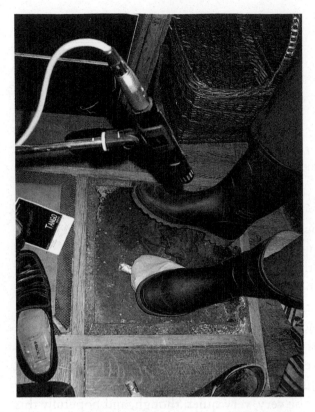

Figure 14.4. Footsteps are a common Foley element. It is important to have a variety of surfaces for the recording. Are the characters walking on wooden floors, carpet, cement? Are they walking in heels, sandals, or barefoot? Are they stomping, tip-toeing or shuffling along?

Figure 14.5. Hard sound effects are created with a variety of sound effect devices. A good Foley artist will have these tools ready prior to each session, or will create their own on the fly.

record it, Foley is most often a representation of exaggerated reality.

The technique tends to hype the effects so that, heard alone, they seem bigger than life, but this is made necessary by the masking effect of having many other sounds playing simultaneously in the final sound mix. For Foley to read through the clutter of all those other sounds, it has to be recorded in this way. Even the lowest-budget films can afford Foley today, because the requirements for doing it well are fairly minimal: first, find a quiet absorbing space—for instance, a high-school stage with all the curtains let down to surround you. Then play the cut video over a picture monitor—possibly with headphones so you can listen to the production sound, although this is optional. With a microphone close to your feet, for example, proceed to record footsteps as necessary, placing them on another medium such as a production field recorder, computer audio interface, or even a separate camcorder. Repeat for other effects as needed.

One principal notion that applies to all types of sound effects is well illustrated by Foley, and that is the concept of layering. If you have a crowd walking on screen, you can get a crowd to walk in the Foley room and use multiple microphones to record them all at once, a technique I found in use at Bejing Film Studios; but if you are only one person, you can record sound that corresponds to one person in the shot, and do this repeatedly over several recordings, ultimately building up the sound of the whole scene. To accomplish this, it is useful to record each take to a separate track of an audio editing system such as Pro Tools or Soundtrack Pro so that each can be recorded in sync as you go. You may also want to have on hand a number of pairs of shoes! If you use a field recorder or other portable device to make your recordings, then every track has to be transferred to an editing system and "sunk" up after the fact. Even for the multitrack recording where each track has been recorded in sync to the picture, getting hard sync often means moving Foley effects forward or backward in time by a small amount, but with this system, the process of getting each recording into near-sync is largely automated.

So far we have discussed dialogue, and with it intercut presence; ambience or backgrounds; and Foley effects. The next major category of sounds is cut or hard effects. These are sound effects, drawn from production sound, sound effects libraries, and original recordings made for the individual film, that typically bear a one-to-one relationship to picture. An anecdote illustrates this best. Some years ago, on the particularly tight postproduction schedule for *Tucker*, the re-recording mixers were spending long, long hours at work. The son of one of them had written his father a postcard that was promptly posted on the meter bridge at the top of the mixing console in the dubbing stage. It said, "Gee Dad, I get it—see a car, hear a car." There could be no better definition of Hollywood postproduction sound cutting than that made by the young kid who missed his father. The Hollywood craft tradition says that anything we see that *can* make a sound, *will*.

Some directors accept the craft tradition that says that everything that can make sound will do so at face value, whereas others question it. A process often found in Hollywood is for sound editors to cut a large number of effects—basically everything they can think of—and then for the director to strip out whatever he or she finds unnecessary on the dub stage. This approach is exactly what sound design means to replace—the idea that decisions should be left for the end of the process and for the director to make. In *The Sum of All Fears*, for instance, an early scene in the film is a tension-ridden bomb shelter scene of the President of the United States commanding forces during a crisis. The phone rings and it's his wife calling with trivialities, and we realize that this is not a real crisis: it's only a drill. The spell is broken by the call. Sound editors provided all kinds of sounds, intended for use in both the screen channels and the surround ones, to embed the viewer in the scene and raise its tension level through engaging the listener. The director, on the other hand, found all of these communication chirps and whizzes distracting, particularly in the surrounds, so he stripped them out, and the scene played without most of them being heard.

For other types of filmmaking, especially where this process is carried out by just one person or by a very small crew, the selection of just what effects to use can take place even before one gets to the mix. There is always some kind of limitation on the number of tracks available in an editing or mixing system. The number of tracks that is desirable seems always to be $n + 1$, where $n$ is the number of tracks available. This begins with the simplest mixes with only a few tracks, and it continues through the largest mixes I have seen, with hundreds of tracks: "but if we could just have one more" is a familiar lament even in Hollywood studios. This is also a factor in sound design—keeping the cut tracks to the available range of equipment and software—and this problem is increasing today as editing processes take on what have traditionally been mixing processes. Plug-ins or filters that run on editing workstations take up some of the available computer horsepower, and it is often difficult to know when limits are being approached and what will happen once those limits are exceeded. Today the limitation is how many plug-ins per channel are allowed before the editing system can no longer run in real time.

Hard effects help illustrate and highlight certain truths about film sound. For instance, although supposedly realistic, those face punches in action films are anything but real for sound. I remember visiting a Hollywood recording stage some years ago on a studio tour. A large-fisted man was hitting a ham as hard as he could to get face punches. While this rather literal recording was better than the real thing, especially for the recipient, it's really not enough for the larger-than-life punches of action-adventure movies. One thing to do is to slow down the original recording in an

Figure 14.6. Walter Murch worked as editor and/or sound design artist for a variety of influential films including American Graffiti, Apocalypse Now, The English Patient, and Godfather II.

effort to make it appear bigger than life. Another is to layer together a whole parcel of sounds to make one enormous splat out of several merely exaggerated ones. Ingredients might include sounds of throwing an old leather jacket onto the metal hood of a fire truck, 4 dropping overly ripe fruit onto concrete and slowing down the recording, or breaking a stalk of celery over one's knee, to name a few examples.

One useful result of layering sounds is concealment of the original sound source used for a particular effect. Recognition is less likely when sounds are heard together simultaneously in time and panned to the same location. Additional concealment occurs with the pitch and time shifting that accompanies off-speed playback, which is often used with such effects to make them seem larger than life. As an aside, it is interesting to note that off-speed playback, particularly of an extreme nature, is much easier to accomplish with analog recorders than digital ones—a reason in itself to keep one analog recorder around equipped with a wide-range varispeed in an otherwise all-digital studio.

What differentiates these kinds of sounds recorded for hard effects from Foley is that no attempt is made during recording to match a previously recorded picture in sync, but rather the object is to gather separately a whole set of ingredient parts that when blended together through editing and mixing take on a life of their own, becoming one auditory object, whether composed of a single ingredient or many layered together.

Walter Murch has stated an important concept in comparing sound design to a three-ring circus. Through evolution in time, big circuses settled on three rings, not two or five. How did they get there? It has to do with how much information can be processed by the brain at any one time. More than a certain amount of information leads to disconnection as the senses are overwhelmed. Yet the whole idea is to fully engage you, so growing to the point of diminishing returns is valuable too. Circuses evolved to the point where three things at once could be featured. Note that each of these three rings could contain many performers acting in concert, so there are many more molecular elements than three, but the molecular components are clustered into three groups, to which we can pay adequate, albeit potentially shifting, attention.

In our case the analogy has to do with being able to pay attention to what are called auditory streams. While we can only pay attention to three things at once, our attention may shift among more, because we can only hold so many in our heads at one time; but we can also shift gears among streams. Note that this means we definitely need more than three individual sound tracks, because a single auditory event may be built up from many different elements, but for any given point in time all of the elements clustered together into blocks form no more than three items we can typically follow or pay attention to.

Taking this idea a bit further, we might say that the three elements we can pay attention to are more easily delineated if they are of different types. Three dialogue tracks operating in overlapping fashion would be like three lion tamers in the three rings: confusing. But dialogue, Foley, sound effects, and music tracks, being rather thoroughly differentiated, are more likely to form separate auditory streams that we can follow.

# Music

## By Robin Beauchamp

## OVERVIEW

The music stem or *score* is perhaps the most difficult component of the soundtrack to describe in words. Ironically, score rather than SFX often drive films that lack dialogue. Each musical entrance in a soundtrack is called a *cue*. A cue can *underscore* a scene or represent a *source* such as a radio or phonograph. In addition to source and underscore, many films use music for title, montage, and end credit sequences. The labeling convention for a cue is 1M1, the first number representing the reel and the last number representing the order in which it occurs. Cues are often given titles representative of the scenes they accompany. The blueprint for the score is created at the *spotting session* that occurs immediately after *picture lock* (no further picture editing). Film *composers* begin scoring immediately after the spotting session and are expected to compose two to five minutes of music each day. If copy-protected music is being considered, a *music supervisor* is brought in at the earliest stage to pursue legal clearance. The *music editor* has responsibilities for developing cue sheets, creating temp tracks, editing, synchronization, and preparing the score for the re-recording mixer. There are many additional roles related to the development of the score such as orchestrators, musicians, music contractors, and recording engineers.

> People sing when they are too emotional to talk anymore.
>
> Lynn Ahrens (*Anastasia*)

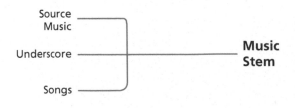

Figure 15.1. Elements in the Music Stem

## UNDERSCORE

During the golden age of animation, underscore was anything but subtle. Most of the action on and off-screen was covered by musical cues that were often indistinguishable from the SFX stem. Composers of this era pioneered the integration of twentieth-century musical styles and performance techniques. Even though they pushed the musical boundaries, their scores remained both playful and accessible. In contemporary animation, the style and approach of underscore is oftentimes indistinguishable from live action cues. Underscore can play through a scene or hit with specific action. Cues that play through a scene provide a linear element in the soundtrack, smoothing edits and creating emotional continuity within a scene. The practice of hitting the action with musical accents is a long established convention. In addition to hitting the action, musical cues occasionally hit with dialogue as well. For example, in the film *Anastasia* (1997), Comrade Phlegmenkoff's line "And be grateful, too" is punctuated with orchestral chords to add emotional weight to the delivery.

> I'm a storyteller … and more or less in the food chain of the filmmaking process, I'm the last guy that gets a crack at helping the story.
>
> James Horner

## SOURCE MUSIC

Source music is the diegetic use of songs to contribute to the implied reality of the scene. To maintain this realistic feel, source music is often introduced "in progress," as if the audience were randomly tuning in. Songs are commonly used as source material, effectively establishing time period, developing characters, or acting as a cultural signifier. Source music also supports

Figure 15.2. Gary Sinise and the Lt. Dan Band *performing in 2009. Source music (where you can actually see what/who is creating the music) is called diegetic sound and contributes to the reality of the scene.*

time-lapse sequences by changing literally with each shot. Source music can be either on-screen (emitting from a radio or phonograph) or off-screen (such as elevator music or a public address system). The songs used in source music are almost always selected for their lyric connection to the narrative. Source music is processed or *futzed* to match the sonic characteristics of implied sound source. Like hard effects, source music is treated like a SFX and panned literally to the on-screen position. Cues often morph or transition from *source to underscore* to reflect the narrative shift in reality typified by montage sequences and other subjective moments.

# SONGS

During the golden age of animation, familiar songs were routinely quoted instrumentally, and the implied lyrics were integral to the sight gags. Original songs such as "Some Day My Prince Will Come" from *Snow White* (1934) blended narrative lyrics with score to create a *musical monologue*. Walt Disney Studios was largely responsible for the animated musical, developing fairy tale stories around a series of songs performed by the characters. These songs are *pre-scored*, providing essential timings for character movements and lip sync. In animated musicals, it is not uncommon for a character's speaking voice to be covered by a voice actor while the singing voice is performed by a trained vocalist. Great care is taken to match the speaking voice with the singing voice. An effective example of this casting approach can be heard in *Anastasia*, where Meg Ryan's speaking voice flawlessly transitions to Liz Callaway's vocals. A more recent trend in animation is the use of pre-existing songs as the basis for the score. This is known as a *song score*; examples of this approach include *Shrek* (2001), *Lilo and Stitch* (2002), and *Chicken Little* (2005). It is sometimes desirable to create a new arrangement of an existing tune as a means of updating the style or customizing the lyrics. An example of this occurs in *Jimmy Neutron: Boy Genius* (2001) in a montage sequence where Thomas Dolby's "She Blinded Me with Science" is covered by Melissa Lefton singing "He Blinded Me with Science" to reflect the POV of Cindy Vortex (Jimmy's female adversary/love interest). Songs continue to play an important roll in short form independent animation, especially if the film does not incorporate dialogue. However, there are potential risks associated with the use of songs in animation. Songs can give a film a dated feel over time, which is why the accompaniments of songs in animated musicals are primarily orchestral. They also introduce the potential for copyright infringement, an issue that will be addressed later in this chapter.

Figure 15.3. Experimental musician Thomas Dolby wrote the original song "She Blinded Me with Science" in 1982. Nineteen years later, Melissa Lefton covered the song for the film Jimmy Neutron: Boy Genius, and changed the lyrics to "HE blinded me with science" to better fit the film's storyline.

> Story is the most important thing … not the song as a song, but the song as development.
>
> Richard Sherman

# TITLE, MONTAGE, AND END CREDIT SEQUENCES

Title, montage, and end credit sequences have a unique function in film and present unique scoring opportunities. Title sequence music can effectively establish the scale, genre, and emotional tone of the film. Composers can write in a more thematic style, as there is little or no

Figure 15.4. *Film Composer JC Basie at Gorky Film Studio. Many studios will have immediate playback options so the composer can see the image that the composition will be matched to as they are mixing.*

dialogue to work around. A good example of title sequence music can be heard in *101 Dalmatians* (1961). Here the music moves isomorphically and frequently hits in a manner that foreshadows the playful chaos that will soon follow. Montage sequences are almost always scored with songs containing narrative lyrics. The linear nature of songs and their narrative lyric help promote continuity across the numerous visual edits comprising a montage sequence. End credit music should maintain the tone and style established in earlier cues while also promoting closure. The end-credit score for animated musicals often consists of musical reprises re-arranged in modern pop styles suitable for radio play.

> You gotta have a montage!—
>
> Gary Johnston (*Team America*)

Figure 15.5. *Musician Danny Elfman has scored a variety of Tim Burton's films, including* Batman Returns. *His original music created a dynamic tempo in the scene featuring the Batmobile racing through the snowy streets of Gotham City.*

# WORKFLOW FOR ORIGINAL SCORE

## Rationale for Original Score

Directors often seek an original score that is exclusive, tailored, and free from preexisting associations. Original music can be an important tool for branding a film. The iconic themes and underscore heard in the Hanna-Barbera animations cannot be emulated without the drawing comparison. Original cues are tailored with hits and emotional shifts that are conceived directly for the picture. In concert music, there are many standard forms that composers use to organize their compositions. If these conventions were used as the basis for film scoring, form and tempo

> I aim in each score to write a score that has its own personality.
>
> Alan Menken

would be imposed on the film rather than evolving in response to the images. Music is known to encapsulate our thoughts and feelings associated with previous experiences. Filmmakers seek to avoid these associations and create unique experiences for their audience. With original score, cues can be written in a similar style without evoking past associations. Even when the music is of a specific style or period, it can be scored to create a timeless feel.

## Temp Music

*Temp music* is perhaps the most effective vehicle for communicating the type of score required for a specific film. As the name implies, a temp (temporary) track is not intended for inclusion in the final soundtrack. Temp tracks are edited from pre-existing music to guide the picture editing process, facilitate test screenings, and provide a musical reference for the composer. The responsibility of creating a temp track often falls on a picture or sound editor. Editors select music that matches the style and dramatic needs as represented in the storyboards or animatic. The music is then edited and synced to create a customized feel for the score. Because the temp track is for internal use, copy-protected material is often utilized. Temp tracks can prove problematic if the director becomes overly attached and has difficulty accepting the original score.

## The Spotting Session

In animation, cues can be source, pre-score, or non-sync underscore. Pre-scored cues must be developed before the animation process begins as the characters are moving in sync to the musical beats. Some composers prefer to begin writing thematic material and underscore for the film as early as the storyboarding stage. However, most underscore cues are decided once the picture is locked. Here, the director meets with the composer and music editor to screen the film and discuss where music can best be contributing. The spotting session is an important opportunity for the director to clarify their vision for their film on a shot-by-shot basis. If a temp score exists, these cues are played for the composer to help clarify the style and intent. During the spotting session, the music editor takes detailed notes related to specific cues. From these notes, the music editor generates cue sheets outlining the parameters of each cue.

Suggestions for identifying cues in a spotting session:

- Determine the importance of music for the scene.

**Music Spotting Log**

Date._____

Page No._____

Project Title: _____     Composer: _____

Music Editor: _____

| Cue #: | Cue Name: | | | Notes: |
|--------|-----------|---|---|--------|
| Start Time: | : | : | : | |
| End Time: | : | : | : | |
| Total Time: | : | : | : | |

Figure 15.6. Spotting Log Template

- Look for opportunities in the scene where music can be brought in without drawing attention to itself.
- Decide when the music should hit, comment, or play through the action.
- Be selective; wall-to-wall music tends to lose its effectiveness.
- Be open to all musical styles; allow the image, rather than personal taste, to influence decisions.

## Writing Original Cues

Film composers must be able to write in all styles and for a wide range of instruments. Chord progressions, rhythmic patterns, and instrumentation are elements that can be emulated to capture the essence of the temp track. They are often used to provide the foundation for an original theme resulting in a similar, yet legal cue. Today, most films are scored to digital video using extensive sample libraries that emulate a wide range of instrumentation. Much of the writing occurs in a project studio utilizing MIDI technologies, recording, and editing capabilities to fully produce each cue. The composer does not work directly with the animator when writing individual cues. Instead, they meet periodically to audition and approve individual cues. Composers use the feedback gained from these sessions to hone in on the musical direction for individual cues. It is important to note that additional picture edits occurring after this point can result in significant qualitative, budget, and scheduling implications. Most scores are created as *works for hire*, requiring the composer to surrender publishing rights to the production company. Creative fees are negotiated based on experience and the amount of music required. Smaller budget projects often require the composer to handle all tasks associated with producing the score. This type of contract is referred to as a *package deal*, and includes: orchestration, part writing, contracting musicians, recording, conducting, and music editing.

> Before you can set out and start scoring ... one's gotta be on the same page with the filmmakers.
>
> Harry Gregson-Williams
> (*Flushed Away*)

*Figure 15.7. Session musicians are often utilized to score films. Scoring sessions involve many people and resources, so planning is an important means of optimizing resources.*

## THE SCORING SESSION

Sample libraries have steadily improved, providing composers with access to a comprehensive set of orchestral, rock, and ethnic samples from which to orchestrate their cues. However, sample-based scoring can be time consuming and lack the expression and feel created with live musicians. Consequently, many larger projects use the traditional approach using live musicians at a *scoring session*. The space where the cues are recorded is called a *scoring stage*. Scoring sessions involve many people and resources, so planning is an important means of optimizing resources. The music editor attends the scoring session(s) to run the clock (synchronization) and to help evaluate individual takes. Due to budget realities and the limited access to qualified musicians, the blending of sequenced music with live musicians is becoming a common practice for a wide range of projects. Once the cues are completed, they are delivered to the music editor for additional editing and sync adjustments. From there, the tracks are delivered to the re-recording mixer in preparation for the final mix.

> My job is to make every moment of the film and every frame of the film come to life.
>
> John Debney

## WORKFLOW FOR PRODUCTION LIBRARIES

### Production Libraries

Hoyt Curtain (composer for Hanna-Barbera) developed a distinctive in-house music library for shows such as *The Flintstones* and *The Jetsons*. The cues contained in this library were re-used in subsequent seasons as well as other series. This provided Hanna-Barbera with a low cost music approach to scoring that also contributed to the continuity while promoting their brand. Commercially available *production libraries* have been developed for similar purpose. The days of "canned music" have long since passed and modern production libraries are providing a high quality, low cost, and expedient means of developing specialized cues or an entire score. The music tracks contained in commercial libraries are *pre-cleared* for use on audio/visual productions. Low-resolution audio files can be downloaded and cut into the temp, allowing the client to approve the cues in context. There are some disadvantages to production music including non-exclusivity, the need for costly editing, and the lack of variation for specific cues. The three types of production libraries are classified by their licensing specifications. *Buy-out* libraries are purchased for a one-time fee and grant the owner unrestricted use. *Blanket licensing* covers a specified use of a library for an entire project. *Needle drops* are the third and most expensive type of library. Needle drop fees are assigned per cue based on variables such as length, territory, distribution, and nature of the use. Most blanket and needle drop libraries provide online search, preview, delivery, and payment options.

### Searching a Library

As with all scores, the process begins with a spotting session to determine where cues are needed and the nature of individual cues. This information guides the music editor in searching production libraries for musical selections that might potentially become music cues. Commercial production libraries can be rather expansive, containing thousands of hours of music. Most production companies have online search engines to assist the music editor in a search. Categories, keywords, and musical styles are the most common type of search modes. Categories are broad and include headings such as Instrumentation, Film Styles, National/Ethnic, and Sports. Keyword searches match words found in titles and individual cue descriptions. Emotional terms prove to be most effective when searching with keywords. Musical styles are also common to production library search engines. Many musical styles are straightforward but others are more difficult to distinguish. This is particularly true of contemporary styles such as rock, pop, and hip-hop. If you are unfamiliar with a particular style, find someone who is and get them to validate the style.

## Managing a Project

Many online libraries contain a project management component in their browsers (Figure 15.6). This feature allows the music editor to *pull* individual cuts from the library and organize them by specific projects and cues. As with original score, there comes a point in the project where the director is brought in to approve the cues. The music editor can open a specific project and play potential cuts directly from the browser. Alternatively, they can download tracks and cut them to picture, allowing the director to audition and approve each cue in context.

## Developing Cues

A skilled music editor can edit cues to create the illusion that the music was scored for a particular scene. They do this by matching the emotional quality of a scene, conforming cues to picture, and developing sync points. Oftentimes, it is the editing that "sells" a particular music selection. Once the cues are developed, the director is brought in to audition and approve the cue.

## Licensing Cues

Once the final placement of the music is determined and the director approves the cue, the music editor or supervisor completes the process by obtaining the necessary licensing. Most production music companies have online quote request forms to assist the music supervisor in defining the nature of the use. It is important to accurately define the extent to which the cue will be used, as this will influence the licensing fee. Licensing parameters can always be expanded at a later time at an additional cost. Once licensing fees are determined, an invoice is issued to the music editor or production company. This invoice constitutes the formal agreement that becomes binding when payment is received.

# WORKFLOW FOR COPY-PROTECTED MUSIC

## Overview

Where animation is subjective, arts law is objective, requiring the artist to fully comply with the international laws pertaining to copyright. The digital age has provided consumers with unprecedented access to digital media. The ease and extent to which this content can be acquired has led to a false sense of entitlement by consumers. It is easy for student and independent filmmakers to feel insulated from issues associated with copyright infringement; however, the potential consequences are substantial regardless of the size or nature of the project. It is the role of the *music supervisor* to clear copy-protected music for use in a film. In Dreamworks' *Shrek* films, the music supervisor cleared an average of 14 copy-protected cues per film. This section is designed to provide guidelines for music clearance. As with any legal endeavor, if in doubt, obtain the services of an arts lawyer.

A verbal contract isn't worth the paper it's written on.

> Every great film composer knows where to steal from.
>
> Richard Stone
> (*Animaniacs*)

## Rights Versus License

When seeking to license copy-protected music, it is important to clarify what specific permissions you are requesting from the copyright holder. For scoring purposes, copyright law only applies to melodies and lyrics. Chord progressions, accompaniment figures, and instrumentation are not protected and can be freely used without risk of copyright infringement. Copyright holders have the exclusive right to reproduce, publish, license, or sell their melodies and lyrics. They also have the right to grant permission, set licensing fees, and establish terms for any music synced to picture. A publisher often controls the synchronization rights and the record companies typically hold the master rights.

## Synchronization, Master, and Videogram License

There are three specific licenses of primary concern to the music supervisor; the *synchronization license*, the *master license*, and the *videogram license*. The synchronization license is the most important of the three, for if this license is not granted, the music cannot be used on the film in any form. The synchronization license grants the right to sync copy-protected music to moving picture. A synchronization license is granted at the discretion of the copyright owner, who is typically the composer or publisher. To use a specific recording of a song requires a master license, which is often controlled by a record company. To make copies of the film for any form of distribution requires videogram licensing. The videogram license must be obtained by both the publisher and record company if a copy-protected recording is used. Licensing can be time consuming and there are no guarantees. Therefore, it is prudent to begin this process as early as possible.

## Public Domain

Works that are public domain can be used freely in an animation. Any music written before January 1, 1923 is public domain. Works written after that date can enter public domain if the term of the copyright expires. Use of the copyright notice (©) became optional on March 1, 1989. It is up to the music supervisor to ensure that a given selection is in fact public domain. One way to establish public domain is to search the selection at www.copyright.gov. Once material is in the public domain, exclusive rights to the work cannot be secured. It is important to differentiate public domain from *master rights*. Although the music contained on a recording might be public domain, the master rights for the actual recording is usually copy protected.

## Fair Use

The authors of the Copyright Act recognized that exceptions involving non-secured permission were necessary to promote the very creativity that the Act was designed to protect. The Copyright Act set forth guidelines governing the use of copy-protected material without securing permission from the copyright holder. These guidelines for nonexclusive rights constitute *fair use*:

The fair use of a copyrighted work ... for purposes such as criticism, comment, teaching ... scholarship, or research, is not an infringement of copyright. In determining whether a specific use applies, consider the following:

- Is the nature of the use commercial value or educational (demonstrating an acquired skill). Even in educational settings, the use of copy-protected music for the entertainment value does not constitute fair use, even if there are no related financial transactions.
- The amount and importance of the portion used in relation to the copyrighted work as a whole.
- The effect of the use on the potential market for, or value of, the copyrighted work. Even if you are not selling the work, distribution, exposure, and unwanted association with a project can have significant impact on the market value of a musical composition.

If an animation complies with these principles, there is strong support for claiming fair use. When claiming fair use, it is still advisable to limit the distribution and exhibition of the work, credit the authors, and display the author's copyright notice within your work. It is important to keep in mind that fair use is not a law but rather a form of legal defense. With that in mind, it is wise to use it sparingly.

## Parody

Parody is an art form that can only exist by using work that is already familiar to the target audience; therefore, provisions had to be made in the Copyright Act for parody or this form of expression would cease to exist. Parody involves the imitation of a recognizable copy-protected

Figure 15.8. Parody involves the imitation of a recognizable work to create commentary. In this example, Grant Wood's iconic painting American Gothic is used as a basis for a 1972 advertisement by RCA Records. Perhaps RCA was commenting on how prevalent music was becoming?

work to create a commentary on that work. The commentary does not have to serve academic purposes; it can be for entertainment value. However, both the presentation and the content must be altered or it is not considered a parody. For example, just changing a few words while retaining the same basic meaning does not constitute parody. Parody must be done in a context that does not devalue the original copy-protected work; therefore, parody is most justifiable when the target audience is vastly different than the original. A parody constitutes a new and copyrightable work based on a previously copyrighted work. Because parody involves criticism, copyright owners rarely grant permission to parody. If you ask permission and are denied, you run the additional risk of litigation if you use it anyway.

In the United States, fair use can be used successfully to defend parody as long as the primary motive for the parody is artistic expression rather than commercialism. A good example of parody can be heard in the *Family Guy* "Wasted Talent" episode (2000) featuring "Pure Inebriation," a parody on "Pure Imagination" from *Willie Wonka & the Chocolate Factory* (1971).

## Music Supervision

When requesting any type of licensing, it is important to define the parameters of your request. Because you will likely pay for licensing based on the scope of the request, it is wise to limit the scope to only that which is needed. The following are basic guidelines when requesting a quote for licensing.

- *Identify the copyright holder.* The publisher usually holds synchronization rights. In most cases, the administrator for this license can be identified through a BMI, ASCAP, or SESAC title search. The master rights are often held by the record company.
- *Define the territory* (e.g., local, regional, national, worldwide, national television, national cable, Internet, film festival). This parameter can be expanded if the film becomes more successful.
- *Define the term.* If you are a student, then your participation in student films typically is limited to 12 months after your graduation date. If you want to have the rights to use the piece forever, you should request "perpetuity for the term." Remember, the greater the request, the more you can expect to pay and the greater the chance your request will be denied.
- *Define the nature of use* (e.g., broadcast, student festival, distribution, or sale). This information should include the amount of the material to be used (expressed in exact time), where it will be placed in the animation, and the purpose for using it (e.g., narrative lyric quality, emotional amplification, or establishing a time period or location).
- *When stating the budget for the project, clarify whether the published figure is for the production as a whole or for the music only.* The distribution of money varies greatly from project to project. Typically, less than 10 percent of the total film budget is available for scoring.
- *Consider these requests as formal documents read by lawyers and other trained arts management personnel.* Use formal language, and proof the final draft for potential errors. Phrase all communication in such a way that places you in the best position to negotiate. Keep in mind that the law demands precision.

*Figure 15.9. Musical tracks from early Disney animation was known to feature harsh dissonance, rapid changes in tempo, exaggerated performance, and quotations from popular tunes.*

# HISTORICAL TRENDS IN ANIMATION SCORING

## The Golden Age

In 1928, Walt Disney released his first sound animation, *Steamboat Willie*, an animated short driven primarily by score. Within a decade, Carl Stalling and Scott Bradley established a unique style of cartoon music through their respective work with Warner Brothers and MGM. This music featured harsh dissonance, rapid changes in tempo, exaggerated performance techniques, and quotations from popular tunes. Stalling and Bradley both had a propensity

---

Licensing Quote Request

Month/Day/Year

To: Director of Licensing (use formal name and title)

From: Name and Title (e.g., Music Supervisor)

Re: Project Title by [Director's Name]

I would like to obtain a quote for synchronization license of [Writer's Name] composition [Song Title] for use on the above-titled animation. The details and parameters of the request are as follows:

Nature of use:

1. Specify whether the project is for commercial or educational use.

2. Specify the length of the cue in minutes and seconds.

3. Specify where the animation will be exhibited (e.g., student festivals, commercial advertising, broadcast, or Internet).

4. Specify all details relating to distribution.

5. Specify whether the request is for exclusive or nonexclusive rights.

Production information:

The soundtrack budget is typically less than 10% of the entire budget. Some license administrators will ask you to state the budget for the project.

Term:

The period of time for which the license applies, such as 1 year (as in the case of student films) or for the life of the copyright (as in the case of a commercial release).

Territory:

Clearly define where the animation will be exhibited such as locally, regionally, nationally, or internationally.

Synopsis:

Provide a *brief* summary of the story and discuss how the song contributes to the story.

Contact information:

Phone

Fax

E-mail

---

*Figure 15.10. Licensing Quote Request. This Form Contains Most of the Information Fields Required when Making a Licensing Request for Synchronization, Master, and Videogram Licensing*

for hitting the action with music, an approach that would become known as *Mickey Mousing*. Though Raymond Scott never scored an animation, his music, especially "Powerhouse," had a profound influence on this musical style and can be heard in many of Carl Stallings scores. Many of the early animations featured *wall-to-wall* (nonstop) music that functioned as both underscore and SFX. Not all animation of the Golden Age featured this approach to scoring. The early Fleisher animations were dialogue driven and contained fewer sight gags. These animations were scored using a more thematic approach associated with live-action films. Winston Sharples and Sammy Timberg composed or supervised many of these scores for films like *Popeye* and *Superman*.

Figure 15.11. Composer Alan Silvestri composed the score for Who Framed Roger Rabbit, *the groundbreaking feature film that seamlessly combined live action and character animation into nearly every scene.*

## The Television Age

The arrival of television in the late 1940s signaled the end of the Golden Age of animation. As animation migrated to television, decreased budgets and compressed timelines gave rise to a new approach to scoring. Hanna-Barbera emerged as the primary animation studio for this emerging medium. They employed Hoyt Curtain to create the musical style for their episodic animations. As a jingle writer, Curtain had a talent for writing melodic themes with a strong hook. He applied this talent to create some of the most memorable title themes, including *The Flintstones*, *Johnny Quest*, and *The Jetsons*. He also created in-house *music libraries* used consistently from episode to episode. These libraries accelerated production time, cut costs, and gave the studio a signature sound.

## The Animation Renaissance

In 1989, Disney released *The Little Mermaid*, which featured an original song score by composer Alan Menkin and lyricist Tim Rice. In that same year, Alan Silvestri composed the score for *Who Framed Roger Rabbit?* Both films were financially successful and renewed studio interest in feature-length animation. In 1995, Pixar released their first feature animation *Toy Story*, scored by Randy Newman. By the mid-1990s, Alf Clausen had established *parody scoring* as a familiar element of *The Simpsons*. Clausen's skill at parody is well represented in the episode entitled "Two Dozen and One Greyhounds," which features the song "See My Vest," a parody of Disney's "Be Our Guest." Feature animation continues to emphasize scoring, attracting A-list composers, editors, and supervisors.

# Animation

## By Angie Taylor

## SYNOPSIS

$\mathcal{T}$he term *motion media* covers several disciplines. During my time as a freelancer, I concentrated on animation but also diversified into doing motion graphic design and visual effects work. These three distinct disciplines each require specialist skills, but they also overlap. The term *animation* is used to describe the process of sequencing drawings, computer-generated artwork, or photographs of models to create the illusion of a moving image. Animation encompasses several categories, including hand-drawn animation, computer-generated animation, and model animation. Each of these can also be broken down into further categories—for example, hand-drawn animation can be divided into cartoon animation and abstract animation. Computer-generated animation  can be split into 2D and 3D animation. Visual effects is the process of applying effects to film, video, or animated footage. Most people think of visual effects in terms of creating amazing 3D creatures, environments, and other CGI elements (computer-generated imagery), but the visual effects umbrella covers several other areas, too. Compositing is the process of combining images and footage together in layers. Keying is the process of removing backgrounds from shots so they can be composited with new ones. Color correction is the process of fixing the color of footage to achieve consistency; it can also be used to apply color treatments to style shots. Within each of these subsets of visual effects it's often necessary to animate values, so animation rules apply here as much as they do in pure animation.

Motion graphic design is a specialized area of TV, video, film, web, and device content production. Motion graphic designers create moving graphic designs—things like opening title sequences for movies, advertisements, interstitial graphics to run between TV shows, animated logos, and web banners—in fact, anything that incorporates text and moving imagery. A motion graphic designer designs layouts, creates animated sequences, incorporates video, and photography to the mix, and adds visual effects. Therefore, they must have an expansive knowledge that encompasses traditional graphic design skills, animation techniques, and visual effects tricks.

It's important that you learn the rules of animation and how to apply them to your work as a motion graphic designer, animator, or visual effects artist. Time and motion are the two things that set motion graphic design apart from any other type of design. Just as color, composition, and typography combine to convey messages in graphic design, the nature of the movement you create when animating elements can also convey a message to the viewer. Animate something bouncing around on the screen quickly, and you'll create a sense of dynamism and energy, or make an object slide or glide to create a more calming or elegant mood.

In this chapter, you'll learn how to understand and control the timing of your animations in order to communicate ideas and feelings to the viewers. You'll also learn how to apply the tried and-tested rules of animation to your motion graphics projects. This will prepare you for recreating all of the time-based trickery you have seen on the big screen and on music videos, including speed ramps, slow motion, video scrubbing, and time warping.

## THE HISTORY OF ANIMATION

*Figure 16.1. A modern replica of child's Victorian-era zoetrope toy. The drum is spun as the viewer looks at the images though the slits, creating the illusion of moving images.*

It's hard to determine exactly when animation began, but the idea of making still drawings come to life has been developed over centuries. This gradual development really gained momentum during the nineteenth and twentieth centuries. Early moving image technology included the magic lantern, which projected sequences of slides upon which an artist would paint or draw. This magical device relied on a phenomenon known as "persistence of vision," where the human eye looks at an image and remembers it for slightly longer than it's actually visible. The magic lantern would project these images in quick succession so the human eye was fooled into interpreting it as a single moving image.

In Victorian times, animation-type games like the flip book and the zoetrope were popular. The flip book allowed the player to draw sequential images on the pages of a small book. The pages were then flicked through quickly to trick the eye into seeing the images move. The zoetrope was a more sophisticated version of the flip book. It was a cylindrical drum with regularly spaced slits that one could look through, revealing a moving image. This "movie" was, of course, just a sequence of images cycled quickly one after the other. When the drum was spun, it would create the same persistence of vision effect.

## TRADITIONAL ANIMATION

Traditional stop-frame animation started in the early 1900s. It was created by photographing a series of drawn images that were then transferred to film and played back to give the optical illusion of a moving image. Originally, it was considered only a novelty for entertaining children and adults until Walt Disney, in the 1930s, developed it into the magical art form it is today. Since then, traditional stop-frame animators have (collectively) developed their skills and techniques over one hundred years. As with most forms of art and design, this has resulted in a well-respected set of rules that should be understood in order to produce successful and compelling animation. We'll be going through these rules in the pages of this chapter to give you a good idea of how to create your own effective animations.

## COMPUTER ANIMATION

Computer animation is a much younger art form and has not yet developed as far as traditional animation. The tendency of untrained computer animators is to rely on the computer's immense capabilities to exactly replicate real-world physics. While this is a good practice if you are a visual effects artist, it's not so good for creating convincing animation, since real life isn't quite dynamic enough to really compel the viewer. When Disney created *Snow White* (1937), the animators had a hard time developing the human characters. Like many computer animators of today, they thought that copying real life would be the solution, so they started by tracing film frames. They soon found that the movements were too "real" to be convincing for an animated film. They learned from this that pushing the possibilities of science and nature to extremes would result in more dynamic and appealing animation.

Don't get me wrong. I love what computers are capable of and have an immense amount of admiration for the creators of visual effects, but animation is a different skill with different rules. My philosophy is not to mimic the real world too much and to try to adapt the rules developed over the years by traditional animators. Here are some of the rules and tips for implementing them in your motion graphic designs and animations.

# ANIMATION TERMS

You can reference this list of commonly used animation terms as you go through the chapter.

- **Stop-frame animation**—Stop-frame animation is also referred to as traditional animation. It involves creating a series of drawings that are played back quickly to give the illusion of a moving image.
- **Cell animation**—Cell animation was so called because it is made up of images drawn or painted onto sheets of clear celluloid, which can be layered on top of one another and moved independently, making the drawings more flexible so they can be reused in different scenes.

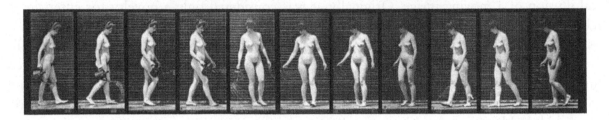

*Figure 16.2. Original footage from Dover Book's Muybridge' Humans in Motion.*

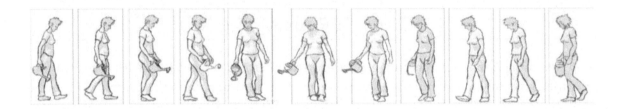

*Figure 16.3. Rotoscoped footage of Muybridge's original footage in Figure 16.2.*

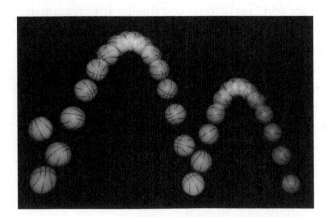

*Figure 16.4. Strobe lights are able to capture more than two dozen images of a basketball bouncing. Which of these images would you choose if you were to create keyframes to animate this action?*

- **Rotoscoping**—Rotoscoping is the process of drawing over individual film or video frames to create a lifelike animation (Figures 16.2 and 16.3). This was originally done by tracing over film frames manually but has been made easier with computer software that can automate a certain amount of the process. However, it's a painstaking and time-consuming process.

## KEYFRAMES

The term keyframe comes from traditional animation. To understand the term, let's look at an example. Imagine Walt Disney wants to create a simple animation of a ball bouncing on the floor. He would make three drawings: the ball at its starting point, the ball as it hits the floor, and the ball at its end point. These are all points where major changes occur in the animation—the most important, or "key," moments of the animation—thus the term keyframes. The term is also used in computer animation, where it refers to a point on the timeline where a change occurs in the selected property.

# TWEENING

Continuing our story, Walt Disney would then hand these keyframes to his assistant animator, who would then create new drawings to fill in all the frames "in-between" the keyframes. The term *tweening* is used to describe this process, and the name *tweener* to describe the person who carries out the process. Computer software assists in this process by automatically generating frames between the keyframes for you.

# INTERPOLATION

*Interpolation* is the term often used in computer software to describe how change occurs between keyframes—that is, how an object travels from one position to the next. If you observe how things move in the real world, you'll notice that they rarely move at a constant speed but will usually vary their speed as they move. They constantly accelerate, decelerate, and vary in speed. Think of a car pulling out of a driveway: It doesn't just take off at 60 miles per hour but starts off at a slow speed and gradually increases in speed over time.

When you animate objects using software, it's very easy to make something move at a constant speed, but your animations will usually look unnatural if you leave them like this. In traditional animation, changes in speed are achieved by creating more drawings when the action is slow and less when the action is fast. With computer software, you can change the interpolation between keyframes by adjusting speed and velocity settings for keyframes in a graph.

Linear, even speeds are represented by straight lines. In Figure 16.5, you can see the speed represented by curves meaning the object starts moving slowly and then gradually accelerates into action. Changing the keyframe interpolation will determine how quickly or slowly an

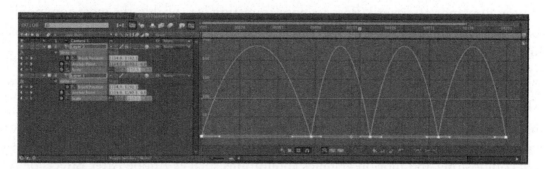

*Figure 16.5. Example of a speed graph in Adobe After Effects.*

object builds speed between keyframes. Using preset timings like "eases" or "smooths," you can also soften the transition from one speed to the next to avoid sudden jumps in speed. Your software manual is the best place to look for instructions on how to control speed in your application of choice. Also, see the bibliography.

# VELOCITY

Velocity describes the rate of change of an object's position as it moves. In computer software the velocity setting usually controls how quickly or slowly an object accelerates or decelerates.

# ANIMATION TYPES

There are three basic animation types listed below.

## Straight-Ahead Animation

Straight-ahead animation is where the animator draws a series of frames in sequence, one after the other, until he or she reaches the end of the animation. This is quite a challenging way to animate because there's no firm plan or schedule in place. But it's the most experimental and creative approach, allowing the animator to make decisions and change ideas as he or she goes. It's nice to allow your animation to evolve as you create it, but can be a risky business, particularly when tight budgets and deadlines are in place. An alternative way that is easier to manage is pose-to-pose animation.

## Pose-to-Pose Animation

This is when the lead animator starts by sketching out ideas and then storyboarding the complete animation before any production takes place. Only after everyone on the production team has approved the storyboard are the main poses in the animation drawn. These are the key moments in the animation and are therefore known as the keyframes. The whole story, plus any music, sound effects, or visual effects, is planned well before the animation stage takes place. Once the key drawings are complete, the assistant animator (or tweener) is then given the job to add the in-between drawings afterward. Pose-to-pose animation is probably the most commonly used approach and the one that most of the big animation studios use today. Everything is planned carefully before proceeding with the animation; formulas are followed to reduce risks.

## Computer-Generated Animation

Much of the animation you see today is created using computers. Many software applications are available that allow you to animate your designs. These can be separated into three basic categories: compositing and motion graphics applications such as Adobe After Effects or Apple's

Motion; 3D applications such as Cinema 4D, 3D Studio Max, or Maya; and web animation packages such as Adobe® Flash or Microsoft® Silverlight applications.

All of these applications use keyframes to mark the key poses in an animation. You just tell the software, "I want this object to start at point A and end at point B," and the software automatically works out all of the steps in-between for you. Unlike a human tweener, the software can't reason, so it doesn't know which path it should take from A to B. Therefore, you must guide the software to determine the steps in-between.

## THE LAWS OF PHYSICS

Before you can create a convincing animation, you need to understand some basic laws of physics. These laws determine how objects look and move in real life; by mimicking these, you can make your animations more believable. This isn't meant to be a comprehensive physics lesson, but I will try to explain why these concepts are important to a motion graphic artist.

## MASS

Mass is the amount of physical matter contained in the object and is determined by a combination of weight, size (or volume), and composition. A cannonball is smaller than a beach ball, but it has more mass because it's made of solid, dense metal. Compare this to a beach ball, which is made from a thin membrane of plastic but largely consists of air. You need to think about the mass of objects when you animate them because it will affect the speed and movement of animated objects.

## GRAVITY

I'm not going to even attempt to explain why gravity works the way it does (if you're really curious, you can Google Newton and find out all about it), but suffice it to say, gravity is a strong force that draws objects toward each other. In terms of animation, gravity is important to consider because it is the force that draws objects toward Earth and so determines how things rise, fall, and move when projected. Gravity also affects the weight of an object (Figure 16.6).

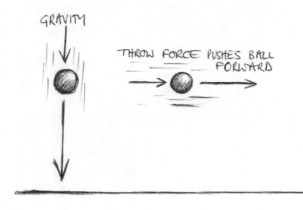

Figure 16.6. Gravity and directional force.

## WEIGHT

Weight is determined by the mass of the object combined with gravitational force. The moon has about 15 percent of Earth's gravitational force, so objects lifted there will appear to be lighter than if lifted on Earth. If you're animating a character picking up an object, then you need to think about how she would feel with that weight in her hands. When animating text, think about the different ways you can suggest weight. You could make the text appear to be very heavy by making it plummet quickly to the ground and making the screen shudder. Or you could make it seem weightless as if in outer space by making it sway slowly and gracefully around the screen. The opening titles for *Barbarella* (by Arcady and Maurice Binder) feature text animation that dances weightlessly around Barbarella in her spaceship. (You can see this online at the wonderful "The Art of the Title Sequence" website at http://www.artofthetitle.com/title/barbarella/)

## DIRECTIONAL FORCE

Some things in life follow a straight path—for example, a ball dropped from above with no force applied will drop in a straight line. It does this because gravity is the only force being applied to it, and gravity will always pull in one direction: downward, toward the center of Earth. Additional directional forces (or "throw forces") can also be applied to objects that can work with or against gravity, depending on their direction (see Figure 16.7). When you're animating objects that are being projected, think about how hard they are being thrown, since that will affect the way they travel and the shape of the path they follow (also known as the arc).

## ARC

If the ball is being thrown from the left, it will be affected by gravity. The result will be the further the ball travels, the nearer it will get to the ground. It is also given an additional force from the person who is throwing. This is known as a left-to-right directional force. When these two forces are combined, this will produce a curved path because the two forces are acting against each other.

The shape of the path that the ball follows is also known as an arc. The shape of the arc will depend on how strong the throw force is compared to the gravity force, which, under normal circumstances, remains constant. This is another important consideration to make when animating. Imagine animating a bouncing ball. You must first consider how hard it's thrown, in what direction it's thrown, and the

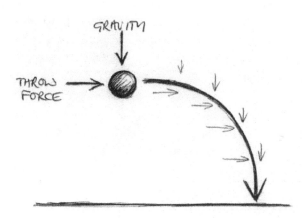

*Figure 16.7. The arc is produced by the two forces of gravity and direction working against each other.*

height it is thrown from. Only after you have considered these factors will you be able to create a believable arc for it to travel along. Then you need to decide how it will bounce. This is not only affected by the weight or mass of the object but also by the damping force of the object it hits when it bounces.

## DAMPING FORCE

When a ball bounces, the object that it bounces against (e.g., the ground) will absorb some of the energy from the ball, and the result is that its bounce will be dampened (lessened, if you like) each time it comes into contact with the ground. In other words, the arc will get gradually smaller each time the ball bounces. The softer the object that it bounces against, the higher the damping force. This means that it will come to a halt quicker after landing on a soft surface than on a hard surface. As an animator you have to try to imagine how the subject of your animation is going to react, depending on how it's affected by its surroundings. A basketball being bounced onto a wooden basketball court (which is fairly hard) will bounce a great deal because the floor will have a fairly low damping force. However, a football bounced on soft grass will bounce less because a higher damping force kind of "soaks up" the bounce.

## ACCELERATION AND DECELERATION

In the real world, objects accelerate as they fall and decelerate as they rise. This is due to the force of gravity acting on the mass of the object. The amount of acceleration or deceleration depends on the weight of the object and the direction it is moving in. If it's working along with gravitational force, it will accelerate more quickly. If it's working against gravitational force, it will accelerate more slowly. Gravity will have more of an effect when working against a beach ball bouncing upward than a heavier basketball because the lighter ball offers less resistance. If the balls are moving along with the direction of gravitational force, the heavier ball will move more quickly. When animating, you can suggest a heavier weight by making an object take longer to come to a halt after moving or by making it take longer to accelerate. Light creatures like birds take off very quickly, whereas heavier creatures, like elephants, take time to accelerate into action.

## RESISTANCE

Resistance is a general term for any force that acts against the movement of an object or force. Resistance can be provided by gravity, directional force, wind, water, or the surface of another object. Imagine you're animating a character walking in a rainstorm. The wind resistance would perhaps make him walk at an angle, leaning into the storm. Or perhaps you want to animate some text to look as though it's traveling through sludge. Then you would make the text or character look as though it's having to work harder to create the feeling of resistance.

# THE RULES OF ANIMATION

Once you understand these basic physics principles, you can apply them to the rules of animation that have been developed over the years by animators. Some of these rules are based on real-life physics, and others on observations and reactions. They provide a set of invaluable "tricks" for animators that have been proven to work in almost every situation. In this section, I use examples of character animation to explain the rules and how they can be applied, but remember that these same principles can be applied to motion graphic design just as effectively.

# TIMING

Timing is not exactly a rule, but it is the most important aspect of animation. It sets animation apart from other drawn art forms. So much of animation is about timing. Messages or feelings that cannot be portrayed by a still picture can be more easily communicated with the addition of timing. One classic example of timing that you see not only in film but also in real life is a dramatic pause. Think of when somebody whispers a secret to a friend. There's a moment, just before they spill the beans, when they hesitate, looking around to make sure no one's listening. This moment makes the anticipation of the secret greater. Exaggerating a dramatic pause can make an event in your animation funnier, more poignant, or more intense. This is only one example of how timing can make a difference. Several others are discussed in the following paragraphs. Think about timing as you implement these rules in your animations.

# SQUASH AND STRETCH

One of the most important rules of animation is the squash and stretch rule. For an object to look convincing, it must "give" when external forces are applied to it. These forces include gravity, directional force, and the mass of the object, as well as other surfaces it comes into contact with.

Let's go back to the example of the bouncing ball. As the ball hits the ground, two forces collide. Gravitational force and the mass of the object come to blows with the surface of the ground, and this will cause the ball to squash. Obviously a softer ball (for example, a beach ball) will squash and stretch a lot, whereas a cannonball will hardly squash and stretch at all. But perhaps what you didn't know is that the ball will also stretch slightly as it falls and rises. Stretching is kind of like the reflex action that comes before and after squashing. To see this in real life, just think

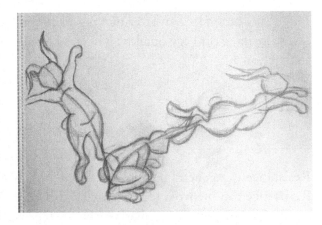

*Figure 16.8. notice that the rabbit squashes as it lands on the ground and stretches as it jumps through the air.*

of a rabbit jumping along the ground: As it hits the ground, it squashes down, and as it jumps again, it stretches along the arc (Figure 16.8).

Going back to our bouncing ball example, the only time the ball should look perfectly round is at the top of each arc, where resistance is at its lowest. You can use squash and stretch techniques to convey an object's density and mass. Often, exaggerating squash and stretch can add to the comedy value of your animations. As I mentioned before, Walt Disney discovered that exaggerating these real-life physical reactions made for much more effective animations. That takes me nicely to the next important rule of animation: exaggeration.

## EXAGGERATION

Another important animation rule is the rule of exaggeration. Exaggeration is literally a method of emphasizing something to increase its significance or draw attention to it. Exaggeration in animation terms is used to emphasize whatever key idea or feeling you wish to portray. For example, imagine you create a character who is smoking a cigarette while dancing. You should exaggerate the action that is most relevant to the scene. If the animation's purpose is to illustrate the joys of dancing (perhaps the cigarette is simply there as a tool to suggest the character is in a bar somewhere), the dancing should be exaggerated. If, however, you want to focus on the fact that the character is smoking (perhaps it's an antismoking ad), you would make him smoke in a very ostentatious way, with his feet making tiny little dancing movements. By exaggerating certain elements, you can guide the viewers' eyes and give them the exact message that you wish to give.

Using our bouncing ball example again, if we squashed the ball by the correct amount, the animation would probably look a little weak. You would hardly be able to see the squash at all because it would be too slight and would happen too quickly. By exaggerating the amount of squash and stretch and exaggerating the pause when it touches the ground, it will make the animation more dynamic. Good use of exaggeration can make an animation come to life, as long as it is done in a balanced way. To make it really work, choose the most important element of the scene, and apply exaggeration only to that. Think carefully about the different elements that can have exaggeration applied to them: movement, facial expressions, squash and stretch, bounce, timing, and facial expressions. By exaggerating one of these elements, you can draw the viewer's attention and make sure that nothing is missed.

## STAGING

Setting the scene (or staging the animation) involves attracting the viewer's attention and focusing it on a particular subject or area of the screen before the action takes place. You must remember that the viewers do not have the luxury of knowing what is about to happen in your animation, so if something moves very quickly, they may not have time enough to realize what is going on (if they blink, they'll miss it!). This is why it is necessary to set the scene for them. It can also set up a mood or feeling that you want the viewer to understand before the main action takes place. Examples of this would be having the subject move suddenly to attract attention, coloring or lighting your subject in such a way that it stands out from the rest of the scene, or using music or sound effects to capture attention.

## ANTICIPATION

Anticipation can also be used to direct the viewer's attention to part of the screen, and it is often intermingled with staging. However, there are differences that make it a rule unto itself. Some anticipation occurs naturally. For example, imagine a mouse is about to hit a cat over the head with a mallet. The mouse has to physically pull the mallet back before plunging it down; the pulling back of the mallet is the anticipation moment. By exaggerating this moment, you can let the viewer know what is about to happen in the scene before it happens. There are other anticipation tricks that do not always happen in nature but are useful in animation. For example, in the old Road Runner cartoons, when the coyote falls off the cliff, he hangs in the air for a second or two before plummeting to the ground. Without the dramatic pause, the viewer would not have time to register the coyote's very fast fall to earth. These pauses are rare moments of stillness in animation, and they can be used to make an action really stand out.

## MOTIVATION

Motivation is also somewhat linked to staging and anticipation. It occurs when one action clearly shows that another action is about to take place. Imagine that you are animating a car speeding off from a crime scene. When the car motor starts, the engine makes the car shudder. You can exaggerate this movement to let the viewer know that the car is ready to explode into action and zoom off the screen.

## SECONDARY ACTION

A secondary action is any type of action that results from the main action (Figure 16.9). Examples of this could include your character's tummy wobbling after he has jumped from a great height or an exaggerated facial expression of agony after Tom has been hit on the toe by Jerry. Like anticipation, secondary actions can also be used to help to strengthen the idea or feeling you are trying to portray. One thing to avoid is making the secondary action more prominent than the main action, since it can then distract the viewer and detract from your intended message.

## OVERLAP

Overlap is when one action overlaps another. It's very important to apply this rule to make your animations flow nicely and have a natural rhythm. If we look at nature again, very seldom

Figure 16.9. The character's face reacts after the telephone gives him an electric shock. Secondary actions reinforce the main action © Angie Taylor 1999.

does one action finish completely before another starts. Imagine you are sitting at the breakfast table; you take a bite of your toast and then have a sip of your tea. You may still be putting the toast back down on your plate with one hand while putting the cup of tea to your lips with the other. These are overlapping actions. If you are new to animation, it may seem natural for you to animate actions in sequence, one after the other. You should avoid doing this because it can make your animations look rigid and unnatural if you don't overlap the actions. This will take some practice, but a good tip is to animate the actions individually first and then try overlapping them by adjusting groups of keyframes along the timeline. With this technique, you don't have to get the timing right the first time.

## FOLLOW-THROUGH

Follow-through is, again, something that occurs in nature but is often exaggerated in animation. Think of a golfer taking a swing at a ball. The golf club doesn't stop suddenly when it comes into contact with the ball; it follows through the same path and then gradually settles back down to a halt. You'll also see follow-through when you observe a cat flicking its tail. After the cat has flicked the base of its tail, a wave of action will follow through to the tip of its tail once the base of its tail has stopped moving. This wave action can be observed everywhere you look in nature. Think of the way fish flip their tails and bodies to swim. People show this kind of wave action in their movement, as well, although not always as elegantly as a cat or fish! The human body also sways as it steps from foot to foot when walking. When you are using natural elements like water, plants, people, and animals in your animations, you should try your best to create fluid waves of movement.

## BALANCE

Balance is crucial for an animation to be truly convincing. You must draw your characters in poses that look real and sustainable (Figure 16.10). You can do this by drawing a center line through your character and making sure that you have equal mass on either side of the line. Balance will change according to the weight or mass of an object; heavy objects will generally

*Figure 16.10. The man on the left is standing upright, making him easy to draw. But if your character leans to one side, you need to make sure that his body adjusts to create balance. Notice that he has moved the barbells more to his right to compensate for his leaning to the left. He is also sticking his leg out to compensate. Think about balance not only with human characters but also with text or other objects in your animations © Angie Taylor 2008.*

take longer to pick up speed. They will also take longer to stop moving than light objects because more resistance is needed to balance their heavier weight.

# RHYTHM

A good understanding of rhythm will help you to work out the timing of your animations. If music is provided as part of the project, you can use this to define the rhythm of the piece. If the project doesn't require music, I often use a soundtrack to help time my animations and then delete it once the animation is completed. Choose a piece of music that conveys the mood you want to convey. You'll be amazed at how the rhythm of the music improves the feel of the whole animation.

# CAMERA MOVEMENT

Camera movement can lend filmic conventions to your animation. Interesting camera angles and animated camera movement can help to represent the point of view of a character. It can add dynamism to an otherwise static scene and can give the viewer a sense of being more involved in the piece.

# RECAP

So you can see that the rules of animation are important, not just for traditional character animation but also when applied to motion graphic design. You can apply the rules when creating time-based effects in very effective ways: retiming edits or simply by adjusting the timing at which events appear to happen.

In this chapter we started by looking at a short history of animation to give us an idea of the origins of traditional animation and how that developed into the world of computer-generated animation that exists today. We examined some common animation terms that you're likely to hear used in the motion graphics industry, and then we discussed the two main animation types: straight-ahead animation and pose-to-pose animation.

We bravely ventured into the world of physics to get an understanding of how things behave in the natural world. We then looked at how the rules of animation bend these laws of physics ever so slightly in the name of entertainment. These included squash and stretch, exaggeration, staging, anticipation, motivation, secondary action, overlap, follow-through, balance, and rhythm.

# Game Play Design

## By Nick Iuppa and Terry Borst

## INTRODUCTION

Determining gameplay is a key component of creative design. But before you undertake this task, the goals and objectives of the serious game (whether a simulation, a persuasive game, a training game, or a promotional game) need to be very clear-cut. If creative solutions to problems are considered prematurely, you may overlook some key elements of the behavior you're trying to teach in favor of those that are more fun to deal with. You may get locked into creative solutions that don't even address your objectives. But once the goals of the game are clear, then the fun begins.

Designing gameplay is an art and a science. It's a science because there are sets of well-known game activities that players can perform in certain stories and environments, and it's important to know them and how they can be used to make your game more fun. It's an art because it is really something like choreography. You have to determine how player-characters move around in the game space and how they react when they encounter elements within the space. You need to figure out the timing of the actions, the related sound and visual effects, and other appropriate game elements. Then you have to polish the game until the interaction between the player, the interface, the player-character/avatar, and other elements in the environment all work together in a smooth and enjoyable way.

The goal is to make it all interesting (and fun) if you can: realistic for a serious game, but also unusual and unexpected. That assures replayability, which contributes to retention.

For example, if your serious game has a learning objective requiring your player to recognize the difference between toxic and nontoxic waste (as ours did in *Spark Island*), then you're into a discrimination (choosing) game. With the gameplay revolving around choosing, how can you make it especially enjoyable while it's under way?

This chapter focuses on selecting kinds of gameplay that match your goals and then talks about how you can tweak them so that your players will get the most fun out of the experience. We're assuming that the instructional designer's job has largely been completed. You know the kind of activities you need. Now it's just a matter of making a great game out of them.

## TRADITIONAL GAMEPLAY NAVIGATION AND INTERACTION

Let 's face it, you aren't really seeing a brand new game every time you open a game box or download a game. When you get inside you find yourself going through activities that you've seen before. On rare occasions, you'll find something utterly new. But mostly you're seeing the latest staging of tried and true game activities. Through all the versions of *Tomb Raider* (the Lara Croft series of games), you're running, dodging, jumping, climbing, crawling, and rolling on the floor: you're navigating the terrain. Then you're aiming and shooting. You're kicking and punching (maybe from many different directions). Sometimes you're being shot at, attacked, and even eaten alive by bears or wolves. Those activities form the basis of the navigation and interactive play of the game. (Figure 17.1 lists common gameplay activities.)

## CLASSIC GAMEPLAY MECHANICS

Even if you use all the basic moves in your game, there are times when a prescripted activity (game mechanic) can offer a major new feature. *Whack-a-Mole* is a classic game in its own right. But there are a million variations: different mole-like creatures to whack, different whacking actions to take. And that is only one activity. Take a look at your favorite game and see how many different kinds of game mechanics you can find. (Figure 17.2 illustrates typical game mechanics.)

| Moving | Swimming | Attacking | Other Actions |
|---|---|---|---|
| Walking | On the surface | Shooting | Grabbing hold |
| Sidestepping | Underwater | Kicking | Climbing |
| Rolling | Dive under | Punching | Pushing/pulling |
| Jumping | | | Looking around |
| Diving | | | Picking up objects |
| | | | Using controls |
| | | | Using puzzles |

*Figure 17.1. Typical Gameplay Activities*

| Vehicle Driven | Sports Driven | Work/Life Driven |
|---|---|---|
| Enter a vehicle | Punch | Flip a burger |
| Start an engine | Swing a baseball bat | Run a maze |
| Drive a vehicle | Kick a football | Operate a radio |
| Ride a skateboard | Swing a golf club | Work a puzzle |
| Fly a plane | Hand fight an opponent | Identify items |
| Jump from a plane | Cast a fishing rod | Whack a mole |
| Drive a boat | Block a ball | |
| Operate a steam shovel | | |

Figure 17.2. Representative game mechanics from popular game sets.

# MATCHING MECHANICS TO OBJECTIVES

Taken together, these navigations and actions, combined with game mechanics, offer a vast array of basic game interactions to consider. The trick is to pick those interactions that match your objectives and content and then to customize them so that they address your objectives most effectively.

In designing the fire control minigame we wanted for *Spark Island*, we determined that it would be best to start small. We began with a small campfire, showed how to build it, and had the player build it. Then we went to a fun minigame. At a new fire, not built according to best practices, sparks began to fly out of the fire and onto the surrounding ground. The player had a hose and had to put out the sparks as soon as they jumped out of the fire. As more and more sparks began to jump, the player was challenged to stop something that could become a raging forest fire.

Figure 17.3 shows the relationship between the objectives and the gameplay solutions that addressed them. Note that the sparks game was only one of several minigames that dramatized

| Objective (after completing FS4K, students will be able to do the following) | Problem Type | Solution Type | Recommended Solution | Comment | Minigame |
|---|---|---|---|---|---|
| 1.1: Know the consequences of fire. 1.2: State examples of fire disasters on homes and villages. | Generalization | Demonstration and prompted exercise | Players need to experience a simulation of a small fire that eventually grows large enough to consume part of the town and possibly their own home. | These objectives are addressed in the first fire lessons with the Dragon Slayer at the fire pits, specifically in the *Sparks* minigame. Also in the *Fire Escape Plan* minigame | *Sparks* Game |
| 1.3: Describe the action of a fire as it spreads. 1.4: Know the effects of smoke, wind, and weather. | Generalization | Demonstration and prompt | Provide several examples of fire as it spreads. | Additional versions of the *Sparks* minigame add wind and a weather component. | *Sparks* Game *Family Escape Plan* Game |

Figure 17.3. Sample objectives and instructional solutions for the Spark Island game.

the danger of fire. The entire *Spark Island* game built to a climax in which the players had to escape from their burning home.

## MAKING GAMES FUN, A PROVEN PROCESS

In the course of creating serious and entertainment games, we've been fortunate to work with some wonderful creative directors who have added their own spin on the creative process. It is this spin that makes their games different and unusual. Phil Campbell has served as creative director on Electronic Art's *Godfather* and *007* franchises and designed several Lara Croft games. He shared his creative process with us, and we'll see how we can apply this to serious games and simulations.

## RESEARCH AND SATURATION

Campbell 's tongue-in-cheek first step is complete immersion in the material. He reads everything he can about the game's subject matter, plays the game, watches videos, and reads the fan blogs and websites. In a serious game, he would become totally familiar with the results of the needs and task analyses. Then he takes a couple of days off, takes his dog to the beach, and lets the information sink in. And then he's ready to start his design.

## CREATIVE BRAINSTORMING

Campbell goes to the first creative meeting and brainstorms with the team. He prefers to brainstorm with the client and key members who have creative ideas about the game. If he gets inspired, he may do his own riff on one or more of their ideas, but he wants key team members to contribute so that everyone will buy into the concepts as they're evolving. Because Campbell is both an architect and a graphic artist, he'll probably start drawing the ideas on the white board. He'll put up as much as he can, tweaking ideas as he goes along. Eventually he'll cover the entire board. He says people will either be inspired or intimidated by this presentation, so it's better not to make the drawings too good or have too final a look. Everyone should know that the ideas will continue to evolve.

## METAPHORS THAT GIVE STRUCTURE

Campbell likes to think of the whole game at once. He wants to see the arc of the game story, especially the beginning and the end. Often he uses metaphors to structure his thinking. For example, he uses a golf course metaphor frequently. The game he's designing (no matter what it is about) can be thought of as a round of golf, he says. The players know the goal of the game:

to get the ball from the tee, onto the green, and into the hole. Sometimes they can see the flag waving at them from the hole. Other times they can't; it's hidden, but they still know where they're going—the purpose of the game. Campbell can pepper the course with obstacles and hazards. He can hide the green or make it visible. But he sculpts the course, building each hole differently, where every hole becomes a level in his game. (Not that he always has 18 levels to each game.)

Next, he gives the player a bag of golf clubs to play with, and those clubs are the mechanics of the game. In a fantasy game, they may be a variety of weapons and spells (invisibility, stealth) as well as tools for climbing and building. Now the entirety of the game has emerged. Campbell sees the whole experience, and, like a golf course, he knows where the traps and hazards are, where things are easy, and where they get difficult.

Another metaphor Campbell likes to use is that of a large building (a nod to his architect training). The building is again a metaphor for the whole game, and the path through the building represents the players ' path through the experience. (See Figure 17.3 for an example.) He sometimes conceptualizes this building to set the mood of the game, so he's always aware of the kind of atmosphere he wants to maintain. How do the players approach the building to get started? What do they see through the windows of the building? What tools do they employ to get in the door? Do they use some kind of stealth and sneak in, or do they pull out a rocket launcher and blow the doors away? This is the kind of wide-range thinking that Campbell uses to get a sense of the whole game, and be it a golf course or complex building serving as a metaphor for an entire world of action or adventure, he's seeking to understand the total player experience.

## GAMEPLAY

Returning to the golf metaphor, Campbell suggests that players can choose their path through the course. Some will choose to charge right down the fairway and get to the hole in as few strokes as possible. That's the way golf is supposed to be played, after all. But other players may want to take the scenic approach to the green, stopping to check out the lake on their way. Still others may want all the challenges they can find, going from trap to bunker to hazard on their way to the hole.

Campbell's point here is that he wants to give the players a course that they can play any way they want to; he gives them different tools so that they can have a variety of experiences as they go along. But he still has them playing in a world that has a beginning, middle, and end; where the direction of the game is never in doubt; and where the players know where they're going at all times, no matter what kind of circuitous path they may take to get there.

## GUIDED PATHS VERSUS BRANCHING

Campbell 's designs do not always require the kind of endless interactive structures and branching that people assume must exist in story-based entertainment games. There may *not* be vast worlds that players can roam around in for hundreds of hours. (Although his *Tomb Raider* games certainly feature such worlds.) But there is always a sense of mission or destiny to these designs. The destiny in the golf game is to get the ball in the hole. And he always tries to create great interactive experiences that can grab players and hold their attention. Players progress from beginning to end along a defined route, but there is still plenty of opportunity to stop and play. " It's kind of sleight of hand, " he says. " We give the illusion of freedom but maintain a grasp on the linear design; the interactivity quotient feels high. " The " guided path " approach doesn't require the building of vast 3D worlds or the creation of many paths through the material. As a result, they're well suited to serious games that have demanding numbers of objectives but limited budgets. It doesn't mean they can't be fun to play. Just that the gameplay is in the activities, not in endless branching.

## THE CLEVER PLAYER

Campbell says that he likes to make the players of his games feel clever: to give them tools, show them how to use them, and then turn them loose. There may be a lot of ways to play the game, but Campbell is always thinking of what the clever player will do. What can he do to challenge and reward that player? He wants his games to be most exciting and rewarding for the players who make the cleverest choices. He lets players see the end of the mission, know where it is all going, but on the way he opens all kinds of windows, opportunities, and options. He doesn't tell them how to play the game though, and in that way he gives them that incredible sense of freedom.

## THE GAMING EXPERIENCE

This is where Campbell and his team get really creative. As he scopes out his terrain (his golf course or the inside of his complex building), he looks for opportunities for traps, hazards, and puzzles, things that the game player has to solve to advance the game. This is where he and his team let their imaginations run wild. We have to build a slight rise in the terrain of our game space, he suggests. So why not add a giant waterfall? The question then becomes, how do players get to the top of the waterfall? Is there a flying horse that they can tame and ride up there? And how do they tame and then ride that beast?

When considering serious games, Campbell asks how game challenges can be used to strengthen skills that fit the objectives of the instructional design. If the challenges fail to strengthen skills, then the serious game won't be fulfilling its mandate.

How do you get through the sand traps? How do you ascend to the next floor of the building? How do you find the hidden gun (or hidden skill set) that will save your life? What are the most creative challenges and answers that you can think of? What would be the trick that would challenge the cleverest players and give them a sense of accomplishment when they solved it?

## APPLYING THIS PROCESS TO SERIOUS GAMES

Let's take a look at how a few of Campbell's approaches apply to serious games:

- Guided paths. The *Leaders* game narrative takes place within one day and is a largely linear story with different " waypoints " that would launch the player toward distinctly new leadership challenges. The player's goal (to successfully complete a food distribution mission) remains the same throughout, but numerous concrete minigoals (e.g., to maintain good relationships with subordinates and superiors, to forge and maintain a good relationship with a local tribal leader) emerge and then must be reached to successfully move toward the primary goal.
- The clever player. Ian Bogost's and Persuasive Games' *Fatworld* (funded and published by the Corporation for Public Broadcasting) gradually introduces the rules of an economy to players. Players are rewarded as they figure out how to apply the rules and better their lot (earn more money, eat better food) throughout the game. Similarly, the Wilson Center's *Budget Hero* allows players to discover how the playing of certain federal budget cards (i.e., budget priorities and variables) may have either minor or major effects on long-term forecasting models.
- The gaming experience. *Fully Involved* continues to amp up the complexities of potential house fires through its levels, revealing new and unexpected challenges that require the use of knowledge gained in earlier firefights.

## CREATIVE QUESTIONS THAT LEAD TO BETTER GAMEPLAY

We talked to some of our other creative director friends who have their own slant on how to make gameplay more fun. Most of their games feature a player-character (an avatar), an environment he or she needs to navigate, objects, and nonplayercharacters (NPCs) that he or she can interact with. Using that basic list of game elements, they recommend getting more creative by asking yourself the following kinds of questions.

## PLAYER-CHARACTERS (AVATARS)

What's fun about a given player-character? What can the avatar do? Does the avatar have powers or limitations? Can you customize what the avatar wears and its other visuals aspects? Does it sound a specific way? Is it a hero or a villain (in relation to the story)? What does the avatar carry? Also, think about the avatar's interactions in the environment. How does the player-character interact with NPCs? Does it have to lead them, convince them, hide from them, kill them, have them follow it somewhere? Just thinking creatively about these basic questions can lead to interesting choices and outcomes.

## NAVIGATION

Ask yourself what's fun about the navigation in this game. Is speed an issue? Can the avatar go too fast? Do doors or gates block its way? Are there vehicles that the avatar can climb on or into, drive or fall out of? What's the terrain? How can you make it more exciting? Does the avatar have to wade through mud? Is the avatar traversing an icy slope that is challenging because of lack of traction? Think about ways that movement within the game world can be more interesting and more fun to understand and get through. The world you're building needs to be believable and tell a story that supports the goals of the game. To make the world make the most sense, pick forms of navigation that suit the story.

Figure 17.4. *Animation technique and sophistication can vary from game to game. When designing objects in a game, ask yourself, "What's fun about interacting the object in this environment?" Is it the look of the vehicle that makes it fun? Or is it the interaction with the environment?*

## OBJECTS

What's fun about interacting with objects in the environment? What's the most creative form these objects can take? How do they relate to the player-character or the navigation of the environment? Do they help or harm the player-character? Do they affect the avatar's performance? Can the avatar carry the objects and move them? Are the objects expendable? Can they be combined into new and more powerful forms? Is the avatar rewarded for finding objects and building sets or collections of them? Are they prizes or symbols of success or symbols of danger and impending doom?

## GAME MECHANICS

Game mechanics are all the things that your characters, environments, and objects are able to do within the game space. (Sometimes they're called the rules of the world .) Think of game mechanics as a toolbox (or, as Phil Campbell suggests, a set of golf clubs). Find the best ones for the job from an established set of pieces you've seen before, and repurpose them to fit the goals of your instructional design, story, and game.

Establish the story you're trying to tell, the goals of the story, and the world the character is in. Then define the things that these different elements do that provide choices with consequences, a heightened feeling of tension and danger, a sense of progress and reward. Create a sense of immersion to pull the players into the game world and make them feel a part of the game. Good designers can do this with very few common pieces, activities, and common rules.

It's easy to get things so complicated that the game will either be hard for the player to learn or so hard for the developer to build that it can't be completed in time.

Another approach here is to take different types of game mechanics and mash them together. Pull the rules from game A and game B together and give them a twist to make something new. Most games are based on features that already exist, but every once in a while something new and revolutionary comes up that's never been done before. (Think of the first time you ever tried Tetris or Guitar Hero .) But don't mash together too many mechanics; your game will lose coherence and become difficult to design and produce.

## KEY GAMEPLAY CONCEPTS

Here are a few gameplay concepts that you should also consider to make your game memorable and rewarding.

## FUN

That gameplay has to be fun goes without saying. What is critical is how you make it fun. See the sections that follow.

## CHOICE

Players need to make decisions. They need to feel that they have the ability to make choices. Some will further their cause, and some will be mistakes. Players should see their choices clearly, be able to execute them intuitively, and then learn from what they did. If they make a mistake, don't punish them. Let them try again with their improved knowledge. Then they will feel they're getting better at making decisions and at the game. The frequency of the choices and the cleverness of the related consequences contribute greatly to the fun of the game.

Choices should have real consequences. If either choice A or choice B leads to the same result, then these are pointless choices. In addition, the consequences should have some weight and meaning. If choice A or choice B leads to trivial or insignificant differences in performance or narrative path, the player will quickly grow frustrated. When choice counts, it's said that players have agency. Players prize agency.

## REWARDS/PROGRESS

You've got to give the player rewards, whether it's to ascend to the next level, obtain new equipment or skill, or add points and progress on a leader board. Whether it's sirens and confetti or messages of congratulations, players have to feel that their decisions further their progress on a moment-to-moment basis. If they earn something tangible from an achievement in the game, they'll want to keep playing to get to the next achievement.

## RISK VERSUS REWARD

Players like rewards, but the rewards are more meaningful when risks are attached to them. The higher the risks taken, the better value will be placed on the reward. Don't be afraid to set up challenges that have real risk (in the context of the game) attached—but if a player fails, be sure the player has opportunities to remedy the failure and learn from the mistake or poor execution.

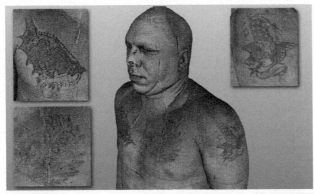

*Figure 17.5. Creating avatars and characters that populate the world help to pull players into the environment. If you put something suddenly out of context into the game world, it makes the game unrealistic and breaks immersion.*

## IMMERSION

How into the game are the players? Do they feel they are the character in the world? Are they pulled into the environment? Do they have an emotional involvement in their decisions and the outcome? Do they feel the tension? We don't necessarily need the emotional pull of *Titanic* or *Gladiator*, but players need investment in the reality of the game world, a feeling they can make a difference, a feeling that it'll be a better (game) world through their experience.

Immersion is easy to break. If you put something suddenly out of context into the game world, it makes the game unrealistic and breaks immersion. The worst example of breaking immersion is a crash bug. Players are ripped out of the experience and feel cheated. But sometimes designers end up breaking immersion themselves by doing something silly, out of context, or punishing in the game. Good games need to pull the player in and keep them there from decision to decision for (ideally) as long as is physically possible for the player, until they have to sleep, eat, or run screaming to the bathroom.

## Further Studies in Gameplay Design

The complexities of designing gameplay can't possibly be covered in a single chapter in a book, when an entire field of study (ludology) and academic degree programs have grown up around the topic. In addition, dozens of books have been written about gameplay design. Two we can recommend are Tracy Fullerton's *Game Design Workshop* (published by Morgan Kauffman) and Jesse Schell's *The Art of Game Design* (published by Focal Press). Take these steps to further improve your grasp of effective gameplay:

- Keep up with the latest developments in gameplay (play a lot of games).
- Understand key components of game mechanics.
- Broaden your study of gameplay to reach beyond videogames (the " prehistory " that includes sideshows, Coney Island – style parks, haunted houses, dioramas, amusement arcades, and much more).

## PILLARS

Pillars are tools to keep the game design under control. You're building a game, and it's an epic project. Ask yourself, what pillars or "tenets" are going to support the project. Identify them, and then use them to measure every decision the team makes. If the decision doesn't support a pillar, it doesn't support the project and it shouldn't be pursued.

There are usually three pillars to a project: never fewer than two and never more than four. For example, a game about fishing could have three pillars: (1) realistic rod-and-reel technique, (2) larger-than-life fish (both in the visual representation and in the timescale in which the player catches them), and (3) a worldwide online fishing competition. With these as the pillars, you could have a constructive discussion about the value of including lots of different types of boats, engines, trucks, and trailers. The game designer should come in at this point and say, "Only those things that further the pillar of realistic rod-and-reel technique should be supported!" As a result, the team would then promptly cut trucks and trailers and some of the boats that don't impact that form of gameplay.

Certainly in serious games, the instructional goals of the project are the tenets. Thus, in a game that didn't just want to simulate a fishing experience but actually wanted to teach fishing, the pillars could include the choice of bait or lure as well as the action of casting and where to cast.

## SUMMARY

- For serious games of all stripes, designing gameplay should take place (as much as possible) after instructional design has been completed—to avoid the premature lock-in of gameplay that fails to support your application's objectives.
- Metaphors for the entirety of the game can help conceptualize gameplay design. We might consider the game as a golf course or as a multilevel building. The ultimate player goal in each instance is clear-cut. But between the tee and the hole, the game designer can add all

kinds of obstacles, hazards, and traps so that the cleverest players will enjoy the challenge of figuring them out.

- Navigation, interaction, and game mechanics are some of the tools (or to extend the golf metaphor, the clubs) in which to assemble gameplay.
- Key elements of effective gameplay include player choice (agency), risk versus reward tradeoffs, immersion, and game pillars.
- Ludology is the study of games from social science, humanities, and engineering perspectives, and the more you study both the theory and practice of gameplay, the better you can contribute to designing unique (and fun!) game experiences.

# Image Credits

Copyright © 2008 by Jorge Royan / www.royan.com.ar / CC BY-SA 3.0

Copyright © 2010 by David Lapetina / Wikimedia Commons / CC BY-SA 3.0

Jacek Filek / Wikimedia Commons / Public Domain

Copyright © 2011 by Vaido Otsar / Wikimedia Commons / CC BY-SA 3.0

Fig 1.1: Copyright © 2011 by Downtown Community Television Center, Inc. / Wikimedia Commons / CC BY-SA 3.0

Fig 1.2: Copyright © 2010 by Tom Raftery / Wikimedia Commons / CC BY-SA 2.0

Fig 1.3: The Expedition of the Donner Party / Wikimedia Commons / Public Domain

Fig 1.4: Copyright © 2008 by Bridget Laudien / Wikimedia Commons / CC BY-SA 3.0

Fig 1.5: Maxfield Barbara / U.S. Fish and Wildlife Service / Public Domain

Fig 1.6: Copyright © 1985 by Miami Dade College Archives / Wikimedia Commons / CC BY-SA 3.0

Fig 1.7: Carlos Latuff / Wikimedia Commons / Public Domain

Fig 1.8: Copyright © 2011 by Joi Ito / Flickr / CC BY 2.0

Fig 2.1: Copyright © 2009 by Linda Spashett / Wikimedia Commons / CC BY 3.0

Fig 2.2: Copyright © 2006 by IllFonic, LLC / Wikimedia Commons / GPLv2 (a copy of this license can be found here: http://www.gnu.org/licenses/old-licenses/gpl-2.0.html)

Fig 2.3: Dominique M. Lasco / U.S Navy / Public Domain

Fig 2.4: Copyright © 2009 by DX Studio / Wikimedia Commons / CC BY 3.0

Fig 2.5: Copyright © 2012 by Surya Prakash / Wikimedia Commons / CC BY-SA 3.0

Fig 2.6: Copyright © 2009 by User:JetskiTradeCenter / Wikimedia Commons / CC BY-SA 3.0

Fig 2.7: Courtesy of Impact Games LLC

Fig 2.8: Copyright © 2012 by Sergey Galyonkin / Wikimedia Commons / CC BY-SA 2.0

Fig 2.10:Copyright © 2011 by Andrew Malone / Wikimedia Commons / CC BY 2.0

Fig 3.1: Copyright © 2008 by User:Paleontour / Flickr / CC BY 2.0

Fig 3.2: Copyright © 2008 by User:_titi / Flickr / CC BY 2.0

Fig 3.3: Copyright © 2011 by Vancouver Film School / Flickr / CC BY 2.0

Fig 3.4: Copyright © 2011 by User:raneko / Flickr / CC BY 2.0

Fig 3.5: Copyright © 2008 by Maik Meid / Wikimedia Commons / CC BY-SA 3.0

Fig 3.6: Copyright © 2010 by Jay Adan / Flickr / CC BY 2.0

Fig 3.7: Copyright © 2007 by Ventura Mendoza / Wikimedia Commons / CC BY 2.0

Fig 3.8: Copyright © 2012 by Milei Vencel / Wikimedia Commons / CC BY-SA 3.0

Fig 3.9: Copyright © 2012 by Paul Stein / Flickr / CC BY-SA 2.0

Fig 5.1: Copyright © 2012 by Blender Foundation and Project Mango / mango.blender.org / CC BY 3.0

Fig 5.2: Rembrandt / Metropolitan Museum of Art, New York / Public Domain

Fig 5.3: Jacek Malczewski / National Museum, Warsaw / Public Domain

Fig 5.4: John Leech / Public Domain

# Index

**SYMBOLS**

2D ANIMATION 139, 217

3D ANIMATION 127, 139, 217, 223, 238

**A**

ABSTRACT ANIMATION 217

ABSTRACT STORYTELLING 42

ACCELERATION 225

ACCENT 49–50, 58–59

ACCENTS 122, 204

ACOUSTIC 48, 51, 75, 77–78

ACOUSTICALLY DEAD 199

ACOUSTIC TREATMENTS 125

ACTION 22, 28, 33, 51–52, 56, 70, 72–73, 131, 133, 152, 160, 162–163, 168, 169, 172, 199, 201, 204, 215, 221, 227–230, 237

ACTION-RESPONSE 32

ACTIVE 11, 24, 27, 32, 44, 163, 170

ACTIVE VERBS 170

ACTS 70–71

ADR 121, 124–125, 127

AESTHETICS 97–98, 102–105, 107, 110, 116, 129, 153

AFFINITY 10, 15, 98–99, 182–189, 193–195

AGON 42

ALTERNATE REALITY GAME (ARG) 89

AMBIENCE 59, 158, 199–200

AMBIENT 59, 76, 198

AMBIENT SONIC QUALITIES 76

ANAGNORISIS 71–73

ANGLE 125, 138–139, 143–147, 150, 153, 182–187

ANIMA/ANIMUS 61, 63, 64

ANIMAL SPEAK 122

ANIMATIC 121, 207

ANIMATION 15, 18, 52, 105, 119–127, 157, 204–207, 210–215, 217–231

ANIMATION, 2D 139, 217

ANIMATION, 3D 127, 217, 223, 238

ANIMATION, ABSTRACT 217

ANIMATION, CARTOON 217

ANIMATION, CELL 220

ANIMATION, COMPUTER 219, 221

ANIMATION, COMPUTER-GENERATED 217, 223, 231

ANIMATION, GOLDEN AGE OF 204–205, 215

ANIMATION, POSE-TO-POSE 222–223, 231

ANIMATION, PRE- 123, 126

ANIMATION, STOP-FRAME 219–220

ANIMATION, STRAIGHT-AHEAD 222, 231

ANIMATRONIC CHARACTERS 44

ANTAGONIST 25, 42, 65, 71

ANTICIPATION 158, 226–230

ARC 21–22, 73, 151, 224–225, 227, 236

ARCHETYPES 16, 61–66

ARRANGEMENT 19, 80–81, 138, 205

ARTIFACT 39–40

ARTIST 3, 9–12, 85–86, 108–109, 117, 157, 200, 202, 210, 218–219, 223, 236

ASPECT RATIO 135–136, 145

ASSETS 37, 90

A-SYNCHRONOUS 120

ATMOSPHERE 40, 54, 58, 158, 199, 237

ATTACK 5, 18, 47–48

AUDIENCE 3–11, 15–20, 23–29, 31, 33–34, 39, 44, 47, 51, 58–59, 71–72, 78, 83–87, 97–99, 107–108, 115–116, 122, 127, 129, 132–136, 142–148, 153, 157–158, 163, 170–171, 189, 191, 194–195, 198–199, 204, 207, 212–213

AUDITORY STREAMS 202

AVATAR 233, 239–240

## B

BACKGROUNDS 6, 98, 121, 199–200, 217

BACKSTORY 18–19

BALANCE 40, 81, 117, 139–140, 198, 230–232

BEGINNING 4, 17–19, 28, 39, 133, 135, 149–150, 199–200, 236–237

BLANKET LICENSING 209

BOOM 148–149

BRANCHING 102, 237–238

BRAND 209

BRANDING 206

BREAKDOWN 69, 124

BROADBAND 89–90

BROKEN OUT 123

BUY-OUT 209

## C

CADENCE 49

CAMERA TAKE 130

CANNED MUSIC 209

CARICATURE 119, 122

CARTOON ANIMATION 217

CATHARSIS 42

CELL ANIMATION 220

CHARACTER 4–10, 20–24, 32–43, 52–54, 61–66, 71–73, 97–99, 107–117, 119, 122–127, 142–152, 162, 167–172, 205, 226–231, 242

CHARACTER ARC 73

CHARACTER DEVELOPMENT 39–40, 61

CHARACTER GOAL 41

CHARACTER JOURNEY 73

CHOICE 7, 33, 38, 59, 125, 139, 141, 146, 195, 241, 244

CHORD 55–56, 76–80

CHORD PROGRESSIONS 76, 208, 211

CHOREOGRAPHY 160, 233

CLOSED FRAME 136–137

CLOSE-UP (CU) 99, 132, 141–142

CLOSURE 120, 173, 176, 206

COLOR 7, 10, 37, 54, 109–117, 173–175, 194, 218

COLOR CORRECTION 217

COLOR THEORY 109

COMB FILTERING 126

COMEDY 4, 6, 227

COMMENTATIVE SOUND 51

COMMUNICATE 6, 12, 16, 35–36, 43, 47, 49, 130, 132–133, 218

COMPETITION 28, 39

COMPLEMENTARY COLORS 110–111

COMPOSER 54, 79–80, 206–209, 211, 215

COMPOSITE PERFORMANCE 125–126

COMPOSITING 126, 223

COMPOSITIONAL STRUCTURE 75

COMPUTER ANIMATION 219

COMPUTER-GENERATED ANIMATION 217, 223, 231

CONCEAL 152–153

CONCEPT ART 124

CONSCIOUS 9–10, 61, 157

CONSONANCE 54–55

CONTEXT 40, 50, 68, 124, 132, 213, 242

CONTEXTUAL SOUND 50

CONTINUITY 54, 133, 199–200, 204, 206, 209

CONTINUUM 8, 40, 50, 78

CONTRAST 10–11, 15, 131, 175–178, 181–195

COPY-PROTECTED MUSIC 203, 210–212

COPYRIGHT ACT 211–212

COPYRIGHT HOLDER 211–213

COPYRIGHT INFRINGEMENT 205, 210–211

COPYRIGHT NOTICE 211–212

CREATIVE DIRECTOR 236, 239

CREATIVE FEES 208

CREATIVITY 3, 6, 12, 16, 83, 87, 91, 112, 165, 211

CREATOR 8, 83–84

CRITIQUE 12, 117

CUE 7, 126–127, 139, 199, 203–210

## D

DAIMON 72

DAMPENING 125

DAMPING FORCE 225

DECAY 47–48, 48, 111

DECELERATION 225

DECISIONS 5–7, 11–12, 15, 33, 81, 103, 201, 208, 222, 241–242

DEEP FRAME 137

DESCRIPTION 159, 161, 162, 165–168, 171

DESCRIPTIVE SOUND 51

DESIGN 16, 39, 48, 50, 56, 58, 98, 102–104, 107, 109–110, 197–198, 201–202, 217–218, 226, 241–243

DIALOGUE 16, 32, 36, 43, 49–50, 58–59, 68, 98, 119–127, 136, 157–159, 162, 166, 169, 199–206, 215

DIALOGUE MENU 36

DIALOGUE MIXERS 125

DIALOGUE STEM 120–121

DIAPHRAGM 126

DIAPHRAGM CONDENSER MICROPHONES 125

DIDACTIC 11

DIEGETIC 50, 204

DIEGETIC SOUND 50, 204

DIGITAL AUDIO WORKSTATION 125

DIRECTIONAL FORCES 224

DIRECTOR 10–11, 121, 126, 146, 152, 162, 197, 199, 201, 207, 210, 236, 239

DISCONTINUITY 199

DISSONANCE 54–55, 214

DOLLY 148–153

DRAMA 4, 6, 19, 28, 33, 35, 42, 44, 49, 59, 72, 171

DRAMATIC PAUSE 226–228

DRAMATIC PUNCTUATION 151

DRAMATIC SEQUENCE 130, 133

DURATION 47–48, 55

DYNAMIC ACCURACY 125

DYNAMIC RANGE 48, 54–55

DYNAMISM 218, 230

**E**

EDITING 78–79, 130–132, 171, 197, 200–203, 207–210

EDUTAINMENT 37, 45, 92

E-LEARNING 92

EMERGENT 102

EMOTION 7, 16, 28, 54, 58, 67, 68, 97, 98, 132, 153, 157, 168, 172

EMOTIONAL IMPACT 23, 27, 39, 55, 140

EMOTIONAL RESPONSE 33, 81, 83, 146

EMOTIONAL TONE 205

EMOTIONAL WEIGHT 204

EMPATHY 23, 25

EMPHASIS 49, 58, 140–141

END CREDIT 203, 205–206

ENDING 4, 10, 23–24, 29

ENERGY 15–16, 42, 93, 111, 115, 151, 170–171, 218, 225

ENGINEERING 125, 244

ENTERTAINMENT GAME 90, 92, 236–237

ENVELOPE 47, 54

ENVIRONMENT 33–40, 51–52, 90, 93, 121, 131, 135–136, 138, 233, 239–240, 242

EPILOGUE 70, 120

EPISODIC TELEVISION 89

ESTABLISHING SHOT 18, 198

EXAGGERATION 158, 227–228, 231

EXPECTATION 4, 68, 72, 98

EXPOSITION 17–19

EXPOSURE SHEET 127

EXTREME CLOSE-UP (ECU) 141

EXTREME LONG SHOT (ELS OR XLS) 141

**F**

FEELING 6, 21, 25, 50, 54, 57–58, 67, 97, 106, 111–112, 137, 140, 142, 144, 149, 157–158, 226–229, 240, 242

FINAL DIALOGUE 121

FINAL MIX 209

FIRST PERSON 120

FIRST-PERSON SHOOTERS 40, 98

FIXED FRAME 145

FLAT FRAME 137

FLIP BOOK 218–219

FOCUS 51–52, 65, 82–84, 106, 120, 125, 138, 139, 143, 189

FOLEY 50, 124, 199–202

FOLLOW-THROUGH 229–230

FORESHADOWS 206

FORM 31, 33, 36, 42, 54, 58, 70, 78, 206, 212, 219, 240

FRAME 98, 105, 130–131, 135–146, 149, 153, 209, 220

FRAME WITHIN A FRAME 145

FREELANCER 217

FREEWARE 90

FREQUENCY 47, 125

FREQUENCY RANGE 125

FREQUENCY RESPONSE 125

FUTZED 204

FX STEM 121

## G

GAME 3–8, 16, 33, 36–37, 39–45, 89–93, 98, 101–106, 158, 233–243

GAME DESIGNER 41, 104, 243

GAME MECHANIC 104, 234

GAMEPLAY 90, 98, 102, 104, 158, 233–235, 238–239, 241, 243

GAMER 33

GAMES OF CHANCE 42

GARAGE GAMES 90

GENERAL AUDIENCE 19

GENRE 3–5, 6, 16–17, 40, 43, 55, 71, 75–77, 81, 83–84, 86, 98, 107, 110, 141, 205

GOAL 7, 15, 19, 21, 24–27, 29, 39–41, 80, 83, 102, 105, 158, 165, 233, 236, 239, 243

GOLDEN AGE OF ANIMATION 204–205, 215

GRANULARITY 40

GRAPHIC DESIGN 217–218, 226, 231

GRAVITY 223–226

GROOVE 83

GROUP ADR 121

GUIDED PATHS 237–238

## H

HAND-DRAWN ANIMATION 217

HARD EFFECTS 201, 202, 204

HARD SYNC 200

HARMATIA 71–73

HARMONY 42, 54–55, 75, 77, 80, 83, 85, 112

HERO 5–7, 10, 16, 21, 23, 26, 42, 61–62, 65–66, 70–73, 165–166, 170–171, 239

HIGH-ANGLE 143

HOOK 215

## I

IMAGE 10, 15–16, 36, 67–68, 97, 131, 133–135, 137–139, 143, 151, 208, 217–220

IMMERSION 34, 158, 236, 240, 242–243

IMMERSIVE 33–35, 44

IMMERSIVE ENVIRONMENT 35

IMPLIED LYRICS 205

INDEPENDENT GAMES 16, 89–92

INDIE GAMES 90

INFLECTION 49, 58, 124

INPUT 32, 90

INSTRUCTIONAL DESIGNER 234

INSTRUMENTATION 4, 9, 98, 208–209, 211

INTELLECTUAL PROPERTY 91

INTERACTION 233, 240, 244

INTERACTIVE DESIGNER 32

INTERACTIVE ENTERTAINMENT 32–33, 36, 39, 45

INTERACTIVE FICTION (IF) 43

INTERACTIVITY 31–33, 35–37, 39–40, 44, 238

INTERCUT 20, 199–201

INTERFACE 200, 233

INTERPOLATION 221

IRONY 159–160

ISOMORPHIC 206

ITV 33, 36–37

## J

JOURNEY 5, 33, 70–73, 83–84

JOYSTICK 8, 33

JUXTAPOSITION 15, 131–134

## K

KEYFRAME 220–223, 229

KEY FRAMING 127

KEYPAD 33

## L

LAUNCH PADS 91

LAYERING 98, 157, 200–201

LEAKAGE 125

LEAN BACK 33

LEAN FORWARD 33

LEFT BRAIN 103

LEGAL CLEARANCE 203

LEVEL 69, 126, 143, 199, 237

LICENSE 211, 213

LICENSING 91, 209–211, 213

LINEAR STORIES 39

LIP SYNC 120–121, 127, 205

LISTENING COMPLEXITY 78

LONG SHOT (LS) 18, 131, 141–142

LOOKING ROOM 140–141

LOUDNESS 47–48, 51, 54–55

LOW-ANGLE 143

LUDOLOGY 244

LYRICAL THEME 77, 83

LYRIC CONNECTION 204

LYRICS 5, 9, 15, 75–81, 98, 205–206, 211

## M

MAIN ACTION 51, 228–229

MAJOR STUDIOS 89

MASKING EFFECT 200

MASS 223–225, 226, 230

MASS AUDIENCE 33

MASTER LICENSE 211

MASTER RIGHTS 211, 213

MATERIAL 18, 21, 28, 31–33, 36, 40, 45, 84, 87, 124, 204, 207, 211, 213, 236, 238

MECHANICS 45, 102–105, 235–236, 237, 240–241, 243

MECHANISM 39, 132

MECHANISM OF GAMING 39

MEDIUM CLOSE-UP (MCU) 141

MEDIUM SHOT (MS) 141

MELODIES 76, 211

MELODY 54–56, 75–77, 79–80, 83, 85

MENTOR 61, 64, 66

METAPHOR 7–8, 51, 236, 237, 244

MIC 199

MICROPHONE 52, 125–126, 200–201

MIDI TECHNOLOGIES 208

MIMICRY 122

MINIGAME 235

MINI-MAJOR 89

MISE EN SCENE 197–198

MISE-EN-SCÈNE 130–135, 153

MIXER 203, 209

MMOG 33, 36

MODEL ANIMATION 217

MONITORS 82, 125–126

MONTAGE 131, 133–134, 153, 198, 203–206

MOOD 6, 49–50, 54, 58, 139, 198, 218, 228, 230, 237

MOOs 43

MORPH 204

MOTIF 77, 157, 181–183, 194–195

MOTION GRAPHIC DESIGN 217–218, 226, 231

MOTION MEDIA 217

MOTIVATION 39–40, 47, 150–152, 228, 231

MOVEMENT 51, 57, 68–73, 122, 133, 140, 141, 147, 153, 165–167, 172, 194, 197, 218–219, 223, 225, 227, 229–230, 240

MUDs 43

MULTIPLE AUDIO TRACKS 126

MULTITRACK RECORDING 200

MUSICAL ACCENTS 204

MUSICAL MONOLOGUE 205

MUSICAL STYLES 4, 56, 59, 158, 204, 208–209

MUSIC CONTRACTORS 203

MUSIC EDITING 208

MUSIC EDITOR 203, 207–210

MUSICIANS 4, 34, 56–57, 78, 203, 208–209

MUSIC STEM 203–204

MUSIC SUPERVISOR 203, 210–211

## N

NARRATION 18, 27–28, 49, 58–59, 120–121

NARRATIVE 4, 17, 19, 22–23, 33–34, 36–41, 44, 50–51, 68, 81, 120, 131, 134, 140–141, 143, 150, 151, 204–206, 213, 239, 241

NARRATIVE SOUND 51

NARRATIVE SPINE 18–19

NATURE OF USE 213

NAVIGATION 36, 93, 234–235, 240–241, 244

NEAR-SYNC 201

NEEDLE DROPS 209

NESTED PLAYLISTS 126

NONDIEGETIC SOUND 54

NONPLAYERCHARACTERS (NPCs) 239

NOTE LENGTH 78

## O

OBJECT 32, 37, 52, 72, 101, 137, 142–143, 165,

174–175, 177–179, 187, 191–195, 202, 218, 221–227, 230, 240

OBJECTIVE 11–12, 24, 26, 233

OBJECTIVITY 79

OBSERVERS 35

OBSTACLES 25, 39, 237, 244

OFF SCREEN 135–136, 153

OFF-SPEED PLAYBACK 202

OMNI-DIRECTIONAL PATTERN 125

OPEN FRAME 136–137

OPEN SOURCE 90

ORCHESTRATION 208

ORCHESTRATORS 203

OUTSOURCE 92

OVERLAP 137, 229, 231

OVER THE SHOULDER (OTS) 146

OVERWRITING 161, 166

## P

PACE 48–49, 51, 53, 57–58, 103

PACKAGE DEAL 208

PAN 132, 146–147

PARODY 7, 212–215

PARODY SCORING 215

PARTICIPANT 31, 33, 35, 44, 51, 149

PART WRITING 208

PASSIVE 24, 27, 33–34, 188, 192

PASSIVE ENTERTAINMENT 33

PERIPETEIA 71–73

PERSISTENCE OF VISION 218–219

PERSONIFY 25

PICTURE LOCK 203

PILLARS 243–244

PITCH 9, 47–49, 54, 85, 126, 202

PITCH VARIATIONS 126

PLAYER 33, 35, 38–41, 104–106, 218, 233–243

PLAYER GOAL 41, 243

PLAY-LISTED 126

PLOSIVES 126

PLOT 16, 17, 20, 22–23, 42–43, 70–73, 120, 165

POLARITY 125

POLAR PATTERN 125

POP-FILTER 126

POSE-TO-POSE ANIMATION 222–223, 231

PRE-ANIMATION 123, 126

PRE-CLEARED 209

PRECONSTRUCTED 40

PRE-SCORED 205, 207

PRESENCE 24, 51, 84, 124, 152, 199–201

PRE-SYNC 120

PREVISUALIZATION 132

PRIMARYCOLORS 110

PRINCIPAL DIALOGUE 120, 126–127

PROCEDURES 102

PROCESSED 202, 204

PRODUCER 75, 77, 79–83

PRODUCTION LIBRARIES 209

PROGRAM 36, 102, 108, 127

PROLOGUE 70, 120

PROPS 44, 116

PROTAGONIST 21, 23–26, 42, 64–65, 71

PUBLISH 211

PUBLISHING RIGHTS 208

PUNCHES 127, 201

PUZZLE 36, 42–43, 238

## R

RECITATIVE 120

RECORDING 50, 52, 77, 80, 121, 123–127, 199–203, 208, 211

RECORDING ENGINEERS 203

RECORDING MIXER 201, 203, 209

RECORDING SCRIPT 121, 123, 126

RECORDING SOFTWARE 125

REFERENCE 116, 120, 122, 141, 143, 149, 207

REFLECTION 126

REGULARITY 48, 78

RELATIONSHIP 8, 12, 15, 32–33, 39, 51, 53, 102, 133, 135, 140–141, 143–144, 195, 197, 201, 235

RELEASE 10–11, 42, 87, 136

REPLACEMENT DIALOGUE 127

REPLAYABILITY 233

REPLICATE 86, 93, 219

REPRISES 206

REPRODUCE 211

RE-RECORDING MIXER 201, 203, 209

RESISTANCE 225–227, 230

RESPONSE 8–11, 32–33, 36, 47–48, 55, 63, 81, 83, 125, 146, 207

RETENTION 233

REVEAL 151–153, 181, 198

REVERBERANT 125

REWARDS 11, 241–242

RHYTHM 47–49, 53–59, 68, 75–76, 78, 80, 83, 85, 126, 229–231

RHYTHMIC PATTERNS 208

RIGHT BRAIN 103

RISK VERSUS REWARD 242–243

ROLE PLAYING GAMES (RPGs) 4

ROOM TONE 199

ROTOSCOPING 220

ROUTE 20, 33, 238

RULE 71–72, 90, 108, 110, 139–140, 160, 169, 226–231

RULE OF THIRDS 139–140

## S

SAMPLE-BASED SCORING 208

SAMPLE LIBRARIES 208

SATIRE 7

SCALE 205

SCENE 10, 32, 51, 54, 56–59, 68, 98, 121–122, 130–134, 141, 144, 147, 150–153, 158–171, 194–195, 197–201, 203–210, 215, 227–228, 230

SCORE 57, 158, 198, 203–210, 214–215

SCORING SESSION 208

SCORING STAGE 208

SCRATCH DIALOGUE 121

SCRATCH TAKES 126

SCREEN 15, 17, 19–20, 27–28, 31, 33, 44, 51, 105, 132, 135–136, 140, 153, 160, 172, 173, 181–182, 187, 200–201, 207, 218, 224, 227

SCREEN LEFT 135

SCREEN PLANE 51

SCREENPLAY 11, 68–71, 159–161, 171

SCREEN RIGHT 135

SCREENWRITER 68, 168

SCREENWRITING 70, 169

SCRIPT 42, 58, 69, 121, 123–125, 136, 159, 162, 165–171

SCRIPT READERS 159

SCRIPT SUPERVISORS 124

SCRUB 127

SECONDARY ACTION 228, 231

SECONDARY COLORS 110

SELL 18, 87, 199, 211

SENSORS 44

SEQUENCE 23, 36, 69–71, 102, 130–134, 182, 184, 194–195, 198, 205–206, 219, 222, 229

SERIOUS GAME 89–93, 233, 236, 238, 243

SFX 50, 121, 203–204, 215

SHADE 113

SHADOW 61–65, 138–139, 169, 174, 192

SHAREWARE 90

SHOT 18, 52, 54, 58, 67–68, 80, 98, 121, 124, 130–154, 178, 181–195, 199–200, 204, 207

SHOT SEQUENCE 130

SIMULATION 37, 39, 91, 93, 233

SIMULATIONS 33, 91, 93, 236

SIZE 3, 10, 36–37, 109, 121, 140, 142, 210, 223

SLOW MOTION 218

SLUG LINE 166, 169

SOLIDARITY 40

SONG 4–12, 15–16, 35, 54, 75–87, 97–98, 158, 205–206, 211, 215

SONG SCORE 205, 215

SONIC EVENTS 127

SONIC SPACE 199

SONIC TIME PATTERN 48

SOUND ABSORPTION 126

SOUND BLANKETS 125

SOUND DESIGN 7, 15–16, 47–48, 58, 158, 197–202

SOUND EDITOR 201, 207

SOUND EFFECTS 28, 47, 50–51, 54–56, 59, 105, 158, 197, 199–200, 202, 222, 228

SOUND ENVELOPE 47

SOUND ISOLATION 125

SOUND PERSPECTIVE 51

SOUNDTRACK 120, 125, 203–204, 207, 230

SOURCE 48, 50, 56, 102, 172, 199–208

SOURCE MATERIAL 204

SOURCE MUSIC 199, 204

SOURCE TO UNDERSCORE 204

SPACE-TIME CONTINUUM 78

SPECTRAL DECONVOLUTION 85

SPEECH PATTERNS 49

SPEED 48, 78, 202, 218, 221–222, 223, 230, 240

SPEED RAMPS 218

SPOTTING SESSION 203, 207, 209

SQUASH AND STRETCH 226–227, 231

STAGING 227, 231, 234

STAKES 28–29, 93

STATIC SHOT 145, 151

STILLNESS 228

STIMULUS 8–9, 10, 36

STIMULUS-RESPONSE EXCHANGE 36

STOP-FRAME ANIMATION 219–220

STORY 4–8, 10–11, 15–29, 33–45, 50–51, 54, 58–59, 62–66, 68, 71–73, 80, 97–105, 110, 113–116, 120–121, 131–133, 139–140, 153, 157–171, 189, 195, 204, 221, 222, 236–240

STORYBOARD 121, 123, 195, 222

STORY/GAME DICHOTOMY 42

STORY REEL 121

STORYTELLER 26, 28, 102, 204

STRAIGHT-AHEAD ANIMATION 222, 231

STRATEGY GAMES 4

STREAMERS 127

STRESS POINTS 127–128

STRUCTURE 5, 22–23, 32, 41, 48–50, 55, 57, 66–70, 75, 77–78, 92, 106, 195, 236–237

STYLE 17, 20, 54–57, 77, 83, 98, 116, 119–120, 133, 135–136, 160–161, 169, 172, 204–207, 210, 214–215, 218, 243

SUBCONSCIOUS 9–10, 98, 115, 157–158

SUBCULTURE 75, 84

SUBJECTIVE 11–12, 204, 210

SUBTEXT 9–10, 97, 157–158

SWEETENERS 122

SYMBOL 165–166

SYNC 20, 120–121, 126–127, 200, 202, 205, 207, 209–211

SYNCHRONIZATION 203, 209, 211, 213

SYNCHRONIZATION LICENSE 211

SYNC POINTS 210

## T

TAG 163–164

TAKE-TO-TAKE 126

TARGET AUDIENCE 78, 87, 107–108, 212–213

TEASER 29

TECHNOLOGY 82, 89, 91–92, 102–105, 139, 218

TEMP MUSIC 207

TEMPO 47–49, 54–59, 68, 85, 98, 206, 214

TEMP TRACKS 203, 207

TENETS 243–244

TENSION 10–11, 17, 25, 27, 59, 144–146, 153, 158, 201, 240, 242

TERM 4, 9, 17, 33, 40, 43, 50–51, 55, 71, 73, 77, 85, 89, 130–131, 147–148, 157, 197, 211, 217, 220–221, 225

TERRITORY 209, 213

TEXT 9, 35–36, 43, 97, 157, 218, 224, 226, 230

TEXTURE 54–56, 98, 139

THEME 5–7, 11, 16, 20, 57, 83, 208

THREE-ACT STRUCTURE 70

THREE SHOT (3S) 142

THROW FORCES 224

TILT 144, 146

TIMBRAL SEPARATION 122

TIMBRE 47–48

TIME CODE 125, 127

TIME-LAPSE 18, 204

TIME-LAPSE SEQUENCES 204

TIME WARPING 218

TIMING 78, 158, 218, 226–231, 233

TINT 113

TITLE 205–206, 213, 215, 218, 224

TITLE CARDS 18

TITLE SEQUENCE 205–206, 218, 224

TONALITY 54

TONE 49, 54–55, 68, 102, 175, 199, 205–206

TRACK 75, 81, 126–127, 147, 158–159, 163, 179–180, 187, 197, 199–200, 207

TRACKING 147–150, 165

TRACK READING 126

TRADITIONAL STORYTELLING 31–32

TRANSIENT RESPONSE 125

TRANSITION 204, 222

TRICKSTER 61, 64–66

TWEENING 221

TWO SHOT (2S) 132, 142

TYPE 65, 159, 163, 207, 213, 218

## U

UNDERSCORE 42, 53, 57, 203–204, 206–207, 215

USER 8–10, 32–45, 158

## V

VELOCITY  221–222

VERB SET  32–33

VIDEO GAME  4–5, 7, 15–16, 33, 36–38, 41–42, 158

VIDEOGRAM LICENSE  211

VIDEO ON DEMAND  37

VIDEO PLAYBACK  125

VIDEO SCRUBBING  218

VIRTUAL OBJECTS  36–37

VIRTUAL REALITY  34, 44, 93

VISUAL EFFECTS  217–219, 222, 233

VISUALIZE  79, 165–166

VOCALIST  77, 205

VOICE ACTORS  119, 121–124

VOICE-OVER  18, 20, 27, 120

VOICING  119

VOLUME  10, 48, 223

## W

WALKING ROOM  140

WALLA  121

WALL-TO-WALL MUSIC  208

WAVEFORMS  81, 126

WEIGHT  80–81, 139–140, 204, 223–226, 230, 241

WIDE SHOT (WS)  98, 141, 151

WIDOWS  170

WILD  126

WORKS FOR HIRE  208

WRITER  33, 35, 42, 49, 75, 77, 79–80, 82–83, 86–87,
        160–161, 168–169, 171, 215

## Z

ZOETROPE  218–219

ZOOM  146–149, 228

CPSIA information can be obtained
at www.ICGtesting.com
Printed in the USA
LVOW02s2020040116

468996LV00007B/29/P

9 781626 612150